Fodor's

LOS CABOS

T0031636

MAPS

Fodor's Features

Contents

Welcome to Los Cabos

With coastline that stretches from the Sea of Cortez to the Pacific Ocean, and 350 sunny days a year, Los Cabos is Mexico's ultimate seaside escape. The sister towns of Cabo San Lucas and San José del Cabo offer endless summer and distinct experiences that range from all-night bar crawls to Thursday-night art walks. Between them the Corridor presents all-inclusive resorts with everything for the perfect vacation. As you plan your upcoming travels to Los Cabos, please confirm that places are still open and let us know when we need to make updates by writing to us at this address: editors@fodors.com.

TOP REASONS TO GO

★ **Beaches:** More than 80 km (50 miles) of gorgeous strands with towering rock formations.

★ **Golf:** Spectacular views from greens designed by the world's best course architects.

★ **Nightlife:** Cabo's after-dark, into-the-dawn party scene draws a loud, festive crowd.

★ **Sportfishing:** Beginners and pros drop a line in the "Marlin Capital of the World."

★ **Whale-Watching:** The gentle giants that migrate here swim right next to the boats.

★ **Spas:** Desert healing treatments in sumptuous resort wellness centers.

Chapter 1

EXPERIENCE LOS CABOS

17 ULTIMATE EXPERIENCES

Los Cabos offers terrific experiences that should be on every traveler's list. Here are Fodor's top picks for a memorable trip.

1 El Arco at Land's End

These towering granite formations let you know you've arrived at the tip of the Baja Peninsula. El Arco ("the Arch") has become the region's emblem. *(Ch. 3)*

2 Todos Santos

This típico town on the West Cape is a perfect day trip and home to a growing expat community, cozy lodgings, and great eateries. *(Ch. 6)*

3 Whale-Watching

Gray whales migrate to Los Cabos every year from December through April, down Baja's coast and up to the east, making for a memorable viewing. *(Ch. 3, 6, 7)*

4 Shopping

Find hand-painted tiles, pottery, cigars, embroidered clothing, hand-blown glass, silver jewelry, and fire opals, plus the iconic beaded crafts of the Huichol people. *(Ch. 3-7)*

5 Sailing

Find Windsurfer and Sunfish sailboats docked at the Cabo San Lucas Marina and take a tour along the region's ultrablue waters. *(Ch. 3-7)*

6 Marina Golden Zone

Peruse upscale shops and enjoy fine dining at Cabo's downtown marina. Stroll along the boardwalk for stunning sea views and dine in a traditional Mexican-style cantina. *(Ch. 3)*

7 Nightlife

A major spring break destination, Cabo is known as a party town, but you can also opt for low-key outings in San José del Cabo. *(Ch. 3-7)*

8 Desert Excursions

Venture through the Baja desert atop a friendly camel, sail across the canyon on a zipline, cruise the sandy basin on a mountain bike, or take a thrilling ATV tour among desert and cacti. *(Ch. 3–5)*

9 Cabo Pulmo National Marine Park

Stretching five miles from Pulmo Point to Los Frailes, this national park encompasses the only living hard coral reef in North America. *(Ch. 6)*

10 Seafood

Cabo is famous for its seafood, especially dishes like chocolate clams, fish tacos, smoked marlin, lobster, and more. *(Ch. 3-7)*

11 Sportfishing

Cabo San Lucas is nicknamed "the Marlin Mecca," but there are over 800 species of fish here. Sportfishing remains one of the area's most popular pastimes. *(Ch. 3-7)*

12 Beaches

In Los Cabos, soft, sandy beaches stretch for about 50 miles beside the turquoise and navy waters of the Pacific Ocean and the Sea of Cortez. *(Ch. 3-7)*

13 Golfing

One of the world's top golf destinations, Los Cabos has courses throughout the area by big-name designers like Jack Nicklaus and Roy Dye. *(Ch. 3-7)*

14 Surfing

Los Cabos, with its warm seas, offers both intense and gentle waves, focused in the Pacific coast, the East Cape, and the Cabo Corridor. *(Ch. 3-7)*

15 Gallery Hopping

Stroll the charming cobblestone streets of San José del Cabo where colorful banners hang over a historic downtown that is home to high-end art galleries and a weekly Art Walk. *(Ch. 5)*

16 Spas

Many come to Los Cabos to relax at one of the many resorts with spas offering scenic outlooks and extensive body and beauty treatments. *(Ch. 3-7)*

17 Farm-to-Table Dining

In Ánimas Bajas, trendy organic restaurants like Flora Farms, Los Tamarindos, and Acre offer the chance to dine right on the picturesque farm where your food was grown. *(Ch. 5)*

WHAT'S WHERE

1 Cabo San Lucas. Cabo has always been the more gregarious, outspoken of the sister cities. The sportfishing fleet is anchored here, and cruise ships anchored off the marina tender passengers into town. Restaurants and bars line the streets and massive hotels have risen all along the beachfront. Here you'll find the towering Land's End Rocks, and the famed landmark, El Arco.

2 The Corridor. Along this stretch of road, which connects San José to Cabo, exclusive, guard-gated resort complexes have taken over much of the waterfront with their sprawling villas, golf courses, and upscale shopping centers such as Las Tiendas de Palmilla, and Koral Center.

3 San José del Cabo. The smaller, quieter, and more traditional of the two regions of Los Cabos has colonial architecture, an artsy vibe, and quality restaurants. Five minutes from the center are golf courses, boutique hotels, and luxury resorts. Drive another five minutes to organic farms that are producing extraordinary dining experiences.

4 Todos Santos. Only an hour north of Cabo San Lucas, Todos Santos lies close enough to be part of Los Cabos experience— but still be that proverbial world away. This *típico* town on the West Cape is home to a growing expat community, as well as some cozy lodgings and restaurants.

5 La Paz. The capital of southern Baja is a "big little" city, one of the most authentic on the peninsula. La Paz is a laid-back community with excellent scuba diving and whale-watching. Its lovely oceanfront *malecón* features a number of good restaurants and hotels.

6 East Cape. One of the last undeveloped stretches of sandy serenity in the area lies east of San José del Cabo along the Sea of Cortez, to north of Punta Pescadero, Los Barriles, and Rancho Buena Vista and is home to the beautiful Cabo Pulmo National Park.

7 Baja California. The beaches and seafood of Rosarito, Ensenada, and Puerto Nuevo in the northern stretches of the Baja peninsula, close to the U.S. border, draw surfers, RV'ers, and the spring break crowd; the Valle de Guadalupe provides respite and fantastic vineyards.

Best Beaches in Los Cabos

LOVER'S BEACH
Water taxis, glass-bottom boats, kayaks, and Jet Skis all make the short trip out from Playa El Médano to this frequently photographed patch of sand, which is backed by cliffs and Cabo's most iconic landmark: El Arco. *(Ch. 3)*

PLAYA EL MÉDANO
Cabo San Lucas' main swimming beach is also one of its most popular. Known as a party beach, it's much like a daylong parade route fueled by buckets of beer, powerful margaritas, and that carefree feeling of being on vacation. *(Ch. 3)*

LA RIBERA
Quiet and off the beaten path, this white-sand beach on the East Cape is perfect for kayaking, paddle-boarding, swimming, and snorkeling away from the crowds. It's also known for its fishing tournaments and proximity to Cabo Pulmo. *(Ch. 6)*

BAHÍA CHILENO
Halfway between San José and Cabo San Lucas, Chileno is easy to find thanks to well-marked signs. It skirts a small, crescent-shaped cove with aquamarine waters perfect for swimming and a reef where you can snorkel among colorful fish or explore tide pools to the east. It is consistently ranked one of the cleanest beaches in Mexico. *(Ch. 4)*

PLAYA COSTA AZUL
Cabo's best surfing beach runs 3 km (2 mi) south from San José's hotel zone along the Corridor and connects to neighboring Playa Acapulquito in front of Cabo Surf Hotel. Surfers usually congregate in summer when waves tend to be the largest. Swimming is not advised due to strong currents and rocks. *(Ch. 4)*

PLAYA BUENOS AIRES
This wide, lengthy, and accessible stretch of beach is one of the longest along Cabo's Corridor. Much of it is unswimmable, but it's a great spot for quiet runs or walks. You can also rent water-sports equipment here and sometimes spot whales breaching from January to March. *(Ch. 4)*

PLAYA LAS VIUDAS
Just west of Bahía Santa María along the Corridor, the small "Widow's Beach" has tide pools, a shallow reef, and rock outcroppings that create private areas and natural tabletops in the sand for beach picnics. *(Ch. 4)*

BAHÍA SANTA MARÍA
Part of an underwater reserve and protected fish sanctuary, this broad, horseshoe-shaped beach has placid waters that are ideal for snorkeling. The cove is surrounded by rocky, cactus-covered cliffs but there's no shade, so you might want to bring an umbrella and your own supplies. *(Ch. 4)*

PLAYA MONUMENTOS
At eastern end of Playa El Médano, this point break popular with surfers is best viewed from Sunset Mona Lisa restaurant perched on the cliff. (True to the restaurant's name, it's a great place to be when the sun goes down). The powerful waves mean it's not a good swmming beach. *(Ch. 4)*

PLAYA ESTERO
At the mouth of San José del Cabo's lush estuary that starts at the north end of Hotel Zone, this beach is home to more than 350 species of wildlife and vegetation and can be explored on foot or via kayak. *(Ch. 5)*

PLAYA LOS CERRITOS
If you're visiting Todos Santos, the best beach nearby is Playa Los Cerritos, famous for its surfing. It's great for beginners thanks to consistent but not overly powerful waves, and wading is possible near shore. The beach conveniently has a restaurant, bathrooms, and surf shops. *(Ch. 6)*

PLAYA PALMILLA
Multimillion-dollar villas and the ritzy One&Only Palmilla resort line this serene beach, protected by a rocky point that makes for calm water and the best swimming near San José. It attracts surfers to the offshore Punta Palmilla farther out to sea. *(Ch. 4)*

What to Eat and Drink in Los Cabos

FARM-TO-TABLE MEALS
Just outside San José you can indulge in fresh, beautifully green organic produce straight from the farms on which the ingredients are grown. Acre, Jazamango, and Flora Farms are top farms to enjoy Baja Sur's magical garden bounty.

GUEMES TAMALES
While tamales may be known across Mexico, the guemes variety are specific to the Baja Peninsula. Made with pork or chicken, olives, and raisins, the steam-cooked corn wrappers are similar to the Cabo version called "fadados" prepared with stewed chicken, corn dough, and local seasonings.

MEZCAL, TEQUILA, AND DAMIANA
A locally made liqueur is the herbacous Damiana, bottled in a woman-shaped container. You'll also find mezcal and tequila tastings easily at top restaurants and resorts. Although there are at least five "local" Cabo tequilas, most of the good stuff hails from Jalisco.

CHILAQUILES
Whatever you do, don't call these breakfast nachos. This traditional Mexican brunch favorite consists of fried tortilla chips smothered in salsa verde, crumbly cotija cheese, and eggs.

CEVICHE
Beautiful presentations of fresh raw fish marinated in lime juice are the perfect way to try Baja's fresh fruits de mer. The poolside favorite is often made with white fish, lime, tomatoes, jalapenos, cilantro, peppers, and sometimes mango and avocado.

PITAHAYA

Bright pink-and-yellow dragonfruit, a cactus fruit that blooms in the desert regions, is served on its own, in cocktails, infused into dishes and even makes its way into jellied candies, jams, and marzipan.

TACOS DE PESCADO

Fish tacos originated in Baja California, so a trip here without eating one or two (or many) is just wrong. Grilled or fried local catches are piled on a corn tortilla and topped with shredded cabbage, cilantro, salsa, lime, and a dribble of a mayo-based sauce.

OAXACAN MOLE

Renowned for the complexity of its flavors, this dark red or brown sauce is typically served over enchiladas, chicken, and tamales. Made with chocolate, nuts, chiles, raisins, and more, it has a smoky, sweet flavor.

Almejas chocolatas
(Chocolate clams)

ALMEJAS CHOCOLATAS

Chocolate clams are neither cooked in nor taste like chocolate; their name derives from their dark brown shells. Although not as decadent as their name implies, the meaty clams are a flavor-packed delicacy often roasted and seasoned with rosemary.

ZARZUELA

You'll find as many recipes for Baja-style seafood stew as there are cooks, who refer to the dish as paella or zarzuela. Any mix-and-match combination of clams, crab, shrimp, cod, sea bass, red snapper, or mahimahi could find its way into your dish, along with requisite white wine, garlic, and spices.

FRIED LOBSTER

Lightly battered fried lobster is a good treat to try alfresco overlooking the sea from which it came. A world-famous version is served in Puerto Nuevo. Poached octopus is another to try if you can't have shellfish.

SMOKED MARLIN

The Sea of Cortez is full of marlin, the most common catch in Cabo, and this ubiquitous treat is served smoked and shredded in tacos or as a dip.

What to Buy in Los Cabos

HANDBLOWN GLASS
Artisans at The Glass Factory of Cabo San Lucas (Fábrica de Vidrio Soplado) turn crushed recycled glass into exquisite figures in deep blues, greens, and reds. It's as fun to watch the glass items being crafted as it is to select a colorful piece to take home.

TAMARINDO CANDIES
Made from tamarind fruit and wrapped in a corn husk, these small, sweet and sour chewy treats are a good way to bring back the local flavor of Mexico. They are traditionally sold on a stick, to be enjoyed as a lollipop, but there are many bite-sized variations. They're a great, sweet pick-me-up if energy is running low, and kids love them.

PAINTED TALAVERA TILES
Colorful Talavera tiles, a craft introduced to Mexico by the Spanish, are usually hand painted and glazed, and come in striking geometric patterns of ochre, cobalt, and scarlet. Like many other souvenirs you will find in Los Cabos, they are usually made elsewhere in Mexico, but they are popular gifts and can brighten up a walkway, porch, or kitchen. You can buy them in the shops of Cabo San Lucas and San José del Cabo.

FIRE OPAL
As its name suggests, this bright red-orange stone dazzles like a fiery flame. You can buy it in various forms of jewelry such as rings, necklaces, and pendants, from local vendors at Plaza Artesanos or in the Gallery District of San José del Cabo.

HAMMOCK
What's a beach trip without lazing away in a hammock, cold drink in hand? The woven hammocks you buy in Los Cabos may well hail from the Yucatán, but they are a useful purchase for the beaches you'll encounter–and your favorite quiet spot back home. Find them at Plaza Artesanos, which beckons with stalls featuring handicrafts and curios.

DAMIANA LIQUEUR
Sure, tequila and mezcal can be found in abundance, and Los Cabos' finest restaurants have tastings that may inspire you to take some home, but if you're looking for something truly local, try *damiana*, a sweet, herbaceous liqueur made here in Baja Sur. The production of the sugar-cane and damiana plant-based liqueur dates back to the time of indigenous inhabitants, who believed it to be an aphrodisiac and relaxation aid. It's bottled in a woman-shaped glass bottle.

FINE ART
Downtown San José's Art District is a must for art lovers. Here, you can stroll through more than a dozen fine art galleries to find the perfect decorative piece. Pick up a one-of-a-kind painting or sculpture from Galeria Corsica, highlighting Mexican artists, during one of the area's art walks, held each Thursday from November to June. Even if you're not in the market, check out the contemporary work at Casa Dahlia.

Huichol crafts

HUICHOL CRAFTS

The Huichol, or "Peyote People," of Nayarit and Jalisco are known for their ceremonial use of the hallucinogenic drug peyote; their visions, thought to be messages from God, are represented in their colorful, intricately beaded and woven designs on votive bowls, jewelry, bags, and prayer arrows. The price of these pieces can range from $5 to $5,000 depending on quality of the materials and the artist's skill. Spot their distinct rainbow of mesmerizing patterns in shops in Cabo San Lucas and San José del Cabo.

HANDMADE RESORT WEAR

A custom-designed bathing suit or dress from a local boutique is the perfect purchase for soaking up the sun here. A favorite boutique for locally made clothing and accessories is Eclectic Array, which has locations in the hotel zone of San José del Cabo, Flora Farms, and the marina in Cabo San Lucas. All of their products are made by local Mexican artisans, and their colorful woven camera straps and dog collars are popular gift items. Pepita's Magic of the Moon is another excellent boutique that's stood the test of time with its one-of-a-kind clothing. Plaza del Pescador is another good stop for clothing shops.

GOODIES FROM FLORA FARMS

Artisanal salts, fresh produce and herbs, plus flowers, candies, pots, and candles can be found at Flora Farms Grocery, the store attached to the well-loved Flora Farms. However, shopping is just part of the experience at the working farm, grocery, kitchen, and spa. You can also get a spa treatment in the open air and dine on fresh produce in a magical garden setting. Flora Farms, along with a host of new farm-to-table dining experiences, is located just a short drive from San José del Cabo in the Ánimas Bajas.

ARTISANAL SOAPS

Santo Cabo's pampering, natural line of beauty and apothecary products are a must for wellness enthusiasts, and perhaps the best way to bring the scents of Los Cabos home with you. The local company is best known for their beautiful bar soaps and hand lotions made using regionally grown organic ingredients (think: aloe and cucumber, peppermint and red reef clay, or rosemary and grapefruit). Shops in San José del Cabo and Cabo San Lucas as well as Flora Farms carry the line.

Cruising to Los Cabos

In March 2020, the COVID-19 pandemic forced all cruise lines into a global suspension with no sailing for 12 months. Once restrictions were lifted, the cruise industry implemented strict health and safety protocols, but some say it will take years before cruise lines will make a full comeback.

Cruise lines with itineraries to Los Cabos and Baja California include Carnival, Celebrity, Crystal, Cunard, Holland America, Lindblad Expeditions, Norwegian, Oceania, Princess, Regent Seven Seas, and Royal Caribbean. Most depart from Los Angeles (Long Beach), San Diego, San Francisco, Seattle, Fort Lauderdale, Miami, New York, San Juan, Vancouver, and even Southampton, England, or Bridgetown, Barbados. Most cruises to Baja dock at Cabo San Lucas, with a few calling at Ensenada, La Paz, and Loreto.

Terrific shopping, dining, beaches, and shore excursions and the unforgettable view of El Arco upon approach make Cabo San Lucas a crowd-pleaser among cruise ports. Ships need to drop anchor and tender passengers to the marina, about a 10-minute trip. Ensenada is a favorite stop on shorter Baja cruises. Its modern Cruise Port Village terminal berths two full-size ships at a time. La Paz, on the Sea of Cortez, wins rave reviews as being the most "authentically Mexican" of Baja's cruise destinations. A few large ships dock at its port of Pichilingue, about 16 km (10 miles) north of town. Smaller boats can berth at La Paz itself. Tenders transport travelers ashore to the port of Loreto, north of Pichilingue.

Carnival. Carnival is known for its large-volume cruises and template approach to its ships, which both help keep fares accessible. Boats in its Mexican fleet have more than 1,000 staterooms. Seven-night Mexican Riviera trips out of Los Angeles hit Cabo San Lucas among other Pacific ports in Mexico. Carnival wrote the book on Baja-only cruises, with three- or four-day itineraries out of Los Angeles to Ensenada. Las Vegas–style shows and passenger participation is the norm. ☎ 800/764–7419 ⊕ www.carnival.com.

Celebrity. Spacious accommodations and modern luxury are hallmarks of Celebrity cruises. Its *Celebrity Infinity* plies the Panama Canal east- and westbound on 15-day itineraries, hitting Cabo San Lucas along the way, with an extensive choice of departure ports (Fort Lauderdale, Los Angeles, or San Diego). ☎ 800/647–2251 ⊕ www.celebritycruises.com.

Crystal. Crystal is known for combining large ships with grandeur, opulence, and impeccable service. Its *Crystal Symphony* calls at Cabo San Lucas on a variety of itineraries from Miami to Los Angeles (16 days). ☎ 866/866-8025 ⊕ www.crystalcruises.com.

Holland America. The venerable Holland America line leaves from and returns to San Diego or Fort Lauderdale. Panama Canal cruises spanning 14- to 23-day itineraries include stops in Cabo San Lucas. ☎ 877/932–4259 ⊕ www.hollandamerica.com.

Lindblad Expeditions. Lindblad's smaller *Sea Lion* and *Sea Bird* take you where the other guys can't go, for an active, nature-themed Baja cruise experience. Five- to 15-day excursions embark in La Paz or Loreto and nose around the islands of the Sea of Cortez. Its kayaks and Zodiacs launch from the ship to provide you with unparalleled opportunity to watch whales, dolphins, and seabirds. ☎ *800/397–3348* ⊕ *www.expeditions. com.*

Norwegian Cruise Line. Its tagline is "whatever floats your boat," and Norwegian *is* known for its relatively freewheeling style and variety of activities and excursions. Seven day cruises on the *Bliss* depart from Los Angeles, with full days in Cabo San Lucas, and Panama Canal cruises on the *Jewel,* and *Encore* from 15 to 16 days all call on Cabo San Lucas. ☎ *866/234–7350* ⊕ *www.ncl.com.*

Oceania. The ships of Oceania are intimate and cozy. Before arrival at Cabo San Lucas or any port, you can attend a lecture about its history, culture, and tradition. The *Regatta* stops here on an 18-day cruise from San Francisco to Miami. ☎ *855/623–2642* ⊕ *www.oceaniacruises.com.*

Princess Cruises. Not so great for small children but good at keeping teens and adults occupied, Princess strives to offer luxury at an affordable price. Seven- to 10-day Mexican Riviera cruises aboard the *Ruby Princess or Majestic Princess* start in Los Angeles or San Francisco and hit Los Cabos and other Pacific ports. Shorter five-day trips out of Los Angeles call at Los Cabos. ☎ *800/774–6237* ⊕ *www.princess.com.*

Regent Seven Seas Cruises. RSSC's luxury liner the *Marnier* offers 18-day trips that originate in Miami to San Francisco and call at Cabo San Lucas. The *Marnier* also has a 12-day round-trip route from Los Angeles with calls in Cabo and other Mexican Pacific ports. ☎ *877/505–5370* ⊕ *www.rssc.com.*

Weddings

Choosing the Perfect Place. Los Cabos is a popular Mexican wedding and honeymoon destination. Many couples choose to marry on the beach, often at sunset because it's cooler and more comfortable for everyone; others opt to marry in an air-conditioned resort ballroom.

Consider booking an all-inclusive, which has plenty of meal options and activities to keep your guests busy before and after the main event.

Beach Wedding Attire. Some brides choose a traditional full wedding gown with veil, but more popular and comfortable—especially for an outdoor wedding—is a simple sheath or a white cotton or linen dress that will breathe in the tropical heat. Some opt for even less formal barefoot attire such as a sundress.

Weddings on the beach are best done barefoot, even when full gowns are worn. Choose strappy sandals for a wedding or reception that's not on the sand. Whatever type of attire you choose, purchase it and get any alterations done before leaving home. Buy a special garment bag and hand-carry your dress on the plane. Don't let this be the one time in your life that your luggage goes missing.

The groom and any groomsmen can take their what-to-wear cue from the female half of the wedding party, but know that Los Cabos has no place to rent formal attire.

Time of Year. Planning according to the weather can be critical for a successful Los Cabos wedding. If you're getting married in your bathing suit, you might not mind some heat and humidity, but will your venue—and your future in-laws—hold up under the summer heat? We recommend holding the ceremony between November and February. March through June is usually dry but extremely warm and humid.

By July the heat can be unbearable for an outdoor afternoon wedding, and summer rains, rarely voluminous in Los Cabos, begin to fall here around the same time. Although hurricanes are rarer along the Pacific than the Caribbean, they can occur August through late October and even early November. For an outdoor wedding, establish a detailed backup plan and purchase wedding insurance in case the weather does not comply. Generally insurance will cover the cost of a wedding tent if your outdoor party experiences rain.

Finding a Wedding Planner. Hiring a wedding planner will minimize stress for all but the simplest of ceremonies. A year or more in advance, the planner will, among other things, help choose the venue, find a florist, and arrange for a photographer and musicians.

The most obvious place to find a wedding planner is at a resort hotel that becomes wedding central: providing accommodations for you and your guests, the wedding ceremony venue, and the restaurant or ballroom for the reception. You can also hire an independent wedding coordinator, which you can find easily online by searching "Los Cabos wedding," and ask them to provide references.

When interviewing a planner, talk about your budget and ask about costs. Are there hourly fees or one fee for the whole event? How available will the consultant and his or her assistants be? Which vendors are used and why? How long have they been in business? Request a list of the exact services they'll provide, and get a proposal in writing. If you don't feel this is the right person or agency for you, try someone else. Cost permitting, it's helpful to meet the planner in person.

Requirements. A bona fide wedding planner will facilitate completing the required paperwork and negotiating the legal requirements for marrying in Mexico. Blood tests must be done upon your arrival, but not more than 14 days before the ceremony. All documents must be translated by an authorized translator from the destination, and it's important to send these documents by certified mail to your wedding coordinator at least a month ahead of the wedding.

You'll also need to submit an application for a marriage license as well as certified birth certificates (bring the original with you to Los Cabos, and send certified copies ahead of time). If either party is divorced or widowed, official death certificate or divorce decree must be supplied, and you must wait one year to remarry after the end of the previous marriage. (There's no way around this

archaic requirement, still on the books, designed to ensure that no lingering pregnancy remains from a former marriage). The two getting married and four witnesses will also need to present passports and tourist cards. Wedding planners can round up witnesses if you don't have enough or any.

Since religious weddings aren't officially recognized in Mexico, a civil ceremony (matrimonio civil) is required, thus making your marriage valid in your home country as well. (It's the equivalent of being married in front of a justice of the peace). Cabo San Lucas and San José del Cabo each have one civil judge who performs marriages, a good reason to start planning months in advance. Often for an extra fee, the judge will attend the site of your wedding if you prefer not to go to an office. Civil proceedings take about 10 minutes, and the wording is fixed in Spanish. Most wedding planners will provide an interpreter if you or your guests don't speak the language. For a Catholic ceremony, a priest here will expect evidence that you've attended the church's required pre-wedding sessions back home. If you're planning a Jewish wedding, you'll need to bring your rabbi with you, as Los Cabos has no synagogues. Another option is to be married in your own country and then hold the wedding event in Los Cabos without worrying about all the red tape.

Same-sex civil unions are either allowed or recognized in every state in Mexico; it is legal in both Baja California and Baja California Sur.

Kids and Families

Los Cabos and Baja don't necessarily leap to mind when planning a vacation with the kids. (This isn't Orlando, after all). It's not that the region is unfriendly to children, but enjoying time with the kids here does take some advance preparation and research.

PLACES TO STAY

Except those that exclude children entirely, many of Los Cabos' beach hotels and all-inclusive resorts cater to families and have children's programs. A few offer little more than kids' pools, but several of the big hotels and their wealth of activities go way beyond that and make fine options for families with kids. Our top picks:

Dreams Los Cabos has an active Explorers Club for children ages 3–12. (The search for a beach treasure is always a crowd-pleaser). Older kids will appreciate tennis, badminton, volleyball, soccer, and movie nights under the stars.

Grand Velas houses the best spots for kids and teenagers in Los Cabos. Exclusively for children ages 4–12, the Kids' Club teaches little ones how to make piñatas, jewelry, masks, and kites. The Teens' Club, for ages 13–18, has a dance club, juice bar, pool table, Ping-Pong, karaoke, and private gaming pods. These supervised services are open all day, and free of charge to hotel guests.

Hilton's Cabo Kids' Club is geared toward kids 4–12, with cookie decorating, arts and crafts, board games, Spanish classes, cinema under the stars, and even spa treatments for kids at Eforea Spa. Babysitting service is also available so parents can get some alone time.

Vacation Rentals: Apartments, condos, and villas are an excellent option for families. You can cook your own food (a big money saver), spread out, and set up a home away from home. If you decide to go the apartment- or condo-rental route, be sure to ask about the number and size of the swimming pools and whether outdoor spaces and barbecue areas are available.

BEACHES

If you have visions of you and your family frolicking in the surf, revise them a bit. Many Los Cabos–area beaches are notoriously unsafe for swimming, so your day at the beach will be relegated to the sand.

The destination has a handful of beaches you can swim in, the most popular (and crowded) being Playa El Médano in Cabo San Lucas. Although it may be good for swimming, there are some quick drop-offs, not to mention the waters can get congested with party people. Other swimmable beaches include Playa Solmar on the Pacific side of Land's End and Santa Maria Beach off the main highway. Chileno Bay is great for families, but part of the cove is now dominated by the recently developed Chileno Bay Resort. Estuary Beach at the north end of hotel row in San José del Cabo is relatively calm, as is Playa Hotelera just east of the San José Estuary. Playa Palmilla, near San José del Cabo, offers tranquil water most days, making it a good spot for stand-up paddleboarding or swimming. Playa Buenos Aires in the Corridor is safest between Hilton and Paradisus Resort, where the man-made Tequila Cove serves as a wave breaker. Playa del Amor (Lover's Beach), at Land's End near Cabo San Lucas, is regarded as okay for swimming on the Sea of Cortez side, but not the Pacific side. (You can't swim in any of the Pacific beaches here).

AFTER DARK

Nightlife here is mostly geared toward grown-ups, but a few kid-friendly dining spots do exist. El Merkado in the Corridor offers an elevated "food court" concept that explores the best of Mexico's gastronomy. Flora Farms, Acre, and Los Tamarindos all have "farm-to-table" dining experiences, meaning kids can explore the grounds while Mom and Dad enjoy live music over a watermelon julep. Most all-inclusives have familiar food that will satisfy the most finicky of eaters, and the U.S. chains are all here, too.

All restaurants in Mexico are nonsmoking (except in outdoor-seating areas). Both San José del Cabo and Cabo San Lucas have modern theaters that show Hollywood movies a few weeks after they premiere back home; note, though, that animated films or G-rated films are often dubbed in Spanish.

BAJA TOP FIVE FOR KIDS

Canyon and Beach Action, Cabo San Lucas: For little adventurers, Baja Outback has bodyboarding, surfing, sand-castle building, stand-up paddleboarding, and more at the beach. For teens Wild Canyon Adventures in the Corridor dishes up desert action with safari camel rides, dune buggies, and ziplining.

La Bufadora, near Ensenada: Literally "the buffalo snort," this natural tidal-wave phenomenon near Ensenada sprays water 75 feet into the air.

Swim with the Dolphins, San José del Cabo: Kids can swim and play with friendly dolphins at the marina in Puerto Los Cabos near San José. A second dolphin center is located at the marina in Cabo San Lucas.

Whale-Watching, Los Cabos, Ensenada, Guerrero Negro, Loreto, Magdalena Bay: You'll find whale-watching venues up and down the peninsula;outfitters here take you out to sea in pangas, small boats that let you get an up close view of the magnificent beasts. No matter what your age, Baja has no greater thrill.

Wild Wet Fun Water Park, Caduaño: It's worth the one-hour drive inland from Cabo San Lucas to this water park with splash zones and water slides, especially for just a $10 entrance fee.

LEGALITIES

All children over the age of two require a Mexican Tourist Card (FMT card) to venture beyond the U.S. border region. Kids 15 and under require only a birth certificate to return to the United States by land from Mexico. If you fly home, everyone, regardless of age, must hold a passport to get back into the United States.

Don't forget Mexico's well-known and stringent laws regarding the entry and exit of children under 18. All minors must be accompanied by both parents or legal guardian. In the absence of that, the parent not present must provide a notarized statement granting permission for the child to travel. Divorce, separation, or remarriage complicate these matters, but do not negate the requirement.

If you are traveling as a full family, multi-ethnic family, or have remarried, adopted, or have different last names, copies of relevant documentation are always beneficial for Mexican immigration officials, just in case there are questions.

Snapshot Los Cabos

WHERE DESERT MEETS SEA

A visitor flying into Los Cabos will readily observe the peninsula's stark, brown terrain—indeed, it feels like you're arriving in the middle of nowhere. You'll realize soon after landing that even though the tip of Baja once also resembled the rest of the dry, inhospitable desert, it has been transformed into an inviting desert oasis. The landscape, where once only cacti and a few hardy palms resided, is now punctuated by posh hotels, manicured golf courses, and swimming pools. As shown by the thousands of sun-worshipping, partying people seemingly oblivious to the fact that true desert lies, literally across Carretera Transpeninsular (Highway 1) from their beachfront hotel, Los Cabos has successfully beaten back the drylands. Pay some respect to the area's roots by taking a hike or tour around the surrounding desert landscape.

A similar phenomenon exists in the northern sector of the peninsula, with the metro area anchored by Tijuana, in reality almost a continuation of U.S. Southern California. Irrigation has turned this desert into one of Mexico's prime agricultural regions.

In between far-northern Baja and Los Cabos—the peninsula logs a distance of just over 1,600 km (1,000 miles), which compares to the north–south length of Italy—expect mostly desert scrubland. Two-thirds of the landmass is desert—a continuation of the Sonora Desert in the southwest United States—and receives about 10 inches of rain per year. The remaining third of the peninsula forms a mountainous spine, technically four mountain ranges. The northernmost of these mountains are pine-forested and might make you think you've taken a wrong turn to Oregon. East of San Felipe, Baja's highest peak, the Picacho del Diablo ("Devil's Peak"), measures 10,150 feet and is snowcapped in winter.

THE BAJACALIFORNIANOS

Geography, history, and economics have conspired to give Baja California a different population mix from the rest of Mexico. The country as a whole is of mixed indigenous and European descent, but only half of *Bajacalifornianos*—the name is a mouthful—can point to any indigenous ancestry. Those native to Baja California Sur are known as *Choyeros*, making up only about 15% of the population. Locals born in Cabo San Lucas refer to themselves as *Cabeños*, while those born in San José del Cabo are known as *Cabo Josefinos*.

Historically, the peninsula was a land apart, a Wild West where only the intrepid dared to venture to seek their fortunes—many Mexicans still view Baja through that prism—and has drawn a more international population. The indigenous population that does live here is a recent addition of migrants from the southern states of Oaxaca and Chiapas drawn to jobs in the border cities.

Baja's population is over 3.5 million, but nearly two-thirds of that number lives near the U.S. border. The 1,600-km (1,000-mile) drive from north to south confirms this is a sparsely populated region of Mexico. The state of Baja California Sur, the southern half of the peninsula, is the country's least populous.

U.S. citizens make up around 10% of the population, with retirees, business owners who have set up shop here, or commuters who live in Mexico but work in the San Diego metro area among them.

A MULTIFACETED ECONOMY

By Mexican standards, the Baja Peninsula is prosperous, but things were not always so. It was only some six decades ago that Mexico even deemed part of the region to be economically viable enough for statehood, creating the state of Baja California north of the 28th parallel in 1953. Baja California Sur became Mexico's newest state in 1974. Prior to that, the region, once considered far-off and neglected, was administered as a territory directly from Mexico City.

This is Mexico, however, and all is relative, even today. Wages here may be double, triple, or quadruple those in the rest of the country, but you pause when you realize that about $6 a day is still the national average. The presence of the *maquiladora* (foreign-run factories in Mexico) economy has brought up the on-paper average level of prosperity to the peninsula. This industry of tariff-free, export-geared manufacturing congregates on the U.S. border with more than 900 factories providing employment for more than 300,000 people, but critics decry the sweatshop conditions. Urban magnet Tijuana—whose population now stands at 1.9 million—attracts people from all over the country looking for jobs.

Agriculture and fishing contribute to Baja's economy, too. Cotton, fruit, flowers, and ornamental plants grow in the irrigated northern region. (Most of the rest of Baja California is too arid and inhospitable to support much agriculture other than vineyards in Valle de Guadalupe). Large populations of tuna, sardines, and lobster support the fishing industry.

And it goes without saying that tourism is a huge business in Baja, with an impressive $1 billion flowing into Los Cabos annually. Historically, the border region has tallied those kinds of numbers as well, but fears of drug-cartel violence have greatly eaten into tourism revenues for that area.

LIVIN' LA VIDA BUENA

Living the good life in Mexico—specifically in and around Los Cabos—seems to get easier year after year. Americans and Canadians are by far the biggest groups of expats, not only at the peninsula's southern tip, but in communities such as Ensenada, Rosarito, Loreto, and La Paz. In addition to those who have relocated to make Mexico their home, many foreigners have part-time retirement or vacation homes here.

Some visitors to Los Cabos and Baja experience "Sunshine Syndrome" and want to extend their stay indefinitely. But many find living in Baja bears little resemblance to vacationing here. Experts suggest doing a trial rental for a few months to see if living the day-to-day life here is for you.

The population of Los Cabos and the larger communities of Baja are a mix of natives and foreigners, so contractors and shopkeepers are used to dealing with those who speak English. Los Cabos has many English-language publications and opportunities for foreigners to meet up for events or volunteer work.

What's New in Los Cabos

COVID-19 RECOVERY

In 2020 Los Cabos (and indeed, much of the world) was gravely impacted by the COVID-19 virus. Restaurants, hotels, shops, bars, and even cultural institutions shuttered in an attempt to curb its spread, and many ended up closing for good. Baja California Sur, a tourism-heavy area, suffered the second-largest employment loss of any Mexican state during the pandemic. If you're planning a visit, expect stricter safety protocols and remember to call ahead to verify the property is still in operation. As a resilient destination, the Baja Peninsula—no stranger to hurricanes and economic downturns—hopes to make their greatest comeback yet.

DESERT GREEN THUMB

Visitors to the region often ask whether they should stay in San José del Cabo, Cabo San Lucas, or somewhere in between. Those looking for action and nightlife have always opted for the flashier Cabo San Lucas, while San José's hoteliers and restaurateurs have stopped trying to compete on San Lucas's terms, opting instead to market their community for what it is—a cultural, historic art center with a relaxed vibe.

The city has truly come into its own. San José's *zócalo* (central plaza) is a bit of a romantic district where couples stroll after leisurely dining; old haciendas have been transformed into trendy restaurants and charming inns. The city's art scene is thriving with a high-season Thursday Night Art Walk, where those interested in art can visit participating galleries and enjoy free drinks and live music. The desert farms on the outskirts of San José, capitalize on the organic food movement with their farm-to-table

restaurants. By adding cooking schools, markets, tours, spas, and lodging, these desert draws provide more of an experience than just an ordinary meal.

SWING INTO ACTION

Golf is the name of the game in Los Cabos. There are multiple courses tied to names that read like a who's who of golf legends and course designers: Jack Nicklaus, Greg Norman, Davis Love III, Phil Mickelson, Tom Weiskopf, Robert Trent Jones II, and Tom Fazio. Baja golf is more than just Los Cabos: courses line the entire peninsula, if not in the same density as at its southern extreme.

THE RISE OF TODOS SANTOS

Once the province of surfers—the breaks are wicked here, making for some amazing waves, but risky swimming—this town overlooking the western cape about an hour north of Cabo San Lucas is home to a growing artists' community. Just don't call Todos Santos Baja's "hot" new destination, because folks here aren't interested in becoming another Los Cabos. The area is refined and preserves its Mexican culture.

BAJA'S BOOMTOWN

People often ask, "Is Los Cabos the next Cancún?" which implies potential detriment to the environment and the local culture. Los Cabos has grown immensely in the past decade, as noted in the Corridor where construction cranes dominate the skyline, multimillion-dollar renovations of existing hotels, and the birth of new ones. Currently Los Cabos has more than 85 hotels with 18,500 rooms, with plans to keep growing. Yet the question remains whether Los Cabos can handle the boom with so little infrastructure in place.

Chapter 2

TRAVEL SMART

Updated by
Marlise Kast-Myers

★ **CAPITAL:**
La Paz (capital of Baja Sur)

☏ **COUNTRY CODE:**
52

⊘ **TIME:**
2 hours behind New York

⚇ **POPULATION:**
804,708 (Baja Sur)

⚠ **EMERGENCIES:**
911

⊕ **WEB RESOURCES:**
www.visitloscabos.travel
www.gringogazette.com
www.discoverbaja.com
www.visitbajasur.travel
www.golapaz.com

💬 **LANGUAGE:**
Spanish

🚗 **DRIVING:**
On the right

$ CURRENCY:
Mexican Peso (U.S. Dollars
accepted)

⚡ **ELECTRICITY:**
120–220 v/60 cycles; plugs
have two or three rectangu-
lar prongs

✈ **AIRPORT:**
SJD

○ Ciudad Constitución

BAJA
CALIFORNIA
SUR

La Paz
○

San Juan
○ de los Planes

○ Punta Pescadero

○ Los Barriles

Todos Santos ○

○ Cabo Pulmo

○ ○ San José del Cabo

Cabo San Lucas

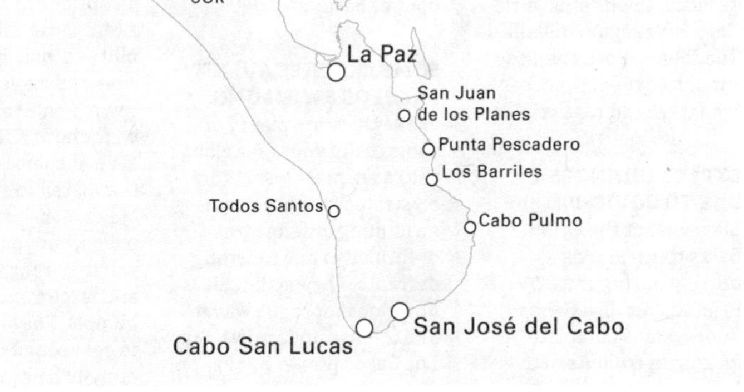

Know Before You Go

Is Baja kid-friendly? Can you drink the water? Do you need special documents to enter the country? You may have a few questions before your trip to Mexico. We've got answers and a few insider tips to help you make the most of your visit, so you can rest easy in paradise.

GET THE LAY OF THE LAND.

Located at the southern tip of the Baja peninsula (Baja California Sur), Los Cabos is comprised of two towns—Cabo San Lucas and San José del Cabo—as well as their connecting "Corridor." Each of these three areas has its own vibe: Cabo San Lucas is a popular nightlife haven; San José del Cabo is quiet and artistic; and the Corrdior is home to a string of luxurious resorts. Many visitors make day trips to nearby destinations, including Todos Santos, La Paz, and East Cape. Note that Baja California Norte at the northern end of the peninsula is not within driving distance of Los Cabos; you will need to fly or take a multiday car trip to reach its beach towns and world-class wine region in Valle de Guadalupe. Both are close enough to the U.S. border for a weekend road trip.

EXPECT CHANGES DUE TO COVID-19.

Like most of the world, Baja's tourism took a beating during the COVID-19 pandemic. Los Cabos underwent a complete lockdown from April to June 2020 and suffered the second-largest employment loss of any Mexican state during the pandemic. More rural areas like Valle de Guadalupe's wine country suffered possibly even more than Los Cabos. In time Baja reopened, putting increased health and safety measures in place, including social distancing and stringent disinfecting practices that will likely continue for months or years to come. In general, you can expect menus to be accessed by digital QR codes on your cell phone, and credit card machines to be wrapped in plastic that is replaced after each transaction. No one knows what the long-term effects to Baja are yet, but you can bet that this resilient destination will bounce back.

SOME BEACHES AREN'T SAFE FOR SWIMMING.

While there are plenty of spots to dip your toes along the coast, most resorts are on stretches of beach where swimming is dangerous or forbidden due to strong currents. The Pacific side is notorious for rogue waves and intense undertows. But Los Cabos proper has 22 swimmable beaches, including Cabo San Lucas' Lover's Beach (the most photographed beach, closest to the iconic "El Arco" arch) and Playa Médano (the party beach). Just southwest of San José, the most popular swimming beaches are Costa Azul and Playa Palmilla. The Corridor's less congested swimming beaches include Las Viudas, Bahía Santa María, and Bahía Chileno. When in doubt, look for green flags that indicate waters are safe for swimming. A red flag will indicate swimming conditions are unsafe.

TIPPING IS EXPECTED.

Tipping is appreciated and expected in Los Cabos. If the service was good, leave 15% to 20% of the bill. Double-check to make sure this amount was not already added to your bill. With tours and private guides, tip accordingly since some depend on tips as their main source of income. When you arrive, it's a good idea to have smaller bills to pay for tips.

A RENTAL CAR CAN BE HANDY.

Rental cars, taxis, and public transportation are all options in Los Cabos, but a rental car will offer flexibility to visit surrounding sites and explore outside of town. Rental agencies can be found at SJD airport and even at some larger hotels. Compared to other parts of Mexico, the roads are nicely paved, but you should still watch out for speed traps and large *topes* (speed bumps). The cheapest way to get around is by bus, but you'll be locked into a schedule and will have to walk or organize additional transportation from the bus stop. If you plan on spending a great deal of time at your resort with few outside excursions, note that many tour operators include transportation in their rates. Taxis are expensive but offer impeccable service and are available 24 hours a day from all hotel lobbies. They don't use meters, but have set rates that are well displayed.

YOU MUST GET CAR INSURANCE FOR RENTALS.

Regardless of the coverage you have from your credit card or travel insurance, you must (by law) have additional Mexican auto insurance to rent a car. This mandatory cost is as much as $40 per day, which is often more than the daily rental fee if you happen to find a good deal online. When renting a car, make sure that your insurance coverage includes an attorney and claims adjusters who will come to the scene of an accident.

KNOWING SOME SPANISH IS HELPFUL.

If you stay within the main tourist areas, nearly everyone will speak English, and if they don't, someone nearby certainly will. In remote towns and areas less visited by travelers, you'll have to speak "Spanglish" or rely on Siri to give you the translation. Speaking the local language is always helpful and appreciated.

IT'S SAFER NOT TO DRINK THE WATER.

Tap water in Mexico is not potable and comes from the surrounding mountains. It's filtered through natural sand beds and then desalinated and purified by major hotels and restaurants. To err on the side of caution, you may want to ask for your beverage *sin hielo* (without ice), as a contaminated piece could ruin a vacation; or opt for bottled water, which is readily available.

HOLD ON TO YOUR TOURIST PERMIT.

You must have a valid passport to enter Mexico and to re-enter the United States. Before landing in Mexico, you'll be given an FMM form (tourist permit) to be stamped at immigration. This allows you to stay in the country for 180 days. Keep this card safe, because you'll need to present it when you leave the country. If you stay longer than the time you were granted or lose your FMM card, you will need to visit an immigration office and pay heavy fines before leaving the country. All foreign visitors are expected to pay an $18 tourism tax at digital kiosks at the airport.

ALL-INCLUSIVE RESORTS HAVE PROS AND CONS.

All-inclusives are like all-you-can-eat buffets— and that has its benefits. You fork over one lump payment and have at it, from food and drink to an expansive pool complex and often water sports and excursions, too. You

might consider this as one way for first-time visitors (especially families) to experience Los Cabos and not to break the bank. But it also means you're less likely to venture off-property to try local food. Note that while some all-inclusives offer endless complimentary amenities, others have a list of exclusions (in fine print) that you'll be billed for in the end.

THERE'S PLENTY OF KID-FRIENDLY ENTERTAINMENT.

From stellar kids' clubs in Cabo San Lucas to epic surf breaks near Rosarito, the entire Baja peninsula has something to appease every age group. Barring the wine region in Valle de Guadalupe, many properties are kid-friendly and go out of their way to entertain children. In La Paz kids can swim with whale sharks and a seal colony. In Cabo there are adrenaline-pumping water activities like Jet Skiing, banana boat rides, snorkeling, surfing, kayaking, and whale-watching (from December–April). Smaller children may prefer a pirate boat tour, camel ride, submarine tour, or interactive program at a Kids' Club. To blend nature and education, visit between August and October when children can see rescued turtle hatchlings.

Getting Here and Around

✈ Air

You can fly nonstop to Los Cabos from Atlanta, Austin, Charlotte, Chicago, Culiacán, Dallas/Fort Worth, Denver, Guadalajara, Houston, Los Angeles, Mexico City, Monterrey, New York, Phoenix, Portland, Sacramento, Salt Lake City, San Diego, San Francisco, San Jose, Seattle, and Tijuana. From most other destinations, you will have to make a connecting flight, either in the United States or in Mexico City. Via nonstop service, Los Cabos is about 2 hours from San Diego, about 2¼ hours from Houston, 3 hours from Dallas/Fort Worth, 2½ hours from Los Angeles, and 2½ hours from Phoenix. Flying time from New York to Mexico City, where you must switch planes to continue to Los Cabos, is 5 hours. Los Cabos is about a 2½-hour flight from Mexico City.

AIRPORTS

Aeropuerto Internacional de San José del Cabo (SJD) is 1 km (½ mile) west of the Carretera Transpeninsular (Highway 1), 13 km (8 miles) north of San José del Cabo, and 48 km (30 miles) northeast of Cabo San Lucas. The airport has restaurants, duty-free shops, and car-rental agencies. Los Cabos flights increase in winter with seasonal flights from U.S. airlines, and, despite growing numbers of visitors to the area, the airport manages to keep up nicely with the crowds.

Aeropuerto General Manuel Márquez de León serves La Paz. It's 11 km (7 miles) northwest of the Baja California Sur capital, which itself is 188 km (117 miles) northwest of Los Cabos.

FLIGHTS

Calafia Airlines flies charter flights from Los Cabos for whale-watching from January through March. Aeroméxico, an airline partner with Delta, has flights to La Paz from Los Angeles, San Diego, Tijuana, and Mexico City.

Alaska Airlines flies nonstop to Los Cabos from Los Angeles, San Diego, Sacramento, San Jose, Seattle, Portland, and San Francisco. American Airlines flies to Los Cabos from Austin, Charlotte, Dallas–Fort Worth, Chicago, Los Angeles, New York (JFK), Phoenix, and Sacramento. British Airways and other European carriers fly to Mexico City where connections can be made for the 2½-hour flight to Los Cabos.

United Airlines has nonstop service from Chicago, Denver, Houston, Los Angeles, and New York. Delta flies to Los Cabos from Atlanta, Los Angeles, and New York. Southwest offers direct flights from San Diego to Los Cabos.

GROUND TRANSPORTATION

If you have purchased a vacation package from an airline or travel agency, transfers are usually included. Otherwise, only the most exclusive hotels in Los Cabos offer transfers. Fares from the airport to hotels in Los Cabos are expensive. The least expensive transport is by city bus Ruta del Desierto ($2) or by shuttle buses that stop at various hotels along the route; fares run $16 to $25 per person. Private taxi fares run from $65 to $100. Some hotels can arrange a pickup, which is much faster and costs about the same as a shuttle. Ask about hotel transfers, especially if you're staying in the East Cape, La Paz, or Todos Santos and not renting a car—cab fares to these areas are astronomical.

Sales representatives from various time-share properties compete vociferously for clients; often you won't realize you've been suckered into a time-share presentation until you get in the van. To avoid this situation, go to the official taxi booths inside the baggage claim or just outside the final customs clearance area and pay for a ticket for a regular shuttle bus. Private taxis, often U.S. vans, are expensive and not metered, so always ask the fare before getting in. Rates change frequently, but it costs about $65 to get to San José del Cabo, $80 to a hotel along the Corridor, and $100 to Cabo San Lucas. After the fourth passenger, it's about an additional $15 per person. Usually only vans accept more than four passengers. At the end of your trip, don't wait until the last minute to book return transport. Make arrangements a few days in advance for shuttle service, and then reconfirm the morning of your departure. Or at least a day in advance, sign up at your hotel's front desk to share a cab with other travelers, reconfirming the morning of your departure.

🚌 Bus

In Los Cabos the main Terminal Central Cabo San Lucas Aguila (Los Cabos Bus Terminal) is about a 10-minute drive west of Cabo San Lucas. There are also terminals in San José del Cabo and La Paz. Express buses, including Aguila and ABC, have air-conditioning and restrooms and travel frequently from the terminal to Todos Santos (one hour) and La Paz (two hours). One-way fare from Cabo San Lucas or San José del Cabo is about $10 (payable in pesos or dollars) to Todos Santos. From either terminal to La Paz will cost around $20. From the Corridor expect to pay about $25 for a taxi to the bus station.

The area's city bus, Ruta del Desierto, has nine stops along the highway between the airport in San José del Cabo and Terminal Aguila in Cabo San Lucas. Although affordable ($2), the trip from the airport to Cabo San Lucas takes over an hour and only departs from Terminal 1 (international flights arrive in Terminal 2). Plus, drop-off points are on Carretera Transpeninsular, meaning you'll still have

to get from the highway to your hotel. If you have time and a sense of adventure, this is your cheapest way into the city.

In La Paz the main Terminal de Autobus is in front of the *malecón*, the seaside promenade.

🚗 Car

Rental cars come in handy when exploring Baja. Countless paved and dirt roads branch off Highway 1 beckoning adventurers toward the mountains, ocean, and sea. Baja Sur's highways and city streets are under constant improvement, and Highway 1 is usually in good condition except during heavy rains. Four-wheel drive comes in handy for hard-core backcountry explorations, but isn't necessary most of the time. Just be aware that some car-rental companies void their insurance policies if you run into trouble off paved roads. If you are even slightly inclined to impromptu adventures, it's best to find out what your company's policy is before you leave the pavement.

GASOLINE

Pemex (the government petroleum monopoly) franchises all gas stations in Mexico. Stations are to be found in both towns as well as on the outskirts of San José del Cabo and Cabo San Lucas and in the Corridor, and there are also several along Highway 1. Gas is measured in liters. Prices run higher than in the United States. Premium unleaded gas (*magna premio*) and regular unleaded gas (*magna sin*) are available nationwide, but it's still a good idea to fill up whenever you can. Fuel quality is generally lower than that in the United States and Europe. Vehicles with fuel-injected engines are likely to have problems after driving extended distances.

Getting Here and Around

Gas-station attendants pump the gas for you and may also wash your windshield and check your oil and tire air pressure. A tip of MX$10 or MX$20 (about 50¢ or $1) is customary depending on the number of services rendered beyond pumping gas.

ROAD CONDITIONS

Mexico Highway 1, also known as the Carretera Transpeninsular, runs the entire 1,700 km (1,054 miles) from Tijuana to Cabo San Lucas. Do not drive the highway at high speeds or at night—it is not lighted and is very narrow much of the way. For a faster option, the toll road begins just after the airport with exit points in San José del Cabo ($2.50) and Cabo San Lucas ($3.50). From there you can jump on Highway 19 to Todos Santos.

Four-lane Highway 19 runs between Cabo San Lucas and Todos Santos, joining Highway 1 below La Paz. The four-lane road between San José del Cabo and Cabo San Lucas is usually in good condition. Roadwork along the highway is common and may cause delays or require detours.

In rural areas roads tend to be iffy and in unpredictable conditions. Use caution, especially during the rainy season, when rock slides and potholes are a problem, and be alert for animals—cattle, goats, horses, coyotes, and dogs in particular—even on highways. If you have a long distance to cover, start early, fill up on gas, and remember to keep your tank full, as gas stations are not as abundant here as they are in the United States or Europe. Allow extra time for unforeseen obstacles.

Signage is not always adequate in Mexico, and the best advice is to travel with a companion and a good map. Take your time. Always lock your car, and never leave valuables in plain sight (the trunk will suffice for daytime outings, but be smart about stashing expensive items in there in full view of curious onlookers).

Your smart phone's map should suffice to get you around, but it's a good idea to stock up on every map your rental-car company has for back up. Gas stations generally do not carry maps. Most car-rental agencies have GPS units available for around $15 per day with regional maps preprogrammed.

ROADSIDE EMERGENCIES

The Mexican Tourism Ministry operates a fleet of more than 350 pickup trucks, known as the Angeles Verdes, or Green Angels. Bilingual drivers provide mechanical help, first aid, radio-telephone communication, basic supplies and small parts, towing, tourist information, and protection. Services are free; spare parts, fuel, and lubricants are provided at cost. Tips are always appreciated ($20–$30 for big jobs, $10–$15 for minor repairs). The Green Angels patrol sections of the major highways daily 8–8 (later on holiday weekends). If you break down, call Green Angels, or if you don't have a cell phone, **pull off the road as far as possible,** lift the hood of your car, hail a passing vehicle, and ask the driver to **notify the patrol.** Most bus and truck drivers will be quite helpful. If you witness an accident, do not stop to help—it could be a ploy to rob you or could get you interminably involved with the police. Instead, notify the nearest official.

SAFETY ON THE ROAD

The mythical *banditos* are not a big concern in Baja. Still, **do your best to avoid driving at night,** especially in rural areas. Cows and burros grazing alongside the road can pose as real a danger as the ones actually in the road—you never know when they'll decide to wander into traffic.

Though it isn't common in Los Cabos, police may pull you over for supposedly breaking the law, or for being a good prospect for a scam. If it happens to you, remember to be polite. Tell the officer that you would like to talk to the police captain when you get to the station. The officer will usually let you go. If you're stopped for speeding, the officer should hold your license until you pay the fine at the local police station, but he will always prefer taking a *mordida* (small bribe) to wasting his time at the police station. Corruption is a fact of life in Mexico, and the $20–$40 it costs to get your license back is supplementary income for the officer who pulled you over with no intention of taking you to police headquarters.

RENTAL CARS

When you reserve a car, ask about cancellation penalties, taxes, drop-off charges (if you're planning to pick up the car in one city and leave it in another), and surcharges (for being under or over a certain age, for additional drivers, or for driving across state or country borders or beyond a specific distance from your point of rental). All these things can add substantially to your costs. Request car seats and extras such as GPS when you book.

Rates are sometimes—but not always— better if you book in advance or reserve through a rental agency's website. There are other reasons to book ahead though: for popular destinations, during busy times of the year, or to ensure that you get certain types of cars (vans, SUVs, sports cars). We've also found that car-rental prices are much better when reservations are made ahead of travel, from the United States. Prices can be as much as 50% more when renting a car upon arrival in Los Cabos. Shockingly low rates through third-party sites usually result in hidden fees when you actually pay for the car on-site. Los Cabos–based

Cactus Car includes insurance, taxes, and unlimited mileage in the quoted rate and have a solid fleet of compact cars, SUVs, and vans. They have some of the best prices in the area and include 30% discounts on local attractions when booking through their website. If you plan on renting a car in the United States and driving it across the border, the only agency that allows (and encourages) this is California Baja Rent-A-Car. Keep in mind that your pickup point is San Diego County.

■ TIP➜ **Make sure that a confirmed reservation guarantees you a car. Agencies sometimes overbook, particularly for busy weekends and holiday periods.**

Taxi fares are especially steep in Los Cabos, and a rental car can come in handy if you'd like to dine at the Corridor hotels, travel frequently between the two towns, stay at a hotel along the Cabo Corridor, spend more than a few days in Los Cabos, or plan to see some of the sights outside Los Cabos proper, such as La Paz, Todos Santos, or even farther afield. If you don't want to rent a car, your hotel concierge or tour operator can arrange for a car with a driver or limousine service.

Convertibles and jeeps are popular rentals, but beware of sunburn and windburn, and remember there's nowhere to stash your belongings out of sight. Specify whether you want air-conditioning and manual or automatic transmission. If you rent from a major U.S.-based company, you can find a compact car for about $60 per day ($420 per week), including automatic transmission, unlimited mileage, and 16% tax; however, having the protection of complete coverage insurance will add another $25 per day, depending on the company, so you should figure the cost of insurance into your budget. You will pay considerably more (probably double) for a larger or higher-end car. Most

Getting Here and Around

vendors negotiate considerably if tourism is slow; ask about special rates if you're renting by the week.

To increase the likelihood of getting the car you want and to get considerably better car-rental prices, make arrangements before you leave for your trip. You can sometimes find cheaper rates online. No matter how you book, rates are generally much lower when you reserve a car in advance outside Mexico.

In Mexico your own driver's license is acceptable. In most cases the minimum rental age is 21, although some companies may tack on a surcharge for drivers under 25. A valid driver's license, major credit card, and Mexican car insurance are required.

CAR-RENTAL INSURANCE

In Mexico the law states that drivers must carry mandatory Third Party Liability, an expense that is not covered by U.S. insurance policies or by credit card companies. To be safe, agree to at least the minimum rental insurance. It's best to be completely covered when driving in Mexico.

If you own a car, your personal auto insurance may cover a rental to a degree, though not all policies protect you abroad; always read your policy's fine print.

Even if you have auto insurance back home, you should buy the collision- or loss-damage waiver (CDW or LDW) from the car-rental company, which eliminates your liability for damage to the car. Some credit cards offer CDW coverage, but it's only supplemental to your own insurance and rarely covers SUVs, minivans, luxury models, and the like. If your coverage is secondary, you may still be liable for loss-of-use costs from the car-rental company. But no credit-card insurance is valid unless you use that card for *all* transactions, from reserving to paying the final bill. In general, U.S. and Canadian auto insurance policies are not recognized in Mexico, and the few that are only cover specific coverage like damage and theft. Rather than fear what *might* happen, it is best to purchase a Mexican liability insurance package from your rental company so you know you're covered.

Ride-Sharing

Ride shares such as Uber and Lyft are not readily available in Los Cabos. Although they can sometimes operate around town, they are not permitted to pick up passengers from the airport.

Taxi

Taxis are plentiful throughout Baja Sur, even in the smallest towns. Government-certified taxis have a license with a photo of the driver and a taxi number prominently displayed. Fares are exorbitant in Los Cabos, and the taxi union is very powerful. Some visitors have taken to boycotting taxis completely, using rental cars and buses instead, the latter of which can be the most time-consuming. The fare between Cabo San Lucas and San José del Cabo runs about $50–$60—more at night. Cabs from Corridor hotels to either town run at least $30 each way. Expect to pay at least $65 from the airport to hotels in San José, and closer to $100 to Cabo.

In La Paz taxis are readily available and inexpensive. A ride within town costs under $5; a trip to Pichilingue costs between $10 and $15. Illegal taxis aren't a problem in this region.

Essentials

🏃 Activities

Los Cabos has something for everyone in a relatively small area. Whether you want a lively beach or a secluded cove, high-speed Jet Ski rides or leisurely fishing trips, deep-sea scuba expeditions or casual snorkeling, the waters off Cabo and the surrounding area offer endless possibilities.

Long stretches of coastline along the Sea of Cortez and the Pacific Ocean make Los Cabos a beautiful spot for a beach vacation. Be careful about where you take a dip, though—many of the beaches border sea waters that are too dangerous for swimming due to strong undercurrents. Nearly 360 warm and sunny days per year make Los Cabos a natural wonderland, where outdoor activities—both land- and water-based—can be enjoyed year-round.

Waterskiing, Jet-Skiing, and sailing are found almost exclusively at Cabo San Lucas's Playa El Médano, where you can also go kayaking. At least eight good scuba-diving sites are near Playa del Amor. The East Cape, which includes the town of Cabo Pulmo, is a great area for kayaking, fishing, diving, and snorkeling. In fact, Cabo Pulmo has the only coral reef in the Sea of Cortez and there are numerous spots to dive—even just snorkeling right off the beach is an experience. Both the Sea of Cortez and the Pacific provide great waves for year-round surfing whether you're a longboarder or a hotshot on a short board. Still, in the spot known as the "Marlin Capital of the World," sportfishing remains one of the most famous and popular water sports.

If you'd like to mix up your Los Cabos experience with some land-based adventures, the area's desert terrain lends itself to all sorts of possibilities, whether you're a thrill seeker or a laid-back bird-watcher. You can explore cactus fields, sand dunes, waterfalls, and mountain forests on foot or horseback. Ziplining, camel rides, dune buggy tours, and electric bikes are all the rage around Arroyo Azul. Back in town you can play beach volleyball on Playa El Médano, tennis at one of the hotels, or golf at one of the many courses available. If you are fortunate enough to be in Los Cabos during the whale migration (December through April)—when the weather is perfect—a whale-watching trip with one of the many tour-boat operators is a must.

⚓ Beaches

Along the rocky cliffs of the Pacific Ocean and the Sea of Cortez lie many bays, coves, and roughly 80 km (about 50 miles) of sandy beach. The waters range from translucent green to deep navy, and even a stunning turquoise on some days of the year.

The destination has 22 swimmable beaches but most people come to Médano's active 3-km (2-mile) stretch for the crowds, since there's no better place to people-watch. Gorgeous Playa del Amor (Lover's Beach) near the famous *El Arco* (the Arch) is five minutes across the bay by water taxi ($10–$15). Do not pay a round-trip fare since the likelihood of your boat returning is slim. There are plenty of boats that will take you back to the mainland. It's a great spot for swimming, though the waters can be somewhat busy with all the *panga* (skiff) traffic. Just southwest of San José, the most popular beaches are Costa Azul and Playa Palmilla. Between Cabo San Lucas and San José del Cabo are the Corridor's less congested beaches of Las Viudas, Bahía Santa María, and Bahía Chileno.

Essentials

No other beaches are within walking distance of either Cabo San Lucas or San José del Cabo; some can be accessed by boat, but most require a car ride (unless you're staying at a Corridor hotel nearby). Since beach service and amenities are limited to hotel guests, it is imperative that you lug extra water, especially if you are adventuring during the searing summer months.

SUN AND SAFETY

If swimming in the ocean or sea is at the top of your vacation checklist, opt for a property on a protected cove, where swimming is permitted. Most resorts in the region are on stretches of beach where swimming is dangerous or forbidden due to strong currents. Look for the beach warning flags posted outside resorts: red means conditions are dangerous, yellow signals to use caution, and green signifies conditions are safe. Barely visible rocks and strong undertows make many of the beaches unsuitable for swimming. Use precaution as tides change from serenely calm or dangerously turbulent, depending on the day or even the hour. The Pacific side is notorious for rogue waves and intense undertows. Also, the sun here is fierce: don't underestimate the need for water-proof sunscreen and a wide-brimmed hat.

BEACH ETIQUETTE

As on most beaches in Mexico, nudity is not permitted on Los Cabos beach-es. If you head to a beachside bar, it's appropriate to put on a cover-up, although you'd be hard-pressed to find a strict dress code at any of these places unless you're at one of the more posh resorts.

As tempting as it is to pick up seashells from the beach, be advised that U.S. Customs commonly seizes these items upon reentry to the United States. Packing a picnic or cooler for a day at the beach is a great idea, as few of the public beaches have restaurants or food vendors. A few beaches have vendors offering umbrella rentals, but if you're really keen on having one for shelter, it's best to take your own.

BEACH FACILITIES

As a general rule, Los Cabos beaches are no-frills, with very few public facilities. There is no established lifeguard program in the entire Los Cabos region. Hotels will often post a red flag on the beach to alert swimmers to strong currents and undertows, but you won't see such warn-ings on the stretches of public beach along the coasts.

More and more of the public beaches have toilets, but you'll still be hard-pressed to find a shower. The picnic tables, grills or fire pits, playgrounds, and other amenities common at U.S. beaches simply aren't part of the scene in Los Cabos. If you want or need anything for your day at the beach, it's best to pack it yourself. If any of the following facilities are present at a beach, we'll list them: food and drink, lifeguards, parking (fee or free), showers, toilets, and water sports.

Mexican beaches are free and open to the public, though some of the resort developments along the Corridor are doing their best to keep their beaches private for guests. Resort boundaries are usually very well marked; any beach after that is free to all.

If you like:	In Cabo San Lucas	Along the Corridor	In San José del Cabo or beyond
Crystal-clear water	El Médano, Playa del Amor	Bahía Santa María	San José del Cabo's main beach (aka Playa del Sol)
Snorkeling/Swimming	Lover's Beach (near the Sand Falls area)	Bahía Santa María, Bahía Chileno	For snorkeling, keep going to the East Cape and Cabo Pulmo area.
Surfing	Monuments Beach (at eastern end of El Médano Beach)	Costa Azul stretch, Acapulquito Beach (at the Cabo Surf Hotel)	Shipwreck, 14½ km (9 miles) northeast of San José; Nine Palms, just beyond
Beachside or ocean-view bars	The Office, Mango Deck, Billygan's at El Médano Beach	Zipper's at Costa Azul, or Acapulquito Beach at 7 Seas at Cabo Surf Hotel	Buzzard's Bar & Grill (east of La Playita) or El Ganzo Beach Club
Undiscovered beaches	El Faro Viejo Beach is difficult to access, with dangerous waves, but is a gem for sunbathing.	A drive along the highway will reveal many "acceso a playa" signs—be wary of waves.	Los Frailes and Cabo Pulmo at Playa Los Arbolitos is distant—a full day's adventure—but pristine for water activities and well worth the time.

Dining

Prepare yourself for a gourmand's delight. The competition, creativity, selection, and, yes, even the prices are utterly beyond comprehension. From elegant dining rooms to casual seafood cafés to simple *taquerías,* Los Cabos serves up anything from standard to thrilling fare.

Seafood is the true highlight here. Fresh catches that land on the menus include dorado (mahimahi), *lenguado* (halibut), *cabrilla* (sea bass), *jurel* (yellowtail), wahoo, and marlin. Local lobster, shrimp, and octopus are particularly good. Fish grilled over a mesquite wood fire is perhaps the most indigenous and tasty seafood dish, while the most popular may be the tacos *de pescado* (fish tacos): traditionally a deep-fried fillet wrapped in a handmade corn tortilla, served with shredded cabbage, cilantro, and salsas. Beef and pork—commonly served marinated and grilled—are also delicious. Many restaurants import their steak,

lamb, duck, and quail from the state of Sonora, Mexico's prime pastureland, and also from the United States, though many of the high-end spots are only using local ingredients.

In San José international chefs prepare excellent Continental, French, Asian, and Mexican dishes in lovely, intimate restaurants. Following in the footsteps of Northern Baja's Valle de Guadalupe, several restaurants on the outskirts of San José del Cabo are offering farm-to-table cuisine, as well as cooking courses and tours. This organic movement has spread from the farmers' market in San José del Cabo to the luxury resorts along the coast that rely on the farms for their daily menu. The Corridor is the place to go for exceptional (and expensive) hotel restaurants, while intense competition for business in Los Cabos means many restaurants go through periodic remodels and reinvention, the Corridor restaurants included.

Essentials

MEALS AND MEALTIMES

Although Mexicans often prefer dining late into the evening, be warned that if you arrive at restaurants in Los Cabos after 10 pm, you're taking your chances. Most places are open year-round, sometimes closing for a month in the middle of the hot Baja summer, and many Los Cabos restaurants close one night a week, typically Sunday or Monday.

RESERVATIONS AND DRESS

Reservations are mentioned when essential, but are a good idea during high season (mid-November to May). Restaurant websites are common, and many let you make online reservations.

Dress is often casual. Collared shirts and nice slacks are fine at even the most upscale places. In formal restaurants men must wear closed-toe shoes, so leave the flip-flops behind. Shirts and shoes (or sandals) should be worn anytime you're away from the beach.

SMOKING AND DRINKING

Mexican law prohibits smoking in all enclosed businesses, including restaurants. The drinking age here is 18. Establishments do ask for IDs.

What It Costs in U.S. Dollars			
$	$$	$$$	$$$$
AT DINNER			
under $12	$12–$20	$21–$30	over $30

⚠ Emergencies

Mexico's emergency number for police and the fire department is 911. The number can be used throughout the state, and there are English-speaking operators. Another option is air medical services—find a provider through the Association of Air Medical Services (AAMS); several of the U.S.-headquartered operations have bases around Mexico so they can reach you more quickly.

✚ Health and Safety

COVID-19

A novel coronavirus brought all travel to a virtual standstill in the first half of 2020. Although the illness is mild in most people, some experience severe and even life-threatening complications. Once travel started up again, albeit slowly and cautiously, travelers were asked to be particularly careful about hygiene and to avoid any unnecessary travel, especially if they are sick.

Older adults, especially those over 65, have a greater chance of having severe complications from COVID-19. The same is true for people with weaker immune systems or those living with some types of medical conditions, including diabetes, asthma, heart disease, cancer, HIV/AIDS, kidney disease, and liver disease. Starting two weeks before a trip, anyone planning to travel should be on the lookout for some of the following symptoms: cough, fever, chills, trouble breathing, muscle pain, sore throat, new loss of smell or taste. If you experience any of these symptoms, you should not travel at all.

And to protect yourself during travel, do your best to avoid contact with people showing symptoms. Wash your hands often with soap and water. Limit your time in public places, and, when you are out and about, wear a cloth face mask that covers your nose and mouth. Indeed, a mask will be required in most places, such as on an airplane or in a confined space like a theater, where you share the space with a lot of people. You may wish to bring extra supplies, such as disenfecting wipes, hand sanitizer (12-ounce bottles were allowed in carry-on luggage at this writing), and a first-aid kit with a thermometer.

Given how abruptly travel was curtailed in March 2020, it is wise to consider protecting yourself by purchasing a travel insurance policy that will reimburse you for any costs related to COVID-19 related cancellations. Not all travel insurance policies protect against pandemic-related cancellations, so always read the fine print.

FOOD AND DRINK

In Mexico the biggest health risk is turista (traveler's diarrhea) caused by consuming contaminated fruit, vegetables, or water. To minimize risks, avoid questionable-looking street stands and bad-smelling food even in the toniest establishments; and if you're not sure of a restaurant's standards, pass up ceviche (raw fish cured in lemon juice). The Mexican Department of Health warns that marinating in lemon juice does not constitute the "cooking" that would make the shellfish safe to eat. Also avoid raw vegetables that haven't been, or can't be, peeled (e.g., lettuce and tomatoes).

In general Los Cabos does not pose as great a health risk as other parts of Mexico. Nevertheless, watch what you eat, and drink only bottled water or water that has been boiled for a few minutes.

Water in most major hotels is safe for brushing your teeth, but to avoid any risk, use bottled water. Hotels with water-purification systems will post signs to that effect in the rooms.

When ordering cold drinks at establishments that don't seem to get many tourists, skip the ice (order it sin hielo). You can usually identify ice made commercially from purified water by its uniform shape.

Stay away from uncooked food and unpasteurized milk and milk products. Mexicans excel at grilling meats and seafood, but be smart about where you eat—ask locals to recommend their favorite restaurants or taco stands, and if you have the slightest hesitation about cleanliness or freshness, skip it. Fruit and licuados (smoothies) stands are wonderful for refreshing treats, but again, ask around, be fanatical about freshness, and watch to see how the vendor handles the food. Mexico is a food lover's adventure land, and many travelers wouldn't dream of passing up the chance to try something new and delicious.

Mild cases of turista may respond to Imodium (known generically as loperamide), Lomotil, or Pepto-Bismol, all of which you can buy over the counter. Keep in mind that these drugs can complicate more serious illnesses. You'll need to replace fluids, so drink plenty of purified water.

Chamomile tea (té de manzanilla) and peppermint tea (té de menta/hierbabuena) can be good for calming upset stomachs, and they're readily available in restaurants throughout Mexico.

It's smart to travel with a few packets of drink mix such as EmergenC when you travel to Mexico. You can also make a salt-sugar solution (½ teaspoon salt and 4 tablespoons sugar per quart of water) to

Essentials

rehydrate. Drinking baking soda dissolved in water can neutralize the effects of an acidic meal and help with heavy indigestion or an upset stomach. It might also help prevent a painful hangover if taken after excessive drinking.

If your fever and diarrhea last longer than a day or two, see a doctor—you may have picked up a parasite or disease that requires prescription medication.

DIVERS' ALERT
■ TIP→ **Do not fly within 24 hours of scuba diving.**

MEDICAL INSURANCE AND ASSISTANCE
Consider buying trip insurance with medical-only coverage. Neither Medicare nor some private insurers cover medical expenses anywhere outside the United States. Medical-only policies typically reimburse you for medical care (excluding that related to preexisting conditions) and hospitalization abroad and provide for evacuation. You still have to pay the bills and await reimbursement from the insurer though.

Another option is to sign up with a medical-evacuation assistance company. Membership gets you doctor referrals, emergency evacuation or repatriation, 24-hour hotlines for medical consultation, and other assistance. International SOS Assistance Emergency and AirMed International provide evacuation services and medical referrals. MedjetAssist offers medical evacuation.

SAFETY
Since 2017 Los Cabos has seen a 90% decrease in violent crime. At the time of writing, there are no travel advisories for Los Cabos other than a global warning related to COVID-19. Stay up to date with travel warnings on the U.S. State Department website ⊕ www.travel. state.gov. While travelers are generally safe, standard precautions always apply : distribute your cash, credit cards, and IDs between a deep front pocket and an inside jacket pocket, and don't carry excessive amounts of cash. Leave your passport, along with other valuables, in your in-room safe—and be sure to make copies of your passport and credit cards to leave with someone back home.

🖊 Immunizations
Although no immunizations are currently required for travel to Mexico, it's a good idea to keep up to date with routine vaccinations and boosters.

🛏 Lodging
Expect high-quality accommodations wherever you stay in Los Cabos—whether at a huge resort or a small bed-and-breakfast. Much of the area's beaches are now backed by major properties, all vying to create the most desirable stretch on the sand. For the privilege of staying in these hot properties, you'll pay top dollar—and more for oceanfront rooms with incredible views.

Sprawling Mediterranean-style resorts of generally 200 to 400 rooms dominate the coastline of Los Cabos, especially on the 29-km-long (18-mile-long) Corridor, but also on the beaches in Cabo San Lucas and San José (the town of San José is not on the coast, but inland just a bit). Currently Los Cabos has more than 85 hotels with 18,500 rooms, including luxurious new properties from Montage, Nobu, and Four Seasons.

Los Cabos resorts are known for their lavish pools and lush grounds in addition to their beachfront access, although the majority of beaches on the densely developed coastline, with the notable exception of Playa Médano in Cabo San Lucas, can have an oddly deserted appearance because of the dangerous currents in the water and the predominance of luxurious pools.

If you're inclined to go beyond the beach-and-party vibe of Cabo San Lucas, it's well worth spending time in Todos Santos *(see Los Cabos Side Trips chapter)* and San José del Cabo. Both towns offer exceptional independent hotels and inns, as well as burgeoning art scenes, great restaurants, and ambience you won't find elsewhere.

ALL-INCLUSIVES

Many of the resorts along the Corridor offer all-inclusive plans that cover everything from the food and drink to an expansive pool complex and often water sports and excursions, too. Choosing that option is good if you want to check into your hotel and stay put for the duration of your stay, but it also means you'll have little reason to venture out and taste some of the diverse and remarkable food available in this region. Guests looking to get a feel for the local culture may find the generic, chain-hotel atmosphere frustrating. On the other hand, first-time visitors might consider this a viable option to whet the appetite without draining the annual vacation fund.

CABOS WITH KIDS

If you're heading down to Los Cabos with the little ones in tow, you're in luck, because many properties are kid-friendly. Unless they are adults-only properties, most of them welcome children with Kids' Clubs. Many of the independent hotels listed don't restrict children, but their size and arrangement suggest more adult-oriented accommodations. We've mentioned these factors in our reviews.

CABO CONDOS

If you're planning to stay a week or more, renting a condo can be more economical and convenient than a hotel. Los Cabos has countless condominium properties, ranging from modest homes to ultraluxurious villas in such exclusive areas as Palmilla near San José del Cabo and the hill-clinging Pedregal neighborhood above Cabo San Lucas and its marina. Many private owners rent out their condos, either through the development's rental pool or property management companies. The price is the same for both, but with the latter you might get a better selection.

Nearly all condos are furnished and have a fully equipped kitchen, a television, bed and bath linens, laundry facilities, and housekeeping service. Most are seaside and range from studios to three-bedroom units. A minimum stay of one week is typically required, though rules can vary by property. Start the booking process at least four months in advance, especially for high-season rentals.

PRICES

Bargains here are few; rooms generally start at $200 a night and can climb into the thousands. For groups of six or more planning an extended stay, condos or villas can be a convenient and economical option, though you should always book early.

Hotel rates in Baja California Sur are subject to a 16% sales tax. Service charges (at least 15%) and meals generally aren't included in hotel rates, except at some all-inclusive resorts. Several of the high-end properties include a daily service charge in your bill; be sure you know the policy before tipping (though additional tips are always welcome). We always list the available facilities, but we don't specify extra costs; so always ask about what's included.

Essentials

RESERVATIONS

With its growing popularity, Los Cabos has a high season that seems to keep gaining months. It's been said that high season is now mid-November through May, though the crowds are a bit more manageable in October and after mid-April. Summers can be scorchers in this desert landscape, reaching temperatures in the 90s and above. No matter what time of year you visit, rain is pretty unlikely. Los Cabos gets most of its rain—about 15 days—between August and September, so book accordingly. Book your trip early—as many as six months in advance for top holidays such as Thanksgiving, the December celebrations, and New Year's and at least three months in advance for other high-season stays. Note that during any holidays, a seven-night minimum stay is required at most high-end resorts.

WEDDINGS

If you decide to get married in Los Cabos, you'll be able to enjoy nuptials with friends and family in a gorgeous setting, and there'll be no worries about heading out for the honeymoon the morning after—you're already there. Los Cabos has a bevy of choices, and prices, for dream destination weddings. If money is no object, look into the big-name properties such as One&Only Palmilla, Las Ventanas al Paraíso, Esperanza, Grand Velas, and the Marquis Los Cabos, where celebs often say "I do." Palmilla and Grand Velas even have official directors of celebrations to assist. At Las Ventanas the romance director has an entire program dedicated to dream weddings, offering everything from a fireworks display to a ring bearer on horseback. But the true champion of weddings has got to be the Dreams Los Cabos property, where as many as five couples get hitched each week. *For more information on planning a wedding, civil ceremony, or civil union in Los Cabos, see Weddings in the Experience chapter.*

What It Costs in U.S. Dollars

	$	$$	$$$	$$$$
HOTELS	under $200	$200–$299	$300–$399	over $399

Money

Mexico has a reputation for being inexpensive, but Los Cabos is one of the most expensive places to visit in the country. Prices rise from 10% to 18% annually and are comparable to those in Southern California.

Prices in this book are quoted most often in U.S. dollars, which are readily accepted in Los Cabos (although you should always have pesos on you if you venture anywhere beyond the walls of a resort). *For information on taxes, see Taxes.*

ATMS AND BANKS

ATMs (*cajas automáticas*) are commonplace in Los Cabos and La Paz. Be sure to inform your bank of upcoming travel so that your card is not declined. If you're going to a less-developed area, though, go equipped with cash. Cirrus and Plus cards are the most commonly accepted. The ATMs at Banamex, one of the oldest nationwide banks, tend to be the most reliable. Bancomer is another bank with many ATM locations.

Many Mexican ATMs cannot accept PINs with more than four digits. If yours is longer, change your PIN to four digits before you leave home. If you've entered your PIN correctly yet your transaction still can't be completed, chances are that the computer lines are busy, the machine has run out of money, or it's being serviced. Don't give up. Expect to pay a $5 withdrawal fee with each ATM transaction.

Where Should I Stay?

	NEIGHBORHOOD VIBE	PROS	CONS
Cabo San Lucas	With lively beaches and a party atmosphere, Cabo continues its meteoric climb into the five-star stratosphere.	Close to the action; nearly every hotel in Cabo has undergone some kind of renovation recently; near swimmable Playa El Médano.	Not for those who want a quiet vacation or a truly authentic lodging experience.
The Corridor	The stretch that connects San José with Cabo San Lucas is booming with luxurious megaresorts made for visitors.	You'll have your choice of golf courses, private villas, and upscale condos. Many resorts have all-inclusive options.	Most beaches on the Corridor are not swimmable; no reason to venture out; lacks local culture of other neighborhoods.
San José del Cabo	The most charming of the Los Cabos region, the area retains its Mexican colonial roots and offers boutique hotels and bed-and-breakfasts.	Closest to the international airport; some areas are very walkable; farthest from the crowds that gravitate toward downtown Cabo San Lucas's fiesta atmosphere.	Some areas are remote from town centers; not as lively as Cabo San Lucas if you're looking for a party.
Todos Santos	Forty-five miles north of Cabo San Lucas, this charming Pueblo Mágico (magical town) has shifted from day-trip town to a destination in its own right.	Local flavor, boutique B&Bs, and great shopping abound in Todos Santos. But the area isn't short on luxury either, thanks to its new Paradero Todos Santos eco-hotel.	It's far enough from Cabo San Lucas that you'll need a car to reach its lively bars and restaurants, although the neighborhood has some great options itself.
East Cape	The "other" side of Los Cabos most visitors don't see, this off-the-beath path area is for adventurers and trendsetters who prioritize natural beauty and quiet over nightlife.	Few crowds flock here, and you're close to the stunning Cabo Pulmo National Park. You can still find luxury at the Four Seasons Resort Costa Palmas.	The East Cape is far from the more developed neighborhoods of Los Cabos and there isn't much nightlife. The roads are often rough and unpaved.

Essentials

CREDIT CARDS

When shopping you can often get better prices if you pay with cash, particularly in small shops. But you'll receive wholesale exchange rates when you make purchases with credit cards. These exchange rates are usually better than those that banks give you for changing money. The decision to pay cash or to use a credit card depends on whether the establishment finds bargaining acceptable, and whether you want the safety net of your card's purchase protection. To avoid fraud or errors, it's wise to make sure that pesos are clearly marked on all credit-card receipts. Keep in mind that foreign transaction fees tack on an additional 3% for every purchase made abroad. If you travel often, consider getting a credit card with no foreign transaction fees and flexible travel rewards.

CURRENCY AND EXCHANGE

The currency in Los Cabos is the Mexican peso (MXP), though prices are often given in U.S. dollars. Mexican currency comes in denominations of 20-, 50-, 100-, 200-, and 500-peso bills. Coins come in denominations of 1, 2, 5, 10, and 20 pesos and 20 and 50 centavos (20-centavo coins are only rarely seen). Many of the coins are very similar, so check carefully; bills, however, are different colors and easily distinguished.

At this writing US$1 was equivalent to approximately MXP 20.04.

🛈 Nightlife

Crowds roam the main strip of Cabo San Lucas every night from happy hour through last call, staggering home just before dawn. It's not hard to see why this is *the* nightlife capital of southern Baja.

It's not all about the parties though; enjoying a fine dinner is a time-honored way to spend a Los Cabos evening. During the slow, sweltering months of August and September, some establishments curtail their offerings or close for a few weeks altogether. Don't fret though: you'll find nightlife here no matter what season you visit.

WHAT'S WHERE

Cabo San Lucas: Cabo is internationally famous (or infamous) for being a raucous party town. If Vegas hadn't already co-opted the "what happens here, stays here" mentality, Cabo San Lucas might have snatched it up. You can experience spring break here, even if you went to college 30 years ago. Quiet Cabo nightlife does exist; you just need to look a bit harder.

The Corridor: This sprawling strip between the two cities is the province of big resorts and their in-house cocktail bars. Expect upscale venues (and patrons). A few nightspots not affiliated with any hotel do exist here and are quite popular.

San José del Cabo: Proprietors here say that you "graduate" to San José del Cabo after you go through your party phase in Cabo San Lucas. For a cozy, romantic, and often cultural evening, nothing beats the quieter and more intimate San José nightlife, where it's all about a good drink and conversation.

WHAT IT COSTS

Baja's very own Tecate beer can be pricier here than at home. Many places compete for the best happy-hour deals, often about $3 for a *cerveza*. Margaritas cost around $7. A glass of wine in an upscale venue should run $10 and up. The rowdy beach bars in Cabo San Lucas have waitstaff blowing whistles while handing out test tubes of vodka. Don't be fooled—there's a charge and tip behind each offer, so expect to pay around $5 for each. Many places add a 15%–20% tip to your tab. (Look for the word *servicio* on your bill.) A big musical event means a nominal cover charge of a few dollars; those are rare.

WHAT'S GOING ON

You'll find copies of Los Cabos publications in hotels, restaurants, and bars all over the city. The most helpful are *Los Cabos Visitors Guide* and *Los Cabos Magazine*. The free English-language newspapers *Gringo Gazette* (⊕ *www.gringogazette.com*) and *Destino: Los Cabos* (⊕ *www.destinomagazine.com*) offer timely and cultural articles on the ever-changing scene. (We especially like the *Gringo Gazette* for its fun-loving, humorous look at expatriate life in Los Cabos.) These publications are available free at many hotels and stores or at racks on the sidewalk.

DRINKING AGE

Mexico's nationwide drinking age is 18. Bars here check IDs at the door if they have any doubts about your age. Consumption of alcohol or the possession of an open beverage container is not permitted on public sidewalks, streets, or beaches (outside of licensed establishments), or in motor vehicles, whether moving or stationary.

Smoking is prohibited in all enclosed businesses, including bars and restaurants. Lighting up is allowed at outdoor-seating areas provided by such venues, but not indoors.

SAFETY

Nighttime is reasonably safe and secure here. Ask the bar or restaurant to call a taxi for you if you're going far. Taxis aren't cheap, but you shouldn't put a price on getting home safely. All the standard precautions apply: stick to well-lighted areas where people congregate. Wandering dark, deserted streets or lonely stretches of beaches is never wise, nor is staggering home in a state of inebriation.

🛂 Passport and Visa

A passport, or other WHTI (Western Hemisphere Travel Initiative) compliant document, is required of all visitors to Mexico, including U.S. citizens who may remember the days when only driver's licenses were needed to cross the border. Upon entering Mexico all visitors must get a tourist card (FMM card). If you're arriving by plane from the United States or Canada, the standard tourist card will be given to you on the plane. They're also available through travel agents and Mexican consulates and at the border if you're entering by land.

■ TIP→ **You're given a portion of the tourist card form upon entering Mexico. Keep track of this documentation throughout your trip: you will need it when you depart. You'll be asked to hand it, your ticket, and your passport to airline representatives at the gate when boarding for departure.**

If you lose your tourist card, plan to spend some time (and about $60) sorting it out with Mexican officials at the airport on departure.

A tourist card costs about $30. The fee is generally tacked onto the price of your airline ticket. If you enter by land or boat you'll have to pay the fee separately. You're exempt from the fee if you enter by sea and stay less than 72 hours, or by land and do not stray past the 26- to 30-km (16- to 18-mile) checkpoint into the country's interior.

Tourist cards and visas are valid from 15 to 180 days, at the discretion of the immigration officer at your point of entry (90 days for Australians). Americans,

Essentials

Canadians, New Zealanders, and the British may request up to 180 days for a tourist card or visa extension. If you're planning an extended stay, plead with the immigration official for the maximum allowed days at the time of entry. It will save you time and money later.

■ TIP→ **Mexico has some of the strictest policies about children entering the country. Minors traveling with one parent need notarized permission from the absent parent.**

If you're a single parent traveling with children up to age 18, you must have a notarized letter from the other parent stating that the child has his or her permission to leave his or her home country. The child must be carrying the original letter—not a facsimile or scanned copy—as well as proof of the parent-child relationship (usually a birth certificate or court document), and an original custody decree, if applicable. If the other parent is deceased or the child has only one legal parent, a notarized statement saying so must be obtained as proof. In addition, you must fill out a tourist card for each child over the age of 10 traveling with you.

🚚 Shipping

DHL has express service for letters and packages from Los Cabos to the United States and Canada; most deliveries take three to four days (overnight service is not available). To the United States, letters take three days and boxes and packages take four days. Cabo San Lucas, San José del Cabo, and La Paz have a DHL drop-off location.

🛍 Shopping

Los Cabos may not have many home-grown wares, but the stores are filled with beautiful and unusual items from all over mainland Mexico. You can find hand-painted blue Talavera tiles from Puebla; blue-and-yellow pottery from Guanajuato; black pottery from San Bartolo Coyotepec (near Oaxaca); hammocks from the Yucatán; embroidered clothing from Oaxaca, Chiapas, and the Yucatán; silver jewelry from Taxco; fire opals from Queretaro; and the fine beaded crafts of the Huichol tribe from Nayarit and Jalisco.

If you're on the hunt for custom or locally made goods, Fábrica de Vidrio Soplado (Blown-Glass Factory) in Los Cabos produces beautiful glassware. Dozens of shops will custom-design gold and silver jewelry for you, fashioning pieces in one to two days. Liquor shops sell a locally produced liqueur called *damiana,* which is touted as an aphrodisiac. A few shops will even create custom-designed bathing suits for you in a day or so. Additionally, national and international artists are opening galleries across the region as part of its burgeoning arts scene in Los Cabos, with many in San José del Cabo's rapidly evolving city center, and even more dotted throughout Todos Santos's historic downtown.

No longer hawking only the requisite T-shirts, belt buckles, and trinkets, Cabo's improved shopping scene has reached the high standards of other Mexican resorts. Its once-vacant streets are today lined with dozens of new shops, from open-air bazaars and souvenir shops to luxury malls and designer boutiques.

HOURS OF OPERATION

Many stores are open as early as 9 am and often stay open until 9 or 10 pm. A few close for siesta at 1 pm or 2 pm, then reopen at 4 pm. About half of Los Cabos' shops close on Sunday; those that do open usually close up by 2 or 3 in the afternoon.

It's not uncommon to find some shops and galleries closed in San José del Cabo or Todos Santos during the hot season (roughly June to September), though very few shops close in Cabo San Lucas. We've noted this whenever possible; however, some shops simply close up for several weeks if things get excruciatingly slow or hot. In any case, low-season hours are usually reduced, so call ahead during that time of year.

A NOTE OF CAUTION

One of the benefits of traveling in Los Cabos is the low crime rate, thanks in part to the large population of expats and year-round tourists, and the *tranquilo* nature of locals. That being said, it's always wise to pay attention to what's going on when money is changing hands. Some tips: Watch that your credit card goes through the machine only once, so that no duplicates of your slip are made. If there's an error and a new slip needs to be drawn up, make sure the original is destroyed. Don't let your card leave a store without you. One scam is to ask you to wait while the clerk runs next door ostensibly to use another business's phone or to verify your number—but really to make extra copies. Again, this area is refreshingly safe and incident-free compared to many areas on the main-land, but it's always wise to be aware.

BEST LOCAL GIFTS AND SOUVENIRS

Cabo San Lucas is a great shopping town. Works of art by local artists make great treasures to take back home—and galleries will usually ship the items for you. T-shirts, resort wear, and clothing from hip Mexican designers will all compete for space in your suitcase.

If you're looking for something truly authentic and *hecho en Cabo* (made in Cabo), check out the blown glass at the intriguing **Fábrica de Vidrio Soplado.** Other fun souvenirs include the new labels of tequila offered from such outlets as Cabo Wabo, Hotel California in Todos Santos, and the Cabo Surf Hotel.

WHAT YOU CAN'T BRING HOME

Don't buy items made from tortoiseshell or any sea turtle products: it's illegal (Mexico's turtle species are endangered or threatened, and these items aren't allowed into the United States, Canada, or the United Kingdom). Cowboy boots, hats, and sandals made from the leather of endangered species such as crocodiles may also be taken from you at customs, as will birds, or stuffed iguanas or parrots. It isn't uncommon for U.S. Customs agents to seize seashells, so those and all sea creatures are best left where you found them.

Both the U.S. and Mexican governments also have strict laws and guidelines about the import/export of antiquities. Check with customs beforehand if you plan to buy anything unusual or particularly valuable.

American visitors are allowed to bring back up to 100 cigars or $800 worth of Cuban cigars without paying a duty. Mexican cigars without the correct Mexican seals on the individual cigars and on the box may be confiscated. For those 21 and older, U.S. customs allows one liter of alcohol per person to be entered into the U.S. duty-free.

Essentials

TIPS AND TRICKS

Better deals are often given to cash customers—even though credit cards are nearly always accepted—because stores must pay a commission to the credit-card companies. If you are paying in cash, it is perfectly reasonable to ask for a 5%–10% discount—though you shouldn't assume you'll be given one.

U.S. dollars are widely accepted in Los Cabos, although most shops pay a lower exchange rate than a bank (or ATM) or *casa de cambio* (money exchange).

Bargaining is common in markets and by beach vendors, who may ask as much as two or three times their bottom line. Occasionally an itinerant vendor will ask for the real value of the item, putting the energetic haggler into the awkward position of offering far too little. One vendor says he asks *norteamericanos* "for twice the asking price, since they always want to haggle." The trick is to know an item's true worth by comparison shopping. It's not necessary to bargain for already inexpensive trinkets like key chains or quartz-and-bead necklaces or bracelets.

HUICHOL SHOPPING TIPS

Beaded items: The smaller the beads, the more delicate and expensive the piece. Beads with larger holes are fine for stringed work, but if used in bowls and statuettes cheapen the piece.

Items made with iridescent beads from Japan are the priciest. Look for good-quality glass beads, definition, symmetry, and artful use of color. Beads should fit together tightly in straight lines, with no gaps.

Yarn paintings: Symmetry is not necessary, although there should be an overall sense of unity. Thinner thread results in finer, more costly work. Look for tightness, with no visible gaps or broken threads. Paintings should have a stamp of authenticity on the back, including artist's name and tribal affiliation.

Prayer arrows: Collectors and purists should look for the traditionally made arrows of brazilwood inserted into a bamboo shaft. The most interesting ones contain embroidery work, or tiny carved icons, or are painted with symbols indicative of their original, intended purpose, like protecting a child or ensuring a successful corn crop.

💲 Taxes

Mexico charges a departure and airport tax of about $65 that is almost universally included in the price of your ticket, but check to be certain.

A 2% tax on accommodations is charged in Los Cabos, with proceeds used for tourism promotion.

All of Mexico has a federal tax, or Value-Added Tax of 16%, called I.V.A. (*impuesto de valor agregado*), which is occasionally (and illegally) waived for cash purchases. Other taxes and charges apply for phone calls made from your hotel room.

💲 Tipping

When tipping in Baja, remember that the minimum wage is equivalent to a mere $6 an hour, and that the vast majority of workers in the tourist industry of Mexico live barely above the poverty line. Nevertheless, there are Mexicans who think in dollars and know, for example, that in the United States porters are tipped about $2 a bag; many of them expect the peso equivalent. Following are some guidelines. Naturally, larger tips are always welcome.

For porters and bellboys at airports and at moderate and inexpensive hotels, $2 (about MX$40) per bag should be sufficient. At expensive hotels, porters expect at least $4 per bag. Leave at least $3 per night for maids at all hotels. The norm for waiters is 15% to 20% of the bill, depending on service (make sure a 15% service charge hasn't already been added to the bill, although this practice is more common in resorts). Tipping taxi drivers is necessary only if the driver helps with your bags; $1 to $2 should be enough, depending on the extent of the assistance. Tip tour guides and drivers at least $5 per half day or 10% of the tour fee, minimum. Gas-station attendants receive 50¢ to $1, more if they check the oil, tires, etc. Parking attendants—including those at restaurants with valet parking—should be tipped $1 to $3.

U.S. Embassy/Consulate

There's an extension of the U.S. Consulate in Tijuana located at The Shoppes at Palmilla in Los Cabos. ⌂ *Las Tiendas de Palmilla L-B221, Km. 27.5 Carretera Transpeninsular* ☎ *(624) 143–3566*

Visitor Information

Avoid tour stands on the streets; they are usually associated with time-share operations. The *Gringo Gazette* newspaper and the *Baja Traveler Guide* are good resources for the Cabo scene, as is *Los Cabos Magazine*. These publications are free and easy to find in hotels and restaurants throughout the region. Discover Baja, a membership club for Baja travelers, has links and info at its website. For information about ecotourism and environmental issues, visit ⌖ *www.planeta.com*.

The Baja California Sur State Tourist Office is in La Paz about a 10-minute drive north of the *malecón*, the seaside promenade. It serves as both the state and city tourism office. There's also an information stand on the malecón across from Los Arcos hotel. The booth is a more convenient spot, and it can give you info on La Paz, Scammon's Lagoon, Santa Rosalia, and other smaller towns. Both offices and the booth are open weekdays 9–5.

When to Go

HIGH SEASON $$$$

Although Los Cabos hotels are often busiest starting in mid-October for the sportfishing season, the high season doesn't technically begin until mid-December, running through the end of Easter week. It's during this busy period that you'll pay the highest hotel and golf rates. Spring break, which can stagger over several weeks in March and April, is also a particularly crowded and raucous time. Downtown Cabo gets very busy, especially on weekends, throughout the year. Whale-watching season (December–April) coincides with high season, but whale-watchers tend to stay in La Paz, not Los Cabos (though there are plenty of tours in Los Cabos, too).

LOW SEASON $

July through October is the so-called short "rainy" season, but most summer tropical storms pass through quickly. This season is prime time for marlin fishing, which is when big-money fishing tournaments take place in Cabo San Lucas. It's also a great time to score deals on hotels that are experiencing low occupancy. Surfing is best in the summer months, and sea turtles lay their eggs at this time, when visitors can watch them scurry to the sea.

Essentials

VALUE SEASON $$

For the best of both worlds–not too expensive, not too crowded–plan your trip during shoulder season in the spring and fall months. November and May are both excellent times to visit, because they still have pleasant weather and just miss the crowds of high season (November precedes the influx of winter snowbirds and May follows the spring break rush in March and April). November through May is also the time for Art Walks in San José (every Thursday from 5 to 9 p.m.)

WEATHER

Los Cabos enjoys a nearly endless summer, with pleasant warm temperatures and sunshine year-round. June is the hottest and most humid month, with temperatures averaging 80 degrees F and reaching into the 90s F. It never really gets cold in Los Cabos, but January is the coolest month with an average temperature of 70 degrees F. The water can be chilly during this time but is generally still pleasant enough for water sports. The rainy season spans late summer and early fall.

HURRICANE SEASON

The Pacific hurricane season mirrors that of the Atlantic and Caribbean, so there is always a slight chance of a hurricane from August through late October. Hurricanes rarely hit Los Cabos head-on thanks to the natural protection it receives from the bay and surrounding mountains, but the effects can reverberate when a large hurricane hits Mexico's Pacific coast. For peace of mind, track Eastern Pacific hurricanes before your trip at ⊕ *www.nhc.noaa.gov* and be sure to heed any and all warnings for evacuation if a storm does come.

On the Calendar

February

Carnaval. Before Lent the streets of La Paz, the capital of Baja California Sur, are awash in colorful Mardi Gras-like celebrations complete with costumes and parades.

March and April

Semana Santa (Holy Week). Banks close during the week leading up to the Christian holiday of Easter Sunday.

June

Gastrovino Baja Food & Wine Festival. Todos Santos celebrates its culinary standouts at this celebration of local food and wine. ⊕ www.gastrovino.mx

Los Cabos Open of Surf. At Mexico's largest surf and music festival, riders catch big waves made by the famously strong currents here. ⊕ loscabosopenofsurf.com

September

Independence Day. Each September 15 starting at 11 pm, Mexico's president rings the country's liberty bell to signal the start of celebrations for Mexico's independence. The next day, September 16, usual festivities include a parade but vary from town to town.

November

Art Walks. On Thursdays from November to June, participating galleries and shops in downtown San José del Cabo stay open until 9 pm and serve drinks and snacks, and many arrange for special events or openings. There is usually music on Plaza Mijares, and it's not uncommon for the streets to be full of people, locals and tourists alike.

Dia de los Muertos (Day of the Dead). November 2 is Mexico's national day for honoring the dead and celebrating the memory of loved ones who have passed. Family altars are decorated elaborately with photos, candles, and food.

Los Cabos Film Festival. Filmmakers from around the world debut their work at this event. ⊕ cabosfilmfestival.com

December

Sabor a Cabo (The Flavors of Cabo). In early December this weeklong celebration of food, drink, and music showcases the area's top restaurants. ⊕ saboracabo.com

Christmas festivities. On December 12 Mexico feasts on Día de Nuestra Señora de Guadalupe (Day of Our Lady of Guadalupe), to celebrate the belief that the Virgin Mary was encountered in Mexico City on December 9 and 12. Las Posadas (The Inns), taking place from December 16 to 25, commemorates the journey of Joseph and Mary traveling from Nazareth to Bethlehem.

New Year's Eve. Fireworks light up the sky over Playa Médano in Cabo San Lucas, where there's always a party.

Whale-watching season. From December to April humpback whales can be spotted migrating in the waters off La Paz. Outfitters such as Baja Expeditions offer a memorable tour. ⊕ bajaex.com

Great Itineraries

Each of these fills one day in Los Cabos. Together they span the area's most quintessential experiences, from boating to El Arco and visiting the blown-glass factory, to grabbing a beer at a local brewpub and discovering Cabo's Marina Golden Zone.

LEARN THE LAY OF THE LAND

On Day 1 take it easy, enjoy your hotel, take a swim in the pool, and get to know the beach in your general area. If staying in Cabo, meander around town, mentally noting the many restaurants and shops on the way that you might wish to sample later. Walking the length of the marina boardwalk will introduce you to Cabo's notorious party central: From the boardwalk's western end beginning near the **Marina Fiesta Hotel**, you'll pass through the marina's Golden Zone (along which is the infamous **Nowhere ¿Bar?**). The marina walk ends at the **Tesoro Los Cabos Hotel**. Here you can catch a boat for sunset cruises, whale-watching, and sportfishing.

TRAVERSING THE CORRIDOR

To see the Corridor and make it over to San José del Cabo from Cabos San Lucas, it's most convenient and least expensive if you rent a car for a couple of days. (Taxis are frightfully expensive, and buses limit you to their schedule and stops.) Shop around for rentals and you'll be amazed at the range; Alamo and Cactus Car include insurance in their rates. Take your time driving along the Corridor, both to enjoy the sights of the coast, as well as to become accustomed to the unique traits of this quirky highway. On- and off-ramps are challenging, as you'll see. About mid-Corridor you pass **Bahía Santa María** and **Chileno Bay,** fun for stops to sun, swim, and snorkel. Bring your own equipment and refreshments.

As you near San José del Cabo, you can't miss the **Koral Center** or **Tiendas de Palmilla** (Palmilla Shopping Center) across from the **One&Only Palmilla Resort.** "Tiendas" comprises upscale shops and some excellent restaurants, including Nick-San. (Walmart, Costco, and Sam's Club have also set up shop along Highway 1 for your more basic shopping needs.) Heading farther east, you'll shortly see a turnout and large parking lot—a great panoramic overlook of the Sea of Cortez. It's a lovely spot to watch the surf at the **Old Man's break,** to your right, in front of the **Cabo Surf Hotel.**

LOS CABOS BEACHES

All hotels provide beach towels, chairs, and umbrellas. To get to the most pristine beaches along the Sea of Cortez, head east out of San José del Cabo by car. At the corner of Boulevard Mijares and Calle Benito Juárez in San José, turn east at the sign marked "pueblo la playa." The paved street soon becomes a dirt road that leads to the small fishing villages of **La Playa** (The Beach) and **La Playita** (The Little Beach), about 1½ km (½ mile) from San José. As the gateway between San José del Cabo and the East Cape coastline, this area known as Puerto Los Cabos is marked by a series of roundabouts that branch to the marina, organic farms (Flora Farms, Acre, and Los Tamarindos), and luxury resorts like Secrets and JW Marriott.

From La Playita, drive 60 km (37 miles) up the coast to the ecological reserve **Cabo Pulmo,** home of Baja Sur's largest coral reef. Water depths range from 15 to 130 feet, and colorful marine animals live among the reef and shipwrecks. When hunger calls, stroll up the beach from Cabo Pulmo to **Tito's** for a fish taco and an ice-cold cerveza. Try to get back to La Playa by late afternoon to avoid driving the East Cape's dirt road at night. Stop for some fresh seafood and a frozen margarita at **Buzzard's Bar and Grill** right near the beach just north of La Playa. San José is 10 minutes away.

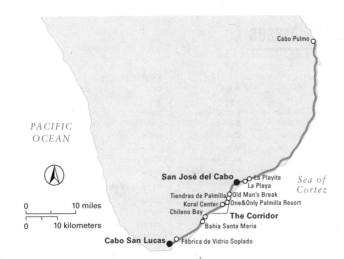

Cabo Pulmo

PACIFIC
OCEAN

San José del Cabo
La Playita
La Playa
Tiendras de Palmilla
Old Man's Break
Koral Center
One&Only Palmilla Resort
Chileno Bay
The Corridor
Bahia Santa Maria
Cabo San Lucas
Fábrica de Vidrio Soplado

Sea of
Cortez

0   10 miles
0   10 kilometers

ARTSY LOS CABOS

Set out from Cabo San Lucas for the **Fábrica de Vidrio Soplado** (Blown-Glass Factory)—a bit hard to find if you're driving yourself. First head toward San José on Avenida Lázaro Cárdenas, which becomes Highway 1. Turn left at the stoplight and signs for the bypass to Todos Santos, then look for signs to the factory. It's in an industrial area two blocks northwest of Highway 1. At the factory you can watch the talented artisans use a process little changed since it was first developed some 4,000 years ago.

From the factory, head east for the 20-minute drive to San José del Cabo. Park at the south end of Boulevard Mijares near the Tropicana Inn, since parking is limited from here on in. Grab some lunch at **Baja Brewing Company**, located on Avenida Morelos. The pub has a tasty San José Especial cerveza, and offers international fare to go along with it. Then stroll through the central plaza, or *zócalo*, directly in front of the **Mision de San José del Cabo Anuiti** (mission church) and peruse the several art galleries north and west of the church.

For dinner, try **Don Sanchez's** in San José proper, where Canadian-born chef Tadd Chapman is elevating the presentation of local ingredients and Mexican wines.

Alternatively, from the glass factory, head north on Highway 19 for the one-hour drive to the laid-back town of Todos Santos. Spend the afternoon visiting in-town galleries near the **Misión de Nuestra Señora de Pilar** (Mission of Our Lady of Pilar) church.

ORGANIC, GREEN, AND GOOD

Start off your morning with green juice and homemade granola at **Lolita Café** in the heart of San José del Cabo. For lunch, join a cooking class at **Los Tamarindos** organic farm, which includes a property tour and four-course meal. If you're in the area on Saturday, be sure to visit **Mercado Organico**, the farmers' market that takes place in San José from 9 am to 3 pm. End the day with a sunset surf session at **Costa Azul Surf Shop** or participate in **Baja Outback** 's evening turtle release program (August to November only). Finish with a healthy dinner at **7 Seas Seafood Grille** restaurant, known for their local prod–ucts, organic oils (instead of butter), and sustainable seafood that has not been impacted by commercial overfishing.

Helpful Phrases

BASICS

Hello	Hola	oh-lah
Yes/no	Sí/no	see/no
Please	Por favor	pore fah-**vore**
May I?	¿Puedo?	**Pweh**-doh
Thank you	Gracias	**Grah**-see-as
You're welcome	De nada	day **nah**-dah
I'm sorry	Lo siento	lo see-**en**-toh
Good morning!	¡Buenos días!	bway-nohs **dee**-ahs
Good evening!	¡Buenas tardes! (after 2pm)	bway-nahs-**tar**-dess
	¡Buenas noches! (after 8pm)	bway-nahs **no**-chess
Good-bye!	¡Adiós!/¡Hasta luego!	ah-dee-**ohss/ah**-stah **lwe**-go
Mr./Mrs.	Señor/Señora	sen-**yor**/sen-**yohr**-ah
Miss	Señorita	sen-yo-**ree**-tah
Pleased to meet you	Mucho gusto	**moo**-cho **goose**-toh
How are you?	¿Cómo estás?	**koh**-moh ehs-**tahs**

NUMBERS

one	un, uno	oon, **oo**-no
two	dos	dos
three	tres	tress
four	cuatro	**kwah**-tro
five	cinco	**sink**-oh
six	seis	saice
seven	siete	see-**et**-eh
eight	ocho	**o**-cho
nine	nueve	new-**eh**-vey
ten	diez	dee-**es**
eleven	once	**ohn**-seh
twelve	doce	**doh**-seh
thirteen	trece	**treh**-seh
fourteen	catorce	ka-**tohr**-seh
fifteen	quince	**keen**-seh
sixteen	dieciséis	dee-**es**-ee-**saice**
seventeen	diecisiete	dee-**es**-ee-see-**et**-eh
eighteen	dieciocho	dee-**es**-ee-**o**-cho
nineteen	diecinueve	dee-**es**-ee-new-**ev**-eh
twenty	veinte	**vain**-teh
twenty-one	veintiuno	**vain**-te-**oo**-noh
thirty	treinta	**train**-tah
forty	cuarenta	kwah-**ren**-tah
fifty	cincuenta	seen-**kwen**-tah
sixty	sesenta	sess-**en**-tah
seventy	setenta	set-**en**-tah
eighty	ochenta	oh-**chen**-tah
ninety	noventa	no-**ven**-tah
one hundred	cien	see-**en**
one thousand	mil	meel
one million	un millón	oon meel-**yohn**

COLORS

black	negro	**neh**-groh
blue	azul	ah-**sool**
brown	café	kah-**fehg**
green	verde	**ver**-deh
orange	naranja	na-**rahn**-hah
red	rojo	**roh**-hoh
white	blanco	**blahn**-koh
yellow	amarillo	ah-mah-**ree**-yoh

DAYS OF THE WEEK

Sunday	domingo	doe-**meen**-goh
Monday	lunes	**loo**-ness
Tuesday	martes	**mahr**-tess
Wednesday	miércoles	me-**air**-koh-less
Thursday	jueves	hoo-**ev**-ess
Friday	viernes	vee-**air**-ness
Saturday	sábado	**sah**-bah-doh

MONTHS

January	enero	eh-**neh**-roh
February	febrero	feh-**breh**-roh
March	marzo	**mahr**-soh
April	abril	ah-**breel**
May	mayo	**my**-oh
June	junio	**hoo**-nee-oh
July	julio	**hoo**-lee-yoh
August	agosto	ah-**ghost**-toh
September	septiembre	sep-tee-**em**-breh
October	octubre	oak-**too**-breh
November	noviembre	no-vee-**em**-breh
December	diciembre	dee-see-**em**-breh

USEFUL WORDS AND PHRASES

Do you speak English?	¿Habla Inglés?	**ah**-blah in-**glehs**
I don't speak Spanish.	No hablo español	no **ah**-bloh es-**pahn**-yol
I don't understand.	No entiendo	no en-tee-**en**-doh
I understand.	Entiendo	en-tee-**en**-doh
I don't know.	No sé	no **seh**
I'm American.	Soy americano (americana)	soy ah-meh-ree-**kah**-no (ah-meh-ree-**kah**-nah)
What's your name?	¿Cómo se llama?	koh-mo seh **yah**-mah
My name is . . .	Me llamo . . .	may **yah**-moh
What time is it?	¿Qué hora es?	keh **o**-rah es
How?	¿Cómo?	**koh**-mo
When?	¿Cuándo?	**kwahn**-doh
Yesterday	Ayer	ah-**yehr**
Today	hoy	oy
Tomorrow	mañana	mahn-**yah**-nah
Tonight	Esta noche	es-tah **no**-cheh
What?	¿Qué?	keh

What is it?	¿Qué es esto?	keh es **es**-toh
Why?	¿Por qué?	pore **keh**
Who?	¿Quién?	kee-**yen**
Where is . . .	¿Dónde está . . .	**dohn**-deh es-**tah**
. . . the bus station?	la central de autobuses?	lah sehn-**trahl** deh ow-toh-**boo**-sehs
. . . the subway station?	estación de metro	la es-ta-see-**on** del **meh**-tro
. . . the bus stop?	la parada del autobus?	la pah-**rah**-dah del ow-toh-**boos**
. . . the terminal? (airport)	el aeropuerto	el air-oh-**pwar**-toh
. . . the post office?	la oficina de correos?	la oh-fee-**see**- nah deh koh-**rreh**-os
. . . the bank?	el banco?	el **bahn**-koh
. . . the hotel?	el hotel?	el oh-**tel**
. . . the museum?	el museo?	el moo-**seh**-oh
. . . the hospital?	el hospital?	el ohss-pee-**tal**
. . . the elevator?	el elevador?	ehl eh-leh-bah-**dohr**
Where are the restrooms?	el baño?	el **bahn**-yoh
Here/there	Aquí/allí	ah-**key**/ah-**yee**
Open/closed	Abierto/cerrado	ah-bee-**er**-toh/ ser-**ah**-doh
Left/right	Izquierda/derecha	iss-key-**eh**-dah/ dare-**eh**-chah
Is it near?	¿Está cerca?	es-**tah sehr**-kah
Is it far?	¿Está lejos?	es-**tah leh**-hoss
I'd like . . .	Quisiera . . .	kee-see-**ehr**-ah
. . . a room	un cuarto/una habitación	oon **kwahr**-toh/**oo**-nah ah-bee-tah-see-**on**
. . . the key	la llave	lah **yah**-veh
. . . a newspaper	un periódico	oon pehr-ee-**oh**- dee-koh
. . . a stamp	un sello de correo	oon **seh**-yo deh korr-**eh**-oh
I'd like to buy . . .	Quisiera comprar . . .	kee-see-**ehr**-ah kohm-**prahr**
. . . soap	jabón	hah-**bohn**
. . . suntan lotion	bronceador	brohn-seh-ah-**dohr**
. . . envelopes	sobres	so-brehs
. . . writing paper	papel	pah-**pel**
. . . a postcard	una postal	oo-nah pohs-**tahl**
. . . a ticket	un billete (travel)	oon bee-**yee**-teh
	una entrada (concert etc.)	oona en-**trah**-dah
How much is it?	¿Cuánto cuesta?	**kwahn**-toh **kwes**-tah
It's expensive/ cheap	Es caro/barato	es **kah**-roh/ bah-**rah**-toh
A little/a lot	Un poquito/mucho	oon poh-**kee**-toh/ **moo**-choh
More/less	Más/menos	mahss/**men**-ohss
Enough/too (much)	Suficiente/	soo-fee-see-**en**-teh/
I am ill/sick	Estoy enfermo(a)	es-**toy** en-**fehr**-moh(mah)

Call a doctor	Llame a un medico	**ya**-meh ah oon **med**-ee-koh
Help!	Ayuda	ah-**yoo**-dah
Stop!	Pare	**pah**-reh

DINING OUT

I'd like to reserve a table . . .	Quisiera reservar una mesa . . .	kee-**syeh**-rah rreh-sehr-**bahr** oo-nah **meh**-sah . . .
. . . for two people.	para dos personas.	**pah**-rah dohs pehr-**soh**-nahs
. . . for this evening.	para esta noche.	**pah**-rah **ehs**-tah **noh**-cheh
. . . for 8 PM	para las ocho de la noche.	**pah**-rah lahs **oh**-choh deh lah **noh**-cheh
A bottle of . . .	Una botella de . . .	oo-nah bo-**teh**-yah deh
A cup of . . .	Una taza de . . .	oo-nah **tah**-sah deh
A glass of . . .	Un vaso (water, soda, etc.) de…	oon **vah**-so deh
	Una copa (wine, spirits, etc.) de…	oona **coh**-pah deh
Bill/check	La cuenta	lah **kwen**-tah
Bread	Pan	pahn
Breakfast	El desayuno	el deh-sah-**yoon**-oh
Butter	mantequilla	man-teh-**kee**-yah
Coffee	Café	kah-**feh**
Dinner	La cena	lah **seh**-nah
Fork	tenedor	ten-eh-**dor**
I don't eat meat	No como carne	noh koh-moh **kahr**-neh
I cannot eat . . .	No puedo comer . . .	noh **pweh**-doh koh-**mehr**
I'd like to order . . .	Quiero pedir . . .	**kee**-yehr-oh peh-**deer**
I'd like . . .	Me gustaría . . .	Meh goo-stah-**ee**-ah
I'm hungry/thirsty	Tengo hambre/sed	**Tehn**-goh **hahm**-breh/seth
Is service/the tip included?	¿Está incluida la propina?	es-**tah** in-cloo-ee-dah lah pro-**pee**-nah
Knife	cuchillo	koo-**chee**-yo
Lunch	La comida	lah koh-**mee**-dah
Menu	La carta, el menú	lah **cart**-ah, el meh-**noo**
Napkin	servilleta	sehr-vee-**yet**-ah
Pepper	pimienta	pee-mee-**en**-tah
Plate	plato	
Please give me . . .	Me da por favor . . .	meh dah pohr fah-**bohr**
Salt	sal	sahl
Spoon	cuchara	koo-**chah**-rah
Sugar	ázucar	ah-**su**-kar
Tea	té	teh
Water	agua	**ah**-gwah
Wine	vino	**vee**-noh

Contacts

✈ Air

AIRPORTS Manuel Márquez de León International Airport. (*La Paz International Airport*). ✉ *Carretera Transpeninsular Km 13, La Paz* ☎ *612/124–6307.* **Aeropuerto Internacional Los Cabos.** (*Los Cabos International Airport*). ✉ *Carretera Transpeninsular Km 43.5, San José del Cabo* ☎ *624/146–5111* ⊕ *www. loscabosairport.com.*

🚌 Bus

Terminal Central Cabo San Lucas Águila. (*Transportes Águila*). ✉ *Av. Hidalgo , Block Ejidal, Cabo San Lucas* ☎ *01800/026–8931 toll-free in Mexico* ⊕ *www. autobusesaguila.com.* **Terminal Central La Paz Águila.** ✉ *Alvaro Obregon 125, entre 5 de Mayo e Independencia, La Paz* ☎ *01800/026–8931 toll-free in Mexico* ⊕ *www.autobusesaguila.com.* **Terminal Central San José del Cabo Águila.** ✉ *Calle Valerio González 1, Colonia Primero de Mayo, Centro* ☎ *01800/026–8931* ⊕ *www.autobusesaguila. com.*

🚗 Car

ROADSIDE EMERGENCIES Federal Highway Patrol. ☎ *624/125–3584.* **Green Angels, La Paz.** ☎ *01800/987–8224 toll-free in Mexico, 078 from any Baja phone.*

RENTAL CARS Cactus Car. ✉ *Carretera Transpeninsular, Km 45, at Aeropuerto Internacional de Los Cabos, San José del Cabo* ☎ *624/146–1839, 866/225–9220 in U.S.* ⊕ *www.cactuscar.com.* **California Baja Rent-A-Car.** ✉ *9245 Jamacha Blvd., Spring Valley* ☎ *619/470–7368* ⊕ *www.cabaja.com.*

🇺🇸 Embassy

Consular Agent in Cabo San Lucas. ✉ *Carretera Transpeninsular, Km 27.5, Shoppes at Palmilla, The Corridor* ☎ *624/143–3566.*

⚠ Emergencies

Highway Patrol. ☎ *624/143–0135 in Los Cabos, 612/122–0429 in La Paz.* **Police.** ☎ *624/142–0361 in San José del Cabo, 624/143–3977 in Cabo San Lucas, 612/122–0477 in La Paz.*

MEDICAL ASSISTANCE COMPANIES AirMed International. ☎ *800/356–2161, 205/443–4840 in Mexico* ⊕ *www.airmed.com.* **Medjet.** ☎ *800/527–7478* ⊕ *www.medjetassist.com.*

➕ Hospitals

AMC American Medical Center. ✉ *Lázaro Cárdenas 911, Playa El Médano* ☎ *624/143–4911* ⊕ *www. amchospitals.com.* **Centro de Especialidades Médicas.** ✉ *Calle Delfines 110, La Paz* ☎ *612/124–0400.*

📍 Insurance

INSURANCE COMPARISON SITES InsureMyTrip. ☎ *800/487–4722* ⊕ *www. insuremytrip.com.* **Square Mouth.** ☎ *800/240–0369* ⊕ *www.squaremouth.com.*

COMPREHENSIVE TRAVEL INSURERS Allianz. ☎ *800/284–8300* ⊕ *www.allianztravel-insurance.com.* **Travel Guard.** ☎ *800/826–4919* ⊕ *www.travelguard.com.* **Travel Insured International.** ☎ *800/243–3174* ⊕ *www. travelinsured.com.*

🛏 Lodging

CONDOS AND VILLAS Cabo Homes and Condos. ☎ *866/321–CABO(2226) in U.S.* ⊕ *www.cabohomesandcondos.com.* **Cabo Villas.** ☎ *855/745–2226 in U.S. and Canada* ⊕ *www. cabovillas.com.*

Chapter 3

CABO SAN LUCAS

3

Updated by
Chris Sands

👁 **Sights** | 🍴 **Restaurants** | 🏨 **Hotels** | 💼 **Shopping** | 🍸 **Nightlife**

★★★★☆ | ★★★☆☆ | ★★★★☆ | ★★★☆☆ | ★★★★☆

NEIGHBORHOOD SNAPSHOT

TOP EXPERIENCES

■ **Land's End:** This must-see area is known for its beautiful beaches, superb snorkeling and diving, and iconic granite monument El Arco (The Arch).

■ **Alfresco Dining:** Feast on Mexican specialties and fresh, local seafood at fine open-air restaurants featuring gorgeous ocean and sunset views.

■ **Whale-Watching:** See the biggest show on earth as migrating humpbacks splash down in spectacular fashion each winter.

■ **Rock Star Parties:** Boisterous downtown nightspots beckon, from rock royalty–approved Cabo Wabo to the lively beachfront Mango Deck.

■ **Marlin Fishing:** Anglers have long been lured to Cabo to fight enormous black and blue marlin that may outweigh them by hundreds of pounds.

GETTING HERE

To reach Cabo San Lucas, fly into the Los Cabos International Airport in San José del Cabo. Getting from the airport to resorts in Cabo San Lucas is easily accomplished thanks to the many local shuttle services, which charge about $20 to $25 per person. Taxi service is also available, as are private SUVs. Some luxury resorts provide their own cars.

Buses do run throughout Los Cabos, but are rarely used by tourists except for service along the tourist corridor between San Lucas and San José (about $3 one-way). Rental cars are a far better bet.

PLANNING YOUR TIME

Cabo San Lucas is a year-round destination, but high season is from October to May, a fact reflected in higher hotel and resort rates. These are the most temperate months of the year, with a nearly endless succession of glorious sunshine and warm (rather than hot) temperatures. Whale-watching is best between mid-December and mid-March, while marlin fishing is best from July to October.

QUICK BITES

■ **Tacos Ramiro's.** The best *suadero* (thinly cut beef) tacos in town—some locals would argue the best tacos, period—are found at this small, off-the-beaten-path restaurant that remains virtually unknown to tourists, but has developed a cult-like following among resident taco aficionados. For a real treat, try the *tuétano* (beef bone marrow), which is served in the bone, but can be scooped out into tacos. ⊠ *16 de Septiembre, between Melchor Ocampo and Zaragoza* ☎ 624/224–1110

■ **El Pollo de Oro.** At this establishment, a half-chicken meal costs about $8. ⊠ *Morelos at 20 de Noviembre* ☎ 624/143–0310 ⊕ elpollodeoro.restaurant-webexperts.com

■ **Los Claros.** This is the place for a quick taco fix; $2 (fish and shrimp) or $5 (lobster) gets you some serious tacos, while $6 will buy you a stellar breakfast. Two-for-one margaritas are served all day, and five beers (Corona or Pacifico) can be had for $10. ⊠ *Zaragoza at 16 de Septiembre* ☎ 624/688–7664

■ **Rico Suave.** Come here for fresh juices and smoothies, as well as a large variety of salads and tortas. ⊠ *Av. Cárdenas between Av. Hidalgo and Calle Guerrero* ☎ 624/143–1043 ⊕ www.rico-suave.com.mx

Lively beaches, legendary nightlife, and buzzy seaside cantinas make Cabo San Lucas the rowdier of Los Cabos' two sister cities, and arguably the most popular destination on the Baja California peninsula. But they're just the tip of the iceberg (or should we say arch?) when it comes to Cabo's myriad enticements. Cabo is also a marlin fishing capital, water sports wonderland, and the home of resorts fit for Hollywood royalty, wrapped into one sun-kissed destination where the Sea of Cortez meets the Pacific Ocean.

The natural attractions of the southern-most community on the Baja California peninsula are on full display from the first glimpse of the half-mile Land's End head-land, with its picturesque beaches and iconic granite formations, including the famous El Arco (the Arch). But beautiful beaches abound here. Playa El Médano, a two-mile stretch of golden sand, serves as the center of the local social scene and is framed by luxury resorts, restau-rants, beach bars, and souvenir shops. Médano Beach also acts as an activities rental center for kayaks, Jet Skis, stand-up paddleboards, and more.

The impressively large and well-equipped marina is headquarters for the charter fishing fleet, as well as tour boats offering everything from snorkeling and diving to sunset sails and seasonal whale-watch-ing. For all the appealing activities possibilities in the marina, the broad, bordering boardwalk promenade offers appeal of a different sort; notably, dining at popular restaurants like Baja Cantina and Solomon's Landing, plus shopping stops galore—from flea market style vendors to the upscale boutiques of Luxury Avenue.

Although not at the level of sister city San José del Cabo in terms of trendy restaurants and art galleries, downtown Cabo San Lucas does promise plenty of great shopping, dining, and nightlife choices. The Van Halen-founded Cabo Wabo and celebrity favorite El Squid Roe headline the nightlife offerings, and both have been leaders of the local party scene for more than 30 years. Shops can be found on every downtown street, and although jewelry stores, pharmacies, and souvenir outlets are the most commonly encountered retail options, discerning shoppers can find everything from folk art to custom-made resort clothing.

Dining is more varied. Taquerías are pervasive, of course, but oddly... so too are Italian restaurants. Freshly caught local seafood is the best bet, however, and nearly every restaurant in town offers "you hook it, we cook it" specials for visiting anglers.

◉ Sights

Land's End is the one must-see attraction in Cabo San Lucas, and it is well worth buying a ticket on a boat tour (or hiring a water taxi just to see its many distinctive features up close. Save a day for the excursion. The town square, Plaza Amelia Wilkes, also merits a visit. Its gazebo and gardens are more beautiful than ever, thanks to a recent refurbishment.

★ Land's End

LOCAL INTEREST | Land's End sightseeing is at the heart of nearly every local boat tour, a small wonder given the many interesting natural attractions found along this half-mile headland. Everybody knows **El Arco** (The Arch), the naturally occurring granite arc estimated to be nearly 80-million-years-old, but there's much more to see, including other granite pinnacles jutting from the sea **(Pelican Rock** and **Neptune's Finger)**; beautiful beaches like **Playa del Amor** (Lover's Beach) and **Playa del Divorcio** (Divorce Beach); **La Lobera** (the sea lion colony); a keyhole shaped opening known as **The Window to the Pacific**; **Scooby Doo Rock** (a rock that looks like the cartoon canine); and a spade-shaped opening on the Pacific side known as the **Pirate's Cave**, reputed to be the site of long-buried treasure. Sightseers will also notice the ruins of the old cannery, which was the center of local commerce before the age of tourism, the three so-called Cannery beaches, and a large hill with a cross on top. This hill is called **El Vigía** ("The Watcher"), and it was a lookout point for the English and Dutch privateers who used to attack the yearly Spanish galleon during the heyday of the Manila Galleon Trade (1565 to 1815). It is also

thought to have been a sun temple and perhaps a sacred burial ground for the Pericú, the indigenous inhabitants of the area, but any evidence of the latter was stolen decades ago. ⊠ *Cabo San Lucas* ✛ *Follow Paseo de la Marina past the navy base toward the old cannery.*

Marina Golden Zone

PROMENADE | Cabo's downtown marina is lined with upscale shops and fine dining, but it's worth coming here just to stroll along the boardwalk and take in glittering marina views. Shopping hot spots include Puerto Paraíso Mall, Marina Fiesta Resort, and Luxury Avenue Boutique Mall. The latter is a collection of shops selling Salvatore Ferragamo, Victoria's Secret, Lacoste, TAG Heuer, and Montblanc, all under one roof. The zone is anchored by the Marina Fiesta Resort & Spa. ⊠ *Marina San Lucas, Cabo San Lucas* ✛ *At Marina Fiesta Resort & Spa* ⊕ *www.goldenzonecabo.com.*

Plaza Amelia Wilkes

PLAZA | Few people in Cabo San Lucas history have been as honored as the town square's namesake, Amelia Wilkes Ceseña. A schoolteacher for 43 years, Wilkes was a tireless advocate for the town, and in 1966 she became the first woman ever appointed to political office in Baja California Sur. Construction on the plaza first began in 1947 on land bounded by Av. Lázaro Cárdenas and Calles Hidalgo, Madero, and Cabo San Lucas. The plaza has been an important landmark ever since (and was named for Wilkes in 1992), but a recent renovation has finally lavished on this historical site the attention it deserves. Its central gazebo has been freshly painted, gardens of colorful flowers have been planted, and new stonework and accents added. A natural history museum is found at the northern end, and on Friday nights the entire plaza comes alive with music, dancing, art, and food between 6 and 10 p.m. ⊠ *Cabo San Lucas* ✛ *Av. Lázaro Cárdenas and Calles Hidalgo, Madero, and Cabo San Lucas.*

⏚ Beaches

There's no shortage of beaches in Cabo San Lucas. Land's End alone has at least five that are named. Playa El Médano (pronounced MEH-dah-no) is two-miles long and easily the biggest and most popular of local beaches; home to everything from luxury resorts and restaurants to shopping and nightlife. Lover's Beach (Playa del Amor) is far and away the most photographed beach (it is particularly prized for destination wedding photography), and arguably the most beautiful.

Many beaches in Cabo San Lucas are swimmable, but the rule of thumb is to avoid Pacific Ocean side beaches due to strong rip currents and occasional rogue waves. Thus, Lover's Beach, which opens onto the Sea of Cortez, is swimmable; while Divorce Beach, which adjoins it but opens onto the Pacific Ocean, is not.

★ **Lover's Beach** (*Playa del Amor*)
BEACH—SIGHT | These days, lovers have little chance of finding much romantic solitude here. The azure cove on the Sea of Cortez at the very tip of the Land's End peninsula may well be the area's most frequently photographed patch of sand. It's a must-see on every first-timer's list. Water taxis, glass-bottom boats, kayaks, and Jet Skis all make the short trip out from Playa Médano to this small beach, which is backed by cliffs. Snorkeling around the base of these rocks is fun when the water is calm; you may spot striped sergeant majors and iridescent green-and-blue parrotfish. Seals hang out on the rocks a bit farther out, at the base of "El Arco," Cabo's famed arched landmark. Swimming and snorkeling are best on the Sea of Cortez side of Lover's Beach, where the clear, green, almost luminescent water is unquestionably the nicest in Cabo San Lucas. Walk through a gap in the rocks to access Divorce Beach on the Pacific side, which is too turbulent for swimming but ideal for sunbathing.

Vendors are usually present, but it's always best to bring your own snacks and plenty of water. The beach is crowded at times, but most people would agree that it's worth seeing, especially if you're a first-timer. To get here, take a five-minute panga water-taxi ride ($10–$15) or the half-hour glass-bottom-boat tour. Opt for the latter if you wish to have some time to photograph the arch from the Pacific-side view. Both boats leave with relative frequency from the Cabo San Lucas marina or Playa Médano. **Amenities:** none. **Best for:** swimming; snorkeling; sunrise; sunset. ⊠ *Cabo San Lucas* ✧ *Just outside Cabo San Lucas, at El Arco.*

Playa El Médano
BEACH—SIGHT | FAMILY | Foamy plumes of water shoot from wave runners and dozens of water taxis buzz through the calm waters off Médano, a 3-km (2-mile) span of grainy tan sand that's always crowded. Bars and restaurants line the sand, waiters deliver ice buckets filled with beer to sunbathers in lounge chairs, and vendors offer everything from silver jewelry to hats, T-shirts, and henna tattoos. You can even get a pedicure. Swimming areas are roped off to prevent accidents, and the water is usually calm enough for small children. Be aware there are quick shoreline drop-offs, so life preservers are a good idea for the little paddlers in your group. Hotels line Médano, which is just north of downtown off Paseo del Pescador. Construction is constant on nearby streets, and parking is virtually impossible. The most popular spot on the beach is around the Mango Deck and The Office, where more than half a dozen bar-restaurants have set up beach chairs and tables. This is a hot spot for people-watching. For something a bit more tranquil, grab a bite at Casa Dorada Resort's oceanfront restaurant Maydan, which is open to the public. Be prepared to deal with the many crafts vendors cruising the beach. They're generally not pushy, so a simple head shake and "*No, gracias*" will do. **Amenities:** food concession. **Best for:** partiers;

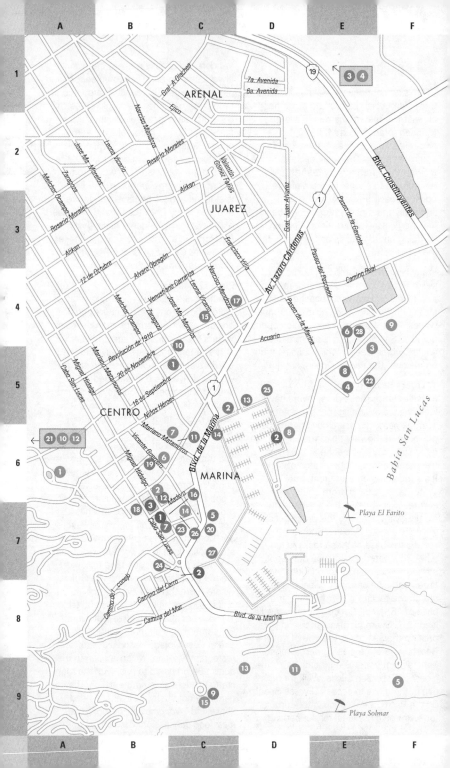

G   H   I

Cabo San Lucas

Playa El Médano

KEY

1 *Exploring Sights*

1 *Restaurants*

1 *Quick Bites*

1 *Hotels*

0 ———— 1,000ft

0 ———— 200m

El Arco
(The Arch)

Lover's
Beach

PACIFIC OCEAN

G   H   I

Sights ▼

1 Land's End **G9**
2 Marina Golden Zone ... **D6**
3 Plaza Amelia Wilkes.... **B7**

Restaurants ▼

1 Alcaravea Gourmet...... **C5**
2 Alexander Restaurant... **C5**
3 Anica **E1**
4 Baja Brewing
   Company.................. **E5**
5 Baja Cantina Marina **C7**
6 Bar Esquina **E5**
7 Crazy Lobster
   Bar & Grill **B7**
8 Edith's Restaurant **E5**
9 El Farallon **C9**
10 El Peregrino **C4**
11 Gordo Lele's
   Tacos & Tortas **C6**
12 Invita Bistro **B6**
13 La Casa Country **D5**
14 Lorenzillo's................ **C6**
15 Los Tres Gallos.......... **C4**
16 Mama's Royal Café **C7**
17 Mariscos Mazatlán...... **C4**
18 Mi Casa **B7**
19 Misiones de Kino **B6**
20 Nick-San................. **C7**
21 Nobu Restaurant
   Los Cabos............... **A6**
22 The Office................. **E5**
23 Pancho's Restaurant &
   Tequila Bar **C7**
24 Romeo y Julieta.......... **C7**
25 Ruth's Chris
   Steak House............. **D5**
26 Salvatore G's **C7**
27 Solomon's Landing **C7**
28 SUR Beach House by
   Bar Esquina **E5**

Quick Bites ▼

1 The Cabo Coffee
   Company................. **B7**
2 California
   Ranch Market............ **C7**

Hotels ▼

1 The Bungalows
   Hotel...................... **A6**
2 Casa Bella **B6**
3 Casa Dorada Los Cabos
   Resort & Spa............. **E5**
4 Grand Solmar at
   Rancho San Lucas....... **E1**
5 Grand Solmar
   Land's End
   Resort & Spa............. **F9**
6 Hotel Mar de Cortez.... **B6**
7 Los Milagros **C6**
8 Marina Fiesta
   Resort & Spa **D6**
9 ME Cabo **F4**
10 Nobu Hotel
   Los Cabos................ **A6**
11 Playa Grande Resort
   and Grand Spa **D9**
12 Pueblo Bonito
   Pacifica Golf and Spa
   Resort **A6**
13 Sandos Finisterra
   Los Cabos................ **D9**
14 Siesta Suites **C7**
15 Waldorf Astoria
   Los Cabos Pedregal **C9**

snorkeling; swimming. ⊠ *Paseo del Pescador, Playa El Médano.*

Playa Solmar

BEACH—SIGHT | Huge waves crash onto the sand on the Pacific side of Cabo San Lucas. This wide, beautiful beach stretches from Land's End north to the cliffs of El Pedregal, where mansions perch on steep cliffs. Swimming is impossible here because of the dangerous surf and undertow; stick to sunbathing and strolling. From December to March, you can spot gray and humpback whales spouting just offshore; dolphins leap above the waves year-round. The beach is at the end of Avenida Solmar off Boulevard Marina—an easy walk from downtown Cabo San Lucas. Five resorts—Solmar, Grand Solmar, Terrasol, Playa Grande, and Sandos Finisterra—are all on this beach, making it easy to stop for a meal if you get hungry. Crowds are minimal, as guests tend to stick to the hotel pools. **Amenities:** none. **Best for:** walking; solitude. ⊠ *Blvd. Marina to hotel entrances, Pedregal.*

🍴 Restaurants

Cabo San Lucas is known for its lively nightlife, and, though much of the fine-dining scene has moved to the Corridor and San José, there are still some solid choices in Cabo. A pedestrian walkway lined with restaurants, bars, and shops anchored by the sleek Puerto Paraíso mall curves around Cabo San Lucas harbor, itself packed with yachts. The most popular restaurants, clubs, and shops are along Avenida Cárdenas (the extension of Highway 1 from the Corridor) and Boulevard Marina, paralleling the waterfront.

★ Alcaravea Gourmet

$$$ | ITALIAN | Alcaravea Gourmet has come a long way from its humble beginnings as a tiny, off-the-beaten-path bistro, and is now considered one of Cabo's top stops for Italian and Mediterranean style cuisine. Enter through a

---

Whale-Watching Tips 👁

Whale-watching season in Los Cabos is officially from Dec. 15 to Apr. 15. The best spot in Cabo San Lucas to watch humpbacks and other whales transit to their winter breeding grounds (other than on a close-up boat excursion) is the tower at the **Sandos Finisterra** resort. Day passes ($40) are usually available for nonguests and include pool access and all-inclusive food and drink. To watch whales from the shore, go to the beach at the Solmar Suites, The Grand Solmar, or lookout points along the Corridor.

---

flower-and-vine-garlanded opening into an intimate dining area. **Known for:** excellent $12 lunch deal; delicious pescado con champiñones; top-tier rib-eye steak. $ *Average main: $25* ⊠ *Zaragoza at 16 de Septiembre, Centro* ☎ *624/143–3730* ⊗ *Closed Sun.*

Alexander Restaurant

$$$ | EUROPEAN | Ideally located along Cabo San Lucas's busy marina walkway, Alexander's is where Switzerland meets México. Pull up a chair at one of the sidewalk tables and start with a meat-and-cheese fondue, a treat for which Swiss chef and owner Alex Brulhart is known. **Known for:** meat-and-cheese fondue; incredible flambéed tequila shrimp; delicious sake lobster. $ *Average main: $30* ⊠ *Plaza Bonita, Cabo San Lucas Marina, Marina San Lucas* ☎ *624/143–2022* ⊕ *www.alexandercabo.com.*

Anica

$$$$ | MEXICAN | At the signature on-site restaurant for Grand Solmar at Rancho San Lucas, terrace seating offers a romantic vantage for sunset views, while a high-ceilinged dining area is very

Did You Know?

Visiting El Arco, a gorgeous rock formation at the southernmost tip of the Baja peninsula, makes for a thrilling day trip from Cabo San Lucas.

stylishly decorated in the rustic *rancho* vein. Even more impressive, however, is the traditional Mexican food from chef Héctor Lucas. **Known for:** Mexican dishes like axiote cabrilla (sea bass); sunset views; exceptional wine list. $ *Average main: $35* ⊠ *Grand Solmar at Rancho San Lucas, Carretera Todos Santos (Hwy 19), Km 120, Cabo San Lucas* ☎ *624/14—0900* ⊕ *ranchosanlucas.com/grand-solmar.*

Baja Brewing Company

$$$ | AMERICAN | A branch of the established San José del Cabo microbrewery, the beers are brewed in San José, meaning what you get here is "20 minutes fresh." No quibbles with the system; the eight house brews and seasonal additions are a flavorful change from the ubiquitous Tecate. The location of this outpost on the rooftop of the Cabos Villas resort on Médano Beach, however, ups the ante with a semi-open-air venue and view of the ocean. **Known for:** ocean views; open-air dining; fresh brews. $ *Average main: $23* ⊠ *Cabo Villas Beach Resort & Spa, Callejon del Pescador, Playa El Médano* ☎ *624/143–9166, 714/625-8769 in the U.S.* ⊕ *www.bajabrewing-company.com.*

Baja Cantina Marina

$$ | MEXICAN | This large, casual, sportfishing-oriented cantina, just around the corner from the Tesoro Los Cabos Resort, draws crowds with its all-day drink specials. Boasting a top marina location near L-M-N Dock, an excellent view of the sportfishing and mega yachts, $2 cervezas all day, affordable eats, and American sports on multiple TVs, it's a favorite of the sportfishing deckhands and boat captains. **Known for:** late-night DJs and dancing; all-day drink specials; budget-friendly eats. $ *Average main: $20* ⊠ *Cabo San Lucas Marina, Dock L-M-N, Marina San Lucas* ☎ *624/143–1111* ⊕ *www.bajacantinamarina.com.*

Bar Esquina

$$$$ | ECLECTIC | Set in Cabo San Lucas's boutique Bahia Hotel, Bar Esquina is making a name for itself as one of Médano Beach's best restaurants. Whether you're craving eggs Benedict in the morning to help you absorb last night's party, a wood-fired pizza, or a burger on a pretzel bun, Bar Esquina is the neighborhood's top option for expertly prepared American-style comfort food. **Known for:** delicious tuna tartare; live music; good food after a night out. $ *Average main: $35* ⊠ *Bahia Hotel & Beach House, Av. El Pescador, Playa El Médano* ☎ *624/143–1890* ⊕ *www.bahiacabo.com.*

Crazy Lobster Bar & Grill

$$ | MEXICAN | Lobster's the thing here, but daily specials like surf-and-turf combos round out the list. Open for breakfast, lunch, and dinner, this typical Mexican sit-down locale has a happy hour that runs from 8 am to 6 pm—and prices are super cheap. **Known for:** excellent people-watching; open-air dining; incredibly cheap and generous food. $ *Average main: $15* ⊠ *Hidalgo at Zapata, Centro* ☎ *624/26—5071* ⊕ *thecrazylobster.mx* ☾ *Closed Sept.*

Edith's Restaurant

$$$$ | MEXICAN | FAMILY | One of the more upscale choices near hectic Médano Beach, Edith's is the sister restaurant to popular The Office on the Beach. The Caesar salad and flambéed banana crepes are prepared table-side at this colorful and popular restaurant. **Known for:** Wally's Special; wine cellar for small private parties; focus on Mexican ingredients. $ *Average main: $50* ⊠ *Camino a Playa El Médano, Playa El Médano* ☎ *624/143–0801* ⊕ *www.edithscabo.com.*

★ El Farallon

$$$$ | **SEAFOOD** | Atop a bluff at the Waldorf Astoria Los Cabos Pedregal, El Farallon provides one of the most breathtaking vantage points in Cabo San Lucas. Chef Gustavo Pinet presents a seafood-heavy menu with a "fresh fish market" displaying the catch of the day. **Known for:** irresistible local chocolate clams; The Champagne Terrace; dishes come with a tasting of the day's three appetizers. [$] *Average main: $125* ✉ *Waldorf Astoria Los Cabos Pedregal, Camino Del Mar 1, Pedregal* ☎ *624/163–4300* 🌐 *www.waldorfastorialoscabospedregal.com.*

El Peregrino

$$ | **INTERNATIONAL** | The name of this restaurant in Spanish means "The Pilgrim," and refers to the power and breadth of knowledge available to intrepid travelers. Fortunately, one needn't be particularly intrepid to find the place, though it is a bit off the beaten track. **Known for:** excellent international fare; cozy dining space; popular slow-cooked barbecue short rib. [$] *Average main: $20* ✉ *Calle Ignacio Zaragoza at 20 de Noviembre, Centro* ☎ *624/688–4872.*

Gordo Lele's Tacos & Tortas

$ | **MEXICAN** | If you're looking for some entertainment to go along with your tacos or *tortas* (sandwiches), listen for the blaring Beatles' tunes at Gordo Lele's, then watch owner Javier Reynoso don his Beatles wig and sing along to "I Want to Hold Your Hand" or "Let It Be." The walls here are filled with Fab Four photos and album covers. Javier's tacos and tortas are made with loving care, and his fans can have two or three ham-and-cheese tortas for what would be the price of one anywhere else, plus an assortment of generously sized tacos. **Known for:** delicious affordable tortas; generously sized tacos; Beatles decor. [$] *Average main: $4* ✉ *Matamoros, Centro* ✥ *Between Lázaro Cárdenas and Niños Héroes* ☎ *624/109–1778* 💳 *No credit cards.*

Invita Bistro

$$$ | **ITALIAN** | **FAMILY** | Go for the delicious complimentary focaccia bread; stay for the fine wines, family-style fare, and charming views of downtown Cabo San Lucas. Chef and co-owner Antonello Lauri shows off his Roman heritage on the menu at Invita, which is overflowing with traditional Italian favorites like the filling eggplant Parmesan made from recipes passed down from his grandmother. **Known for:** views of town square; serious wine selection; traditional Italian recipes. [$] *Average main: $21* ✉ *Calle Miguel Hidalgo, Centro* ✥ *Across from Plaza Amelia Wilkes* ☎ *624/143–1386* 🌐 *www.invitabistro.com.*

La Casa Country

$$$ | **STEAKHOUSE** | For a good steak in a rustic atmosphere accented by wood tables and leather stools, head to La Casa Country. Serving breakfast, lunch, and dinner with sports games playing on oversize TVs in the background, La Casa is the spot for toothsome *carne* at reasonable prices, and a wide variety of Mexican fare. **Known for:** marina views; abundant steak options; generous breakfast menu. [$] *Average main: $22* ✉ *Cabo San Lucas Marina, Marina San Lucas* ✥ *Next to Puerto Paraiso Shopping Mall* ☎ *624/105–1999.*

Lorenzillo's

$$$$ | **SEAFOOD** | Gleaming hardwood floors and polished brass give a nautical flair to this second-floor dining room, where fresh lobster is king. Lorenzillo's has long been a fixture in Cancún, where lobster is raised on the company's farm. **Known for:** Xtabentun cocktail with Mayan liqueur, anise, honey; specialty flaming coffee cocktails; pirate- and marine-themed entrées. [$] *Average main: $50* ✉ *Av. Cárdenas at Marina, Marina San Lucas* ☎ *624/105–0212* 🌐 *www.lorenzillos.com.mx.*

Baja's Tropical Treats 🍴

Tropical fruits like mango and guava are abundant in Los Cabos, and in addition to providing fresh, healthy juices at regional resorts and restaurants, they serve as the key ingredient in many delicious desserts.

Pancho's Restaurant & Tequila Bar, a Cabo San Lucas restaurant famed for its traditional Mexican cuisine, makes a memorable mango mousse; and **Casa de Brasa,** at the Four Seasons Los Cabos Resort at Costa Palmas, serves an applause-worthy guava cheesecake made from aged local cheese.

Then there's the annual **Mango Festival** in Todos Santos, which happens each year in late July or early August (when the fruit ripens), and is notable for its competition to see who can make the best mangate, a mango-based dessert typical of the region. The winners? Everyone who gets to sample the entries, of course.

★ Los Tres Gallos

$$$ | **MEXICAN** | A romantic courtyard shaded by fruit trees, classic *rancheras* (Mexican folk music), and traditional preparations of regional Mexican specialty dishes are the hallmarks at Los Tres Gallos. Discover their delicious heritage dishes such as *cochinita pibil* (slow-roasted pork) and *molcajetes* (stone bowls) filled with flank steak, shrimp, chorizo, nopal, and panela cheese. **Known for:** old-fashioned charm; delicious flan for dessert; tribute to stars of Mexico's golden age of cinema. [$] *Average main: $25* ✉ *Calle Leona Vicario at 20 de Noviembre, Centro* ☎ *624/130–7709* 🌐 *www.lostresgallos.com.*

Mama's Royal Café

$ | **MEXICAN** | Claiming to have "the best damn breakfast restaurant in the entire country," Mama's is a casual, lively, indoor-outdoor spot in Cabo San Lucas that serves bountiful plates of omelets and poached eggs with avocado and ham, and finger-licking fried potatoes. Mama's lives up to their claim of having the "World's Best French Toast"—a treasure stuffed with cream cheese, strawberries, mangoes, bananas, and pecans, and topped with orange liqueur. **Known for:** "World's Best French Toast"; homemade salsas; fresh-squeezed juices. [$] *Average main: $10* ✉ *Calle Hidalgo at Zapata, Centro* ☎ *624/143–4290* 🌐 *www.mamasroyalcafeloscabos.com* 🕒 *Closed Sept.*

Mariscos Mazatlán

$$ | **SEAFOOD** | Ask a local where they go for dinner, and they inevitably mention Mariscos Mazatlán. The crowds of Mexicans lunching at this simple seafood restaurant lend credibility to the claim, as do the huge stuffed fish mounted on the colorfully painted walls. **Known for:** affordable authentic cuisine; local favorite; delicious seafood. [$] *Average main: $20* ✉ *Narciso Mendoza at 20 de Noviembre, Arenal* ☎ *624/143–8565.*

Mi Casa

$$ | **MEXICAN** | **FAMILY** | One of Cabo San Lucas's top restaurants is in a cobalt-blue adobe building painted with murals. Interior decorations range from Day of the Dead statues and silver crosses and hearts, to T-shirts and tequilas. **Known for:** regional Mexican specialties; must-try mole poblano; live mariachi band. [$] *Average main: $20* ✉ *Av. Cabo San Lucas at Lázaro Cárdenas, Centro* ☎ *624/143–1933* 🌐 *www.micasarestaurantcabo.com.*

Misiones de Kino
$$ | MEXICAN | You may feel like you discovered a well-kept secret when you find this palapa-roof house with adobe walls, just a few blocks off the main strip and around the corner from the Mar de Cortez Hotel. Sit on the front patio or in a backyard hut strung with weathered lanterns and photographs of the Mexican Revolution. **Known for:** coconut shrimp; pasta and Italian options; small bar with photos of the Mexican Revolution. $ *Average main: $17* ✉ *Calle Vicente Guerrero at 5 de Mayo, Centro* ☎ *624/105–1408* 🌐 *www.misionesdekino.com* 🕒 *Closed Sun.*

★ **Nick-San**
$$$ | SUSHI | Nick-San may very well be Cabo San Lucas's top restaurant. Owner Angel Carbajal is an artist behind the sushi counter (he also has his own fishing boats that collect fish each day), and his creative fusion menu of Japanese and Mexican cuisines truly sets his masterpieces apart. **Known for:** tuna specialties; reservations recommended; divine sauce on the cilantro sashimi. $ *Average main: $25* ✉ *Plaza de la Danza, Blvd. Marina, Marina San Lucas* ✥ *Next to Tesoro Los Cabos Hotel* ☎ *624/143–2491* 🌐 *www.nicksan.com.*

Nobu Restaurant Los Cabos
$$$$ | JAPANESE FUSION | Celebrity chef Nobu Matsuhisa became famous integrating Peruvian ingredients into traditional Japanese cuisine, and now adds a bit of Los Cabos to the mix at his eponymous eatery at Nobu Hotel Los Cabos. Sleek Japanese wood furnishings and terrace seating overlooking crashing Pacific Ocean waves provide a suitable setting for the chef's delicious offerings, ranging from his signature black cod with miso to destination-appropriate Nobu tacos featuring king crab, lobster, and Wagyu beef. **Known for:** Japanese fusion cuisine; trendy seaside dining; expensive prices. $ *Average main: $40* ✉ *Nobu Hotel Los Cabos, Polígono 1. Fracción D, Diamante, Cabo San Lucas* ☎ *624/689-0160* 🌐 *loscabos.nobuhotels.com* 🕒 *Closed Tues.*

The Office
$$$$ | MEXICAN | At least once during your visit to Los Cabos, you should visit The Office, the original breakfast spot on Médano Beach's sandy shore. The Office screams "tourist-trap," bedecked with tiki torches and colorful tablecloths, but it's all in good fun, and it's always packed with revelers enjoying the near-perfect views of El Arco. **Known for:** strong Mexican coffee; views of El Arco; Cabo breakfast staple. $ *Average main: $35* ✉ *Playa El Médano* ☎ *624/143–3464* 🌐 *theofficeonthebeach.com.*

Pancho's Restaurant & Tequila Bar
$$$ | MEXICAN | FAMILY | Owner Juan Calderoni has an enormous collection of tequilas, and an extensive knowledge of the stuff. His restaurant is something of a tequila museum, with a colorful array of hundreds of the world's top tequilas—many no longer available—displayed behind the bar. **Known for:** nearly 300 types of tequila; Oaxacan decor; tequila tasting menus. $ *Average main: $22* ✉ *Calle Hidalgo, Centro* ✥ *Between Zapata and Camino del Conejo* ☎ *624/143–2891, 624/143–0973* 🌐 *www.panchos.com.*

Romeo y Julieta
$$$ | ITALIAN | At this longtime local establishment near the entrance to Pedregal, diners are delightfully surprised to find an elegant dining area that's open to the stars. The alfresco courtyard is as wonderful as the fine Italian cuisine, highlighted by traditional favorites such as linguine frutti di mare and gnocchi di ricotta. **Known for:** romantic courtyard; fine Italian cuisine; live music. $ *Average main: $25* ✉ *Blvd. Marina at Camino del Cerro, Centro* ✥ *By California Ranch Market* ☎ *624/143–0225* 🌐 *www.restaurant-romeoyjulieta.com.*

Ruth's Chris Steak House

$$$$ | STEAKHOUSE | If you need a break from tacos and have a hankering for a steak like they cook 'em back home, Ruth's Chris at the Puerto Paraíso mall facing the marina is your best bet. It's known for its wide range of meaty cuts from fillets to porterhouse, and also serves veal, chicken, fish, and lamb. **Known for:** mouthwatering steak; range of cuts; specialty cocktails. $ Average main: $60 ⊠ Puerto Paraíso, first floor, Boulevard Lázaro Cárdenas 1501, Marina San Lucas ☎ 624/144–3232 ⊕ www. ruthschris.com.

Salvatore G's

$$ | ITALIAN | The local gringo cadre has nothing but bueno things to say about this affordable and dependable little Italian spot, located by the pool at the Siesta Suites Hotel in downtown Cabo San Lucas. Baked rigatoni, osso buco, chicken Parmigiana, lasagna, and lamb ravioli are just some of the many Italian staples offered at this funky little spot. **Known for:** large portions; reasonably priced; tasty traditional Italian cuisine. $ Average main: $18 ⊠ Emilio Zapata S/N, Centro ✛ Between Vicente Guerrero and Miguel Hidalgo ☎ 624/105–1044 ⊕ salvatoregs. com ⊗ No lunch Sun.

Solomon's Landing

$$$ | SEAFOOD | FAMILY | Chef and owner Brian Solomon runs one of the most popular restaurants on the Cabo San Lucas Marina, supplementing great seaside views with first-class service and an enormous range of quality food and beverage. Fresh local seafood is the specialty of the house, but pastas, steaks, and traditional Mexican favorites are also staples of the lunch and dinner menus. **Known for:** live music on Saturday; monthly food and wine events; fresh local seafood. $ Average main: $22 ⊠ Cabo San Lucas Marina, Marina San Lucas ✛ Behind Tesoro Los Cabos Resort ☎ 624/143–3050 ⊕ www.solomonslanding.com.mx.

SUR Beach House by Bar Esquina

$$$$ | SEAFOOD | Less than two blocks from its affiliate restaurant Bar Esquina at Bahia Hotel & Beach House, SUR is a picturesque mix of casual chic appointments and breezy seaside ambience set on Playa El Médano. The specialties of la casa are pan-Pacific fusions featuring fresh local seafood, from ceviches and sushi to tacos and Peruvian-style tiraditos (raw fish similar to crudo). **Known for:** pan-Pacific fusions; SUP board rentals; Peruvian-style tiraditos. $ Average main: $35 ⊠ Playa El Médano, at Calle Cormoranes, Playa El Médano ✛ Next to The Sand Bar ☎ 624/143–1890 ⊕ www. surcabo.com.

☕ Coffee and Quick Bites

Street stands offer quick, low-cost fine food in Cabo San Lucas. If there's a crowd of locals, it's probably fresh and prepared well. Best bets include quesadillas, fish tacos, corn on the cob, and tortas (sandwiches). Some restaurants have a comida corrida (prepared lunch special), a three-course meal that consists of soup or salad, an entrée with rice and vegetables, coffee, and a small dessert. It's not gourmet, but you'll be sated, and at a reasonable price.

In Cabo San Lucas, head for the taco stands in the couple of blocks behind Squid Roe and Avenida Cárdenas, and the backstreets inland from the marina.

★ The Cabo Coffee Company

$ | CAFÉ | Many of the area's best restaurants source their coffee blends from Cabo Coffee Company. The café, just off the Plaza Amelia Wilkes town square, serves a wide array of espresso drinks made from organic beans grown in Oaxaca's cloud forest. **Known for:** local hangout; free Wi-Fi; tasty fresh pastries. $ Average main: $3 ⊠ Calle Miguel Hidalgo at Francisco I. Madero, Centro ☎ 624/105–1754 ⊕ www.cabocoffee.com.

California Ranch Market

$ | **MEXICAN** | In addition to its great selection of beer and wines, as well as organic and frozen foods, healthy and low-calorie offerings, and cheese, this corner shop carries familiar products and brands from the United States. A second location has been added at The Shoppes at Palmilla. **Known for:** excellent prices; extensive beer and wine selection; healthy and organic options. [$] *Average main: $5* ✉ *Blvd. Marina at Camino del Cerro, Marina San Lucas* ✣ *At the western end of Marina San Lucas* ☎ *624/143–1947* 🌐 *californiaranchmarket.com* 🕒 *Closed Sun.*

Hotels

In Cabo San Lucas, there's a massive hotel on every available plot of waterfront turf. A pedestrian walkway known as the Marina Golden Zone is lined with restaurants, bars, and shops. It's anchored by the sleek Puerto Paraíso mall that curves around the entire perimeter of Cabo San Lucas harbor, itself packed with wall-to-wall sportfishing and pleasure yachts. Unfortunately, a five-story hotel complex at one edge of the harbor blocks a small portion of the water view and sea breezes from the town's side streets, but it can't be denied that Cabo is a carnival and a parade, all at once. The short Pacific coast beach just over the rocky hills at the west end of the marina has a more peaceful atmosphere, though monstrous hotel projects have gobbled up much of the sand here, too. If being right on the water isn't a primary concern, it is well worth checking out some of the smaller, independently owned hotels sprinkled around the downtown area. Several offer gracious, hacienda-style accommodations with a personal touch that huge hotels cannot match. For a tranquil setting close enough to all the action, opt for one of the resorts near Land's End.

★ The Bungalows Hotel

$ | **B&B/INN** | If solitude and a reasonable room rate are more important than being in the center of the action, Bungalows is your place. **Pros:** oasis-like property; excellent value; outstanding breakfasts. **Cons:** noise from traffic and surrounding neighborhood; a bit off the beaten path; 10 blocks to beach. [$] *Rooms from: $165* ✉ *Blvd. Miguel Angel Herrera, Arenal* ☎ *624/143–0585* 🌐 *www.thebungalowshotel.com* 🛏 *16 rooms* 🍴 *Free Breakfast.*

★ Casa Bella

$ | **B&B/INN** | The Ungson family had been in Cabo for more than four decades before turning their home across from Plaza San Lucas into the classiest and friendliest inn in the neighborhood. **Pros:** property feels totally secluded; private home atmosphere; stunning bathrooms, some with gardens. **Cons:** no TVs or phones in the rooms; some street noise; not kid-friendly. [$] *Rooms from: $160* ✉ *Calle Hidalgo 10, Centro* ☎ *624/143–6400, 818/392–8874 In U.S.* 🌐 *www.casabellahotel.com* 🛏 *11 rooms* 🍴 *Free Breakfast.*

Casa Dorada Los Cabos Resort & Spa

$$ | **RESORT** | **FAMILY** | Through the dramatic entry on the stone facade you'll find this seven-floor, all-suites combination hotel-timeshare has it all. **Pros:** beautifully appointed rooms; ocean views from every room; located at the heart of Playa El Médano. **Cons:** noise from bars and clubs on beach in front of the hotel; timeshare salespeople are aggressive; extra charge for Wi-Fi. [$] *Rooms from: $250* ✉ *Playa El Médano, Av. del Pescador, Playa El Médano* ☎ *624/163–5700, 866/448–0151 toll-free in U.S.* 🌐 *www.casadorada.com* 🛏 *150 suites* 🍴 *Free Breakfast.*

Grand Solmar at Rancho San Lucas

$$$ | **RESORT** | **FAMILY** | Impressive in every respect, this new Rancho San Lucas resort commands well over a mile (2 km) of Pacific Ocean coastline north of Cabo San Lucas, with an 18-hole golf course from Greg Norman, five large pool areas (including a water park for kids), four

bars, an excellent on-site restaurant called Anica, and a beachfront spa. **Pros:** stylish suites with upscale furnishings; family-friendly amenities; preferred tee times at Rancho San Lucas Golf Course. **Cons:** far from downtown Cabo San Lucas; can get windy by the beach; only one restaurant so far. [$] *Rooms from: $340* ✉ *Carretera Todos Santos (Hwy 19), Km 120, Cabo San Lucas* ☎ *624/143–0900, 844/645–2292 in the U.S. and Canada* 🌐 *https://grandsolmarranchosanlucas.solmar.com/* 🛏 *130 suites* 🍴 *No meals.*

Grand Solmar Land's End Resort & Spa
$$$$ | **RESORT** | **FAMILY** | Architecture melds perfectly with natural surroundings as luxury villas dramatically hug cliff and sea and subterranean stone passages open to infinity pools framed by cactus gardens and raked sand. **Pros:** ocean views; as close to El Arco as you can get; villas give a sense of home and isolation. **Cons:** beach not safe for swimming; hefty charge for in-room coffee, water, and Wi-Fi; also a timeshare. [$] *Rooms from: $676* ✉ *Av. Solmar 1A, Centro* ✥ *Next to Solmar Resort* ☎ *624/144–2500* 🌐 *www.grandsolmarresort.com* 🛏 *263 suites* 🍴 *All-inclusive.*

Hotel Mar de Cortez
$ | **HOTEL** | Another one of Cabo's original hotels, Hotel Mar is just four blocks from the marina, a block from the main square, near *muchos* restaurants, bars, clubs, and shopping. **Pros:** clean rooms and pleasant surroundings; good value; free Internet. **Cons:** noisy air-conditioning units; surrounding streets are busy and loud; spotty Wi-Fi. [$] *Rooms from: $85* ✉ *Av. Lázaro Cárdenas, Cabo San Lucas* ✥ *Between Vincente Guerrero and Matamoros* ☎ *624/143–0032, 800/347–8821 in U.S.* 🌐 *www.mardecortez.com* ⏲ *Closed Sept.* 🛏 *88 rooms* 🍴 *No meals.*

Los Milagros
$ | **HOTEL** | A mosaic sign (crafted by co-owner Ricardo Rode) near the entrance hints at the beauty inside this small stylish inn offering a relaxed atmosphere and boutique feel without the boutique cost. **Pros:** quiet inn located close to everything in Cabo; one room is wheelchair accessible; free Wi-Fi and TVs in every room. **Cons:** air-conditioning units in rooms can be loud; pool is small and not heated; daily fee for parking in private lot. [$] *Rooms from: $85* ✉ *Mariano Matamoros 3738, Cabo San Lucas* ☎ *624/143–4566* 🌐 *www.losmilagros.com.mx* 🛏 *15 rooms* 🍴 *No meals.*

Marina Fiesta Resort & Spa
$ | **RESORT** | Though this colonial-style building is not ocean-side, most rooms have a pleasant view of the clover-leaf-shaped pool and the yacht-filled marina. **Pros:** close to popular bars and shops; walking distance to Playa El Médano; all-inclusive plan gives access to restaurants on marina. **Cons:** aggressive timeshare salespeople; no ocean views; center rooms are dated. [$] *Rooms from: $165* ✉ *Marina, Lots 37 and 38, Marina San Lucas* ☎ *624/145–6020, 844/278–6596 in U.S.* 🌐 *www.marinafiestaresort.com* 🛏 *155 rooms* 🍴 *All-inclusive.*

ME Cabo
$$$ | **RESORT** | In the middle of Médano's most popular beach is the ME, the Meliá brand's posh offering in Cabos San Lucas with its huge pool areas—including the most popular swim-up bar in Cabo—and hot tubs under the palms is a playground for adults (although children are allowed). **Pros:** great for adults and singles; situated on one of the few swimmable beaches in Los Cabos; comfortable rooms with modern amenities. **Cons:** affordable rooms are limited; crowded pool area with loud music; meals not included. [$] *Rooms from: $350* ✉ *Playa Médano, Cabo San Lucas* ☎ *624/145–7800, 877/954–8363 in U.S.* 🌐 *www.melia.com* 🛏 *150 rooms* 🍴 *No meals.*

Nobu Hotel Los Cabos
$$$$ | **HOTEL** | Japanese design and Pacific Ocean views distinguish Nobu Hotel Los Cabos, the trendy lodging from brand partners Nobu Matsuhisa, Meir Teper, and Robert De Niro. **Pros:** trendy poolside

A Note on Timeshares

For some families who frequently like to get away to resorts, the timeshare concept can be an economical way to vacation. Timeshares are a big business in Los Cabos, and the offers are constant, especially as you walk through the town of Cabo San Lucas. Timeshare representatives at the airport and in many hotel lobbies will try to entice you to attend a presentation by offering free transportation, breakfast, and activities, or even attractive amounts of cash. These salespeople are a major downside to many expensive lodgings where you wouldn't expect to be harassed. Don't feel obligated to accept—presentations often last two hours or more and can be draining. If you're staying in a hotel that has timeshare units, aggressive salespeople may call your room every morning asking you to attend a free breakfast. If you're not interested, ask to be removed from their call list. Or simply say, "I live here," and they'll leave you alone.

scene; superb on-site dining; access to world-class golf courses. **Cons:** a bit too trendy for most families, despite Kids' Club; pricey food and drinks; far from downtown Cabo San Lucas. $ *Rooms from: $500* ✉ *Polígono 1. Fracción D. Fraccionamiento Diamante, Cabo San Lucas* ☎ *624/689-0160* ⊕ *loscabos.nobu-hotels.com* ➥ *200 rooms* ¶◎¶ *No meals.*

Playa Grande Resort and Grand Spa
$$ | RESORT | FAMILY | This large, multicolor all-suite resort complex on the beach looks a bit Las Vegas, even by Cabo standards, but it's got all kinds of activities and facilities, making it a great family vacation option. **Pros:** Playa Grande Spa is huge; putt-putt golf course and play structures; fabulous pools. **Cons:** fitness center and Internet charges apply; getting to and from rooms is time-consuming and confusing; expensive spa services. $ *Rooms from: $200* ✉ *Av. Playa Grande 1, Cabo San Lucas* ☎ *624/145-7524, 800/344-3349 in U.S.* ⊕ *www.solmar.com* ➥ *358 suites* ¶◎¶ *No meals.*

Pueblo Bonito Pacifica Golf and Spa Resort
$$$$ | RESORT | Considered a resort within a resort, Pueblo Bonito's gem is The Towers at Pacifica, which makes up the VIP section of the larger property, with a separate lounge bar, premium liquor, and spacious suites with living rooms and modern amenities. **Pros:** adults only; luxurious accommodations and service; beautiful views and cactus gardens. **Cons:** $40 charge for use of beach beds (no charge for guests in suites); beach is not swimmable; thin walls. $ *Rooms from: $600* ✉ *Predio Paraiso Escondido, Cabo San Lucas* ☎ *624/142-9696, 800/990-8250 in U.S.* ⊕ *www.pueblobonitopacifica.com* ➥ *215 rooms* ¶◎¶ *All-inclusive.*

Sandos Finisterra Los Cabos
$$$$ | RESORT | One of the first hotels built in Cabo, this all-inclusive resort retains a loyal clientele with great service, property upgrades, and a superb location perched on a hill overlooking the marina and the Pacific. **Pros:** fantastic location; rooms have either bay or ocean view; short walk to the marina. **Cons:** beach is not swimmable; pushy timeshare pitch; spotty Wi-Fi. $ *Rooms from: $500* ✉ *Blvd. Marina, Cabo San Lucas* ☎ *624/145-6700* ⊕ *www.sandos.com* ➥ *272 rooms* ¶◎¶ *All-inclusive.*

Siesta Suites

$ | HOTEL | The owners keep a close eye on this four-story hotel—a calm refuge two blocks from the marina—and dispense great insider advice to visitors. **Pros:** friendly staff; barbecue area to cook catch of the day; quiet, simple, and affordable. **Cons:** limited off-street parking; no elevator; pool is small and is surrounded by tables from Salvatore's restaurant at night. $ *Rooms from: $75* ⊠ *Calle Zapata at Guerrero, Centro* ☎ *624/143–2773, 866/271–0952 toll-free in U.S.* ⊕ *www.siestasuitescabo.com* ⇨ *20 rooms* ⧉ *No meals.*

★ Waldorf Astoria Los Cabos Pedregal

$$$$ | RESORT | The majestic Waldorf Astoria Los Cabos Pedregal lies on Cabo San Lucas's most coveted parcel of land—an extraordinary, 24-acre site at the southern tip of the peninsula accessible only through the longest private tunnel in México, a chandelier-lit passage through sheer granite that opens into an open-air lobby backed by gorgeous Pacific Ocean vistas. **Pros:** every room has a plunge pool; outstanding spa; exceptional service and a staff that calls you by name. **Cons:** Pacific-side beach is not swimmable; not ideal for children; El Farallon restaurant is very expensive. $ *Rooms from: $695* ⊠ *Camino del Mar 1, Pedregal* ☎ *624/163–4300, 844/487–3391 in the U.S.* ⊕ *www.waldorfastorialoscabospe-dregal* ⇨ *115 rooms* ⧉ *No meals.*

▼ Nightlife

The epicenter of Cabo San Lucas nightlife is along the Marina San Lucas and the two streets that run parallel beyond it. You'll walk past a gauntlet of servers waving menus in your face, but the sidewalk bars along the marina between Plaza Bonita and Puerto Paraíso are great during happy hour and late into the night. Many bars also serve during the day several times a week when cruise ships are in port.

Watch out for the tequila shooters and Jell-O shots forced upon revelers by merry waiters—they usually cost at least $5 each. Topless bars and "gentlemen's" clubs are abundant (their "showgirls" signs give them away). Single men are often accosted outside San Lucas bars with offers of drugs and sex. Be careful in this area, and be aware that the police may be behind some of these solicitations.

BARS

Baja Brewing Co

BARS/PUBS | The Cabo San Lucas branch of the microbrewery in San José del Cabo shares the same menu and selection of beers on tap. Yet the open space atop a seaside hotel lends a decidedly different, relaxed vibe. Perfect after a day at the beach, "BBC" has pub fare and fresh local seafood, as well as the beer samplers and terrific views. Live music is offered most weekends. ⊠ *Rooftop of Cabo Villas Beach Resort, Médano Beach, Callejon del Pescador S/N, 7th Fl., Playa El Médano* ☎ *624/143–9166* ⊕ *www.bajabrewingcompany.com.*

Billygan's Island

BARS/PUBS | The once boisterous Billygan's Island on Médano Beach is now one of the more tame spots on the sand. The bikini dance contests may be a thing of the past, but you can still get great deals on margaritas and buckets of beer, as well as seafood favorites like coconut shrimp and octopus. ⊠ *Playa El Médano* ☎ *624/144–3908.*

★ Blue Marlin Ibiza

DANCE CLUBS | Miami meets Cabo at this restaurant, bar, and club with an over-the-top feeling of luxury. White gauze canopies shade plush sunbeds and lounge chairs around multiple swimming pools, while DJs spin until 6 pm daily. Their sushi menu pairs well with a fruity cocktail and will help keep the buzz under control. ⊠ *ME Cabo Hotel, Playa Médano, Cabo San Lucas* ☎ *624/145–7800* ⊕ *www.bluemarlinibizaloscabos.com.*

A Shot of Tequila

What once was the drink of the Mexican farmer is now produced *en masse* and enjoyed internationally, with countless varieties crowding shelves across the world. Unfortunately, lower-quality brands make up the bulk of exports, so if the thought of sipping this heady liquor turns your stomach, take some time to seek out some of a higher quality while you're in Los Cabos.

Tequila must contain at least 51% blue agave, a plant related to the lily. The best tequilas are 100% blue agave. Liquid is distilled from the sap of 7- to 10-year-old plants and fermented. If you buy tequila with a worm, it was probably bottled in the United States, and is likely not a good-quality tequila.

Most of the good stuff is made in Jalisco in the town of Tequila, near Guadalajara. Labels bearing *reposado* indicate up to a year of aging; *añejo*, from one to three years. The longer tequila ages, the smoother it tastes.

Even though tequila is not widely produced in Los Cabos, taste-testing is easy to do. Every bar will have at least a couple of bottles on the shelves, of course, but you should also visit at least one establishment that specializes in tastings.

Pancho's Restaurant & Tequila Bar has an impressive collection that numbers in the hundreds of bottles, some of which are rare and no longer manufactured. Pancho's offers tequila tastings by reservation twice a day, with various samplers and pairing options included on a separate tasting menu. In San José del Cabo, owner, chef, and certified tequilier Tadd Chapman of **Habanero's Gastro Grill & Tequila Bar** has done an exceedingly good job of curating a selection of premium tequilas, which the restaurant is happy to integrate into multicourse pairing menus.

Luxury resorts have also taken the tequila concept to another level. The **Tequila & Ceviche Bar** at Las Ventanas al Paraíso whets appetites with an upscale menu of top-shelf tequilas, but also spotlights a special 90-minute Tequila Sign program that utilizes blind tastings to define the taster's palate and personality, then provides appropriate tequilas based on the profile reading.

The recently opened and stylishly designed **Tequila & Mezcal Bar** at Grand Velas Los Cabos, meanwhile, offers over 140 varieties of tequila and mezcal (México's other national spirit), as well as guided tastings and master classes with the resort's on-site master sommelier (who also developed Grand Velas' excellent wine list).

If your tequila tastes run more to margaritas than straight sippers, try the regional variation with Damiana taking the place of triple sec (or Controy). Damiana is a liqueur made from an herb native to the Baja California peninsula.

Fenway Bar

BARS/PUBS | A unique sports bar concept—unique for Cabo San Lucas, anyway—this Red Sox bar features all the live sporting events on close to a dozen TVs, plus plenty of eye-catching Red Sox decor. Owner Ignacio "Nacho" Padilla Rivas grew up in Aguascalientes, México, but is a die-hard fan of the Boston team and has furnished this funky little hole-in-the-wall on Calle Zapata with a replica Green Monster scoreboard, Pesky Pole, and memorabilia galore. The house drink special is the Carajillo, made with espresso and Licor 43 over ice. Food specials are also offered daily, and the bar staff will order in food from pretty much any place in town. ⊠ *Calle Emiliano Zapata, between Guerrero and Hidalgo, Centro* ✛ *Across from Siesta Suites Hotel and Salvatore G's Restaurant* ☎ *624/355-8015* ⊕ *fenwaybarcabo.com.*

Las Varitas

BARS/PUBS | Las Varitas, one of Cabo's most popular clubs, is a branch of the La Paz rock club favored by young Mexicans. Local and internationally famous Latin rock bands perform here almost every night, and the establishment even boasts its own label of house tequila. ⊠ *Paseo de la Marina, Cabo San Lucas* ✛ *Near corner of Camino Viejo San José* ☎ *624/143-9999* ☉ *Closed Sun.*

Mango Deck

BARS/PUBS | Feel like getting a little bit rowdy and dancing in the sand? Mango Deck may reach its peak during spring break, but this beachfront party mecca is always packed. ⊠ *Playa El Médano* ✛ *At the western end of El Médano Beach, near the Casa Dorada resort* ☎ *624/143-0901* ⊕ *www.mangodeckcabo.com.*

Nowhere ¿Bar?

BARS/PUBS | Locals sip beers while exuberant tourists have too much fun at the Nowhere ¿Bar? Two-for-one drinks and a lively dance floor are a big draw here. Don't be at all surprised to see people dancing on the tables from early evening on. Sushi and tacos are served from adjacent restaurants. ⊠ *Plaza Bonita, Blvd. Marina 17, Marina San Lucas* ☎ *624/143-4493* ⊕ *www.nowherebar.com.*

The Office

BARS/PUBS | The Office began as a place to rent water sports equipment, and expanded into a bar/eatery now famous for its seafood and goblet-size margaritas. Despite the fact that the floor here is the sand, this place is a tad more upscale than the other venues on Médano Beach. ⊠ *Médano Beach, Playa El Médano* ✛ *Between Mango Deck and Billygan's* ☎ *624/143-3464* ⊕ *www.theofficeonthebeach.com.*

★ Slim's Elbow Room

BARS/PUBS | Slim's calls itself "the world's smallest bar," and you'll be lucky to get a seat at this kitschy four-seat space that plays honky-tonk music and serves $3 beers and tequila shots. Signed dollar bills line the walls and ceiling, and a buzzing, standing crowd loiters out the door and onto the Boulevard Marina sidewalk each evening, vibing off its energy. ⊠ *Plaza de los Mariachis, Blvd. Marina, Centro* ☎ *624/172-5576* ⊕ *www.slimscabo.com.*

Tanga Tanga

BARS/PUBS | Tanga Tanga, which has both an outdoor and indoor bar, is a hot and popular spot, especially for expats, to listen to live music, and watch sports on big-screen TVs. Local reggae and rock groups play here on Friday and Saturday. Margaritas are plentiful, and the wings are extra spicy! ⊠ *Plaza de la Danza, Blvd. Marina, Marina San Lucas* ☎ *624/143-1511.*

Uno Mas

BARS/PUBS | This tiny palapa bar outside Cabo Wabo is the type of place you stumble on—and you might wind up stumbling out of it after "una mas" cold one. Grab a bar stool and order your favorite cocktail made with fresh squeezed juice. Pace yourself as these drinks have been known to pack a punch—not to mention the

Hagar's Hangout: Cabo Wabo ⓨ

According to local lore, in the mid-1980s former Van Halen lead singer Sammy Hagar and a friend were walking along the beach in Cabo San Lucas when they passed a drunk man stumbling. Hagar remarked, "Hey, he's doing the Cabo Wabo." A few years later in 1990, Hagar and the rest of Van Halen opened the bar called Cabo Wabo—establishing one of the premier stops on the Cabo party circuit. When the group broke up in 1996, all but Hagar sold their shares in the bar.

Mexican and American rock bands perform every night. Almost always packed, the place erupts during Hagar's birthday celebration around October 13, when the legend himself

drops in to play. When not on tour, Hagar stops in at Cabo Wabo up to 10 times throughout the year. Visit the club's website for an events calendar. ⊕ www.cabowabo.com.

Often accompanying Hagar are his musician friends, like Chris Isaak, Kirk Hammett of Metallica, David Crosby, Slash, Rob Zombie, the Cult, and the Sex Pistols.

The lighthouse replica at the entrance makes the bar easy to spot from afar. Designed by architect Marco Monroy, Cabo Wabo has cavernous ceilings and walls adorned with painted zebra stripes and psychedelic neon patterns. Hagar liked Monroy's work so much that he had the bar's design re-created for his set on the Red Voodoo tour.

3

Cabo San Lucas

bartender starts shaking 'em up before noon. ⊠ Plaza del Sol, Blvd. Marina, Marina San Lucas ☎ 624/105–1877 ⊕ www.unomascabo.com ☞ Closed Sun.

DANCE CLUBS
El Squid Roe

DANCE CLUBS | Anything goes at this four-story party spot, including lots of dancing, Jell-O shots, beer-chugging contests, and dancers undulating in a makeshift penitentiary. During spring break or high season, more than 3,000 revelers come here on any given night—and many stay until sunrise. Feeling out of place? Head for one of the balconies on the third and fourth floors (which can be reached by elevator) where the scene is a bit less lurid. Around the corner stands the bar's souvenir shop with humorous T-shirts. El Squid Roe also has a full menu, serving pastas, steaks, and salads. ⊠ Av. Lázaro Cárdenas, Cabo San Lucas ⊹ Between Zaragoza and Morelos ☎ 624/226–7130 ⊕ www.elsquidroe.com.

Giggling Marlin

DANCE CLUBS | Giggling Marlin predates Cabo's tourism explosion, though its gimmicks remain popular. Watch brave (and inebriated) souls be hoisted upside down at the mock fish-weighing scale, or join in an impromptu moonwalk between tables. Many fun (albeit risqué) floor shows relax people's inhibitions. The age of the clientele varies, as does the music, but the dance floor is usually jammed. Daily two-for-one drink specials pack 'em in 9 am–5 pm. ⊠ Blvd. Marina at Matamoros, Cabo San Lucas ☎ 624/143–1182 ⊕ www.gigglingmarlin.com.

Mandala

DANCE CLUBS | At this popular upscale spot, be prepared to wait in line, or pay $200 for a VIP table. Drinks are pricy, but the large dance floor and DJs spinning hip-hop and Latin music just might be worth the disco splurge. ⊠ Av. Lázaro Cárdenas 1112, Centro ☎ 624/143–2056 ⊕ mandalacabos.com.

Rose Bar

BARS/PUBS | Located inside ME Cabo, this bar draws DJs from around the world who come to play their sets and fuel the cozy, neon club. ⊠ *ME Cabo , El Médano Beach, Cabo San Lucas* ☏ *624/145–7800* ⊕ *www.melia.com.*

ROCK CLUBS

Cabo Wabo

MUSIC CLUBS | Depending on when you visit Cabo Wabo, you might just witness a jam session with owner Sammy Hagar and some of his legendary musician friends, who stop by a few times throughout the year. Plan way in advance to attend Hagar's Birthday Bash Week— usually the second week in October—as tickets sell out. The bar's design—high cavernous ceilings, zebra stipes, and psychedelic neon patterns—was re-created for the set of Hagar's Red Voodoo tour. ■**TIP**➔ **Make dinner reservations to avoid the long lines to get in the club.** Lunch and dinner are served with extensive menus, and a taco grill cooks up tasty munchies outside if you wish to cool off after dancing. Shops on-site or at the international airport sell Cabo Wabo souvenir clothing. ⊠ *Calle Guerrero, between Madero and Av. Lázaro Cárdenas, Centro* ☏ *624/143– 1188* ⊕ *www.cabowabocantina.com.*

Hard Rock Cafe

MUSIC CLUBS | After an absence for several years, Hard Rock Cafe is back in Cabo San Lucas, barely a stone's throw from the old location on Av. Lázaro Cárdenas. The new iteration of the global chain is a bit sleeker, and there's now an alfresco dining terrace, but otherwise the focus remains much the same: plenty of comfort food and cocktails, an on-site souvenir store, and walls chock-a-block with rock-and-roll memorabilia, from glitzy stage outfits to custom, rock star–wielded guitars. The Original Legendary Burger with applewood smoked bacon, cheddar cheese, lettuce, tomato, and onion ring is the must-try menu item, while signature cocktails like the Hurricane and Classic Caribbean Mojito come with their own collectible glasses. Check the website calendar for live music and other upcoming events. ⊠ *Av. Lázaro Cárdenas, esq. Av. Morelos, Cabo San Lucas* ☏ *624/143- 4740* ⊕ *www.hardrockcafe.com.*

SUNSET CRUISES

Several companies run nightly cruises for dinner or drinks that capture stunning sunsets as their vessels round the cape. Stands around the marina act as agents and can book excursions for you, but some manage to rope you into a timeshare visit in the process. Better to book through your hotel's front desk or directly through the company.

Caborey

THEMED ENTERTAINMENT | Caborey offers a nightly 2½-hour sunset-dinner cruise on a three-deck catamaran. The cost is $129 and includes a full prix-fixe dinner with your choice of one of six main courses, an open bar for domestic beverages, and a Las Vegas–style show of Mexican music. Departure time is 5 or 6 pm, depending on the timeof year. Check online for discount tickets. ⊠ *Hotel Tesoro Los Cabos, Blvd. Marina, Marina San Lucas* ☏ *624/143-8060, 866/460–4105 in North America* ⊕ *www.caborey.com* ☞ *Tours depart from main cruise ship terminal at Cabo San Lucas Marina.*

Tropicat

THEMED ENTERTAINMENT | Jazz plays nightly as passengers aboard the Tropicat watch the sun set over the 65-foot catamaran, which departs at either 5 or 6 pm, depending upon the time of year. The two-hour excursion is $92 per person and includes premium wines and hors d'oeuvres. The catamaran departs from Dock No. 4, between the cruise ship pier and the dolphin center. ⊠ *Main Dock Gate 4, Cabo San Lucas Marina, Marina San Lucas* ☏ *624/143-3797, 619/446– 6339 in U.S.* ⊕ *www.pezgato.com.*

🛍 Shopping

Cabo San Lucas has the widest variety of shopping options in Los Cabos area, with everything from intriguing Mexican folk art and designer clothing to beer holsters and touristy T-shirts. Bargains on typical Mexican tourist items can be found in the dozens of shops between Boulevard Paseo de la Marina and Avenida Lázaro Cárdenas.

If you get hungry when you're shopping, it's worth trying the inexpensive taco and juice stands tucked into the mini–flea markets that stretch between streets.

Many of the shops in malls like Puerto Paraíso are typical of those you'd find in any mall in the United States—with prices to match. All over the downtown and marina areas, however, are great shops and galleries with unique and compelling items.

ART GALLERIES
Sergio Bustamante

ART GALLERIES | The talented artist from Guadalajara has a shop in the Puerto Paraíso mall. Bustamante's works initially focused on painting and papier-mâché. His sculptures in resin and bronze, many reflecting animal themes, can be purchased at this wonderful gallery and store. Ceramic sculptures and an extensive line of exquisite jewelry in bronze, gold, and silver, many set with precious and semiprecious stones, are found here as well. Don't balk at the price tags: each piece belongs to a limited edition and is created by hand. ⊠ *Puerto Paraíso mall, Boulevard Lázaro Cárdenas 1501, Cabo San Lucas* ☎ *624/144–4894* ⊕ *www. sergiobustamante.com.mx.*

CLOTHING
Almarte Boutique

CLOTHING | This lovely boutique sells designer clothing, silver jewelry, candles, art, books, and more at Waldorf Astoria Los Cabos Pedregal. If you've been admiring the glass-blown hearts dangling from leaf-barren Torote Trees throughout Cabo, this is the place to buy them. The women's line of beach-elegant clothing includes linens, silks, hats and loose-knitted flowing wraps. Some of their highly recognized designers include Chan Luu, Gillian Julius, Minnie Rose, Tom Ford, Jade Tribe, and Roberto Tirado. The store is open to the public; simply notify security at the main gate. ⊠ *Waldorf Astoria Los Cabos Pedregal, Camino del Mar 1, Pedregal* ☎ *624/163–4300* ⊕ *www. waldorfastorialoscabospedregal.com.*

Dos Lunas

CLOTHING | Dos Lunas is full of trendy, colorful sportswear and straw hats, as well as a large selection of handcrafted accessories, bags, and gifts. ⊠ *Plaza Bonita, Blvd. Marina, Cabo San Lucas* ☎ *624/143–1969* ⊕ *www.loscabos-tourism.com/cabo/doslunas.*

Pepita's Magic of the Moon

CLOTHING | A favorite among locals and Cabo regulars, Magic of the Moon features clothing designed by Pepita Nelson, the owner. If you can't find anything that fits you or your style, she will design an outfit for you and finish it in three days. Fabrics are mainly sourced from Mexico, athough the linen is from Brussels and the silk used for her hand-painted creations is also imported. Also check out the handmade ceramic jewelry, beaded bustiers, and colorful bathing suits. ⊠ *Francisco I Madero 7, Centro, Cabo San Lucas* ✛ *Between Guererro and Blvd. Marina, next to J&J* ☎ *624/143–3161* ☉ *Closed Sun.*

DUTY-FREE SHOP
Ultrafemme

PERFUME/COSMETICS | Ultrafemme is the quintessential duty-free shop offering prices that can be up to 30% off designer cosmetic and perfume lines, and name-brand selection of fine jewelry and watches (Rolex, Cartier, and Omega). ⊠ *Luxury Ave. Boutique Mall, Ave. Lázaro Cárdenas, Marina San Lucas* ☎ *624/163–4280* ⊕ *www.ultrafemme.com.*

A Cavalcade of Stars

With Los Cabos' proximity to Southern California (it's a 2½-hour plane ride from L.A.), the southern tip of Baja has become a fabled getaway for all manner of Hollywood celebs. Stars like John Wayne and Bing Crosby vacationed here a half century ago and put Los Cabos on the map; today, some stars opt for the flash and glitz of Cabo San Lucas, while others prefer quieter San José del Cabo with its selection of small inns and intimate restaurants.

Sammy Hagar, the former Van Halen frontman who opened the famous Cabo Wabo bar, is the celebrity most associated with the region, but the list of those who have vacationed here is impressive: Leonardo DiCaprio, Jennifer Lopez, George Clooney, Oprah Winfrey, Brad Pitt, Beyoncé Knowles, Michael Douglas, Catherine Zeta-Jones, Michael Jordan, Brooke Shields, Madonna, Demi Moore, Ashton Kutcher, Meg Ryan, Adam Sandler, Celine Dion, Gwyneth Paltrow, Spike Lee, Jennifer Aniston, Bono, Charlize Theron, Halle Berry, Jessica Simpson, Sarah Jessica Parker, Salma Hayek, Goldie Hawn, Kurt Russell, Sylvester Stallone, Katy Perry, Justin Bieber—and that's just to name a few. Ryan Seacrest often pops over for an afternoon lunch at Las Ventanas.

Many fly into a small airstrip near Cabo San Lucas that handles private jets, as does one terminal at Los Cabos International Airport. You never know who you might see after you arrive, though, so keep your eyes peeled. Paparazzi commonly hire local fishermen to taxi them in pangas just offshore where they photograph celebrities basking in the sun. Remember that "be cool" is one of Los Cabos' cardinal rules: gawking, staring, and taking photos is frowned upon.

LOCAL ART

★ Cobalto Pottery and Tiles

CERAMICS/GLASSWARE | The biggest (and best) pottery collection in Los Cabos is at Cobalto, a colorful boutique set near the town square in Cabo San Lucas that specializes in Talavera-style pottery and tiles from Puebla and Guanajuato. Owner Raquel Pantoja regularly travels the country looking for new pieces, including incredible ceramics by local artisans that were hand-painted with needles to form intricate patterns. All pottery on-site is lead-free and dishwasher safe. ⊠ *Plaza Alamar, Calle Madero, between Guerrero and Hidalgo, Centro* ✛ *Around the corner from Cabo Wabo* ☎ *624/105–0046.*

★ The Glass Factory

(*Fábrica de Vidrio Soplado*)

CERAMICS/GLASSWARE | A beautiful glass mosaic over the entrance to Fábrica de Vidrio Soplado (Blown-Glass Factory) welcomes Los Cabos' most famous artisans every day. Founded in 1988 by engineer Sebastian Romo, the factory uses a glassmaking process close to the one first developed in western Asia four thousand years ago, later refined into glassblowing during the Roman empire. At the factory, 30 artisans produce more than 500 pieces a day from hundreds of pounds of locally recycled glass. Visitors watch while crushed recycled glass is liquefied in gas-fired ovens and, seconds later, transformed into exquisite figures. Secrets for making the thick glassware's deep blues, greens, and reds—the result of special mixtures of metals and gold—are passed from generation to generation. You are sometimes invited to make your own glassware by blowing through a hollow rod to shape a glob of molten glass at the end. ✉ *Calle General Juan Álvarez, Centro* ✛ *Between Capitán Manuel Pineda and 7ª Ave.* ☏ *624/143–0255* ⊕ *www.glassfactory.com.mx* ☉ *Factory closed Sat. and Sun.; gift shop closed Sun.*

Zen-Mar Gallery

CRAFTS | This friendly place carries hundreds of masks, Day of the Dead figures, rugs, glassware, bark-paper wall hangings from Puebla, and all sorts of other fun and captivating items. This is one of Cabo's more comprehensive folk-art shops. ✉ *Av. Lázaro Cárdenas, Centro* ✛ *Between Matamoros and Ocampo* ☏ *624/143–0661.*

FOOD
The Cabo Coffee Company

FOOD/CANDY | The aroma of roasting coffee lures locals and visitors alike into The Cabo Coffee Company, where you can also find refreshing smoothies, cookies, and muffins. The organic green coffee beans are flown fresh from Oaxaca, where they are roasted and bagged for sale. The store sells a number of Starbucks-like flavored coffee drinks and chai tea, as well as ice cream. There is also a book exchange with a few good beach reads. ✉ *Calle Miguel Hidalgo, Cabo San Lucas* ☏ *624/105–1754* ⊕ *www.cabocoffee.com.*

California Ranch Market

FOOD/CANDY | The area's best organic grocery store, California Ranch Market, offers a good selection of imported wines, cheeses, and other gourmet delicacies, as well as American food brands. Freshly squeezed juices and handmade paninis are also available at their second location, in the Corridor-based shopping center The Shoppes at Palmilla. ✉ *Camino del Cerro at Blvd. Marina, Marina San Lucas* ☏ *624/143–1947* ⊕ *www.california-ranchmarket.com.*

GIFTS
Waboutique

GIFTS/SOUVENIRS | Associated with the funky Cabo Wabo bar, Waboutique sells memorabilia, excellent tequila, and souvenirs such as baseball hats, shot glasses, and mugs with the Cabo Wabo logo. ✉ *Calle Guerrero, Centro* ✛ *Between Madero and Lázaro Cárdenas* ☏ *624/143–1188* ⊕ *www.cabowabocantina.com.*

JEWELRY
Diamonds International

JEWELRY/ACCESSORIES | Certified master jewelers are on staff at Diamonds International. This store sells impressive diamonds, designer jewelry, and luxury timepieces. ✉ *Corner of Vicente Guerrero and Blvd. Paseo de la Marina, Centro* ☏ *624/145–8812 Vincente Guerrero location, 624/143-4436 Puerto Paraíso Mall* ⊕ *www.diamondsinternational.com.*

Ultrajewels

JEWELRY/ACCESSORIES | Rolex, Cartier, Tiffany & Co., Mikimoto, TAG Heuer, Omega, Montblanc, and many other top names are offered at Ultrajewels, often at discounted prices. ✉ *Luxury Avenue Boutique Mall, Av. Lázaro Cárdenas, at Malecón corner, Marina San Lucas* ☏ *624/163–4280* ⊕ *www.ultrajewels.com.*

MALLS
Luxury Avenue

SHOPPING CENTERS/MALLS | An indoor mall housing luxury boutiques like Carolina Herrera, Salvatore Ferragamo, Ultrafemme, Ultrajewels, Longchamp, Montblanc, and Lacoste, Luxury Avenue is your one-stop shopping for upscale items in Cabo. It's open daily 10 am–9 pm. There is a second branch in Cancún, Mexico. ✉ *Av. Lázaro Cárdenas, Marina San Lucas* ✛ *Adjacent to Puerto Paraíso mall* ☏ *624/163–4280* ⊕ *www.luxuryavenue.com.*

Plaza Bonita

SHOPPING CENTERS/MALLS | Plaza Bonita is a pleasant place to stroll; it's located at the western edge of the marina and has a few shops ranging from leather and clothing to local artwork and souvenirs. You'll also find an ATM, pharmacy, and Starbucks. ⊠ *Blvd. Marina at Av. Cárdenas, Marina San Lucas.*

Plaza del Sol

SHOPPING CENTERS/MALLS | This open-air market has vendors selling local souvenirs like sarongs, sombreros, bathing suit cover-ups, and beaded necklaces. It's also home to the popular palapa bar, Uno Mas. ⊠ *Blvd. Paseo, Marina San Lucas* ✛ *At the corner of the marina, across the street from Cabo Wabo.*

Plaza Gali

SHOPPING CENTERS/MALLS | It should come as no surprise that Plaza Gali is souvenir central. After all, it's located right in front of the cruise ship terminal. Jewelry, souvenir T-shirts, enormous sombreros, and Cuban cigars abound, as do sundries stores, restaurants, and watering holes. Señor Frog's, a ubiquitous chain in tourist destinations, has a bar and grill here. But souvenirs and margaritas aren't the only attractions. The boutique Mayan Monkey Hostel and Bar is also on-site, as are the check-in offices for two of the best local activities companies: Manta Scuba Diving and Cabo Sails. ⊠ *Blvd. Paseo de la Marina, Marina San Lucas* ✛ *In front of the cruise ship terminal.*

Puerto Paraíso

SHOPPING CENTERS/MALLS | As Los Cabos continues on its upscale trajectory, it's safe to declare that this region has arrived and the shopping here has gone palatial. There is no better, or more apt, way to describe Puerto Paraíso, the city's thriving, air-conditioned, three-story marble- and glass-enclosed mall. With well more than one hundred stores, boutiques, restaurants, galleries, and services, it's quickly becoming the social center of San Lucas. Paraíso offers a dizzying selection of stores. You can have a steak at **Ruth's Chris Steak House;** custom-design your own bikini; shop for beautiful art glass; or enjoy cocktails in a recliner at a movie theater—almost anything is possible in this shopper's paradise. **Sergio Bustamante,** an acclaimed silversmith and sculptor, has a store here, and clothing shops include **Tiki Lounge featuringTommy Bahama, ¡Ay Güey!,** and beachwear boutiques such as **Bari Swimwear, Cabo Style, Ocean Blue, Beach House,** and **Zingara.** A 10-screen movie-theater complex provides cinematic respite, and the second floor is home to a food court and play area for children. Puerto Paraíso is connected to Luxury Avenue, a string of designer boutiques offering top brands like Victoria's Secret and Montblanc. ⊠ *Av. Lázaro Cárdenas 1501, Marina San Lucas* ☎ *624/144–3000* ⊕ *www.puertoparaiso.mx.*

TOBACCO AND LIQUOR

J&J Casa de los Habanos

TOBACCO | This is the best place to find quality Cuban and international cigars, lighters, and ashtrays as well as tequila and Cuban rum. You can schedule a tequila tasting or try one of their signature mojitos while you shop for cigars. ⊠ *Madero at Blvd. Marina, Centro* ☎ *624/143–9845* ⊕ *www.jnjcabo.com.mx.*

⚐ Activities

BOATING

The themes of Los Cabos boat tours vary, but all tours follow essentially the same route: through Bahía Cabo San Lucas, past El Arco and the sea-lion colony, around Land's End into the Pacific Ocean, and then eastward through the Sea of Cortez along the Corridor. Costs run about $90 per person; all tours include an open bar and some offer lunch and snorkel tours. Many of these operators offer whale-watching trips as well.

Glass-bottom boats take passengers to Cabo's top attractions, including Land's End and El Arco.

Cabo Adventures

TOUR—SPORTS | Cabo Adventures has a luxury day sailing trip and a sunset sailing trip on deluxe Beneteau sailboats, during which the crew will teach you some basic sailing maneuvers, or you can simply sit back and enjoy the scenery—the boats pass Lover's Beach and El Arco. The four-hour trip includes food, drinks, snorkel gear, and stand-up paddle-boards. ⊠ *Blvd. Paseo de la Marina, Lot 7, Marina San Lucas* 🕾 *624/173–9500, 888/526–2238* ⊕ *www.cabo-adventures. com* 🖭 *$129.*

Cabo Expeditions

TOUR—SPORTS | **FAMILY** | Winter-season whale-watching (December–April) in the Sea of Cortez with Cabo Expeditions is done from small, customized, inflatable Zodiac boats that allow passengers to get close to gray and humpback whales. Fifteen passengers are allowed per tour; ages five and up. ⊠ *Blvd. Marina S/N, Plaza de la Danza Local 6, Marina San Lucas* 🕾 *624/143–2700* ⊕ *www.caboex-peditions.com.mx* 🖭 *$83.*

Caborey

TOUR—SPORTS | Enjoy incredible views of Los Cabos including the famous arch, Lover's Beach, Santa Maria Bay, Chileno Bay, and the Old Lighthouse aboard the *Caborey.* Set sail from 5 to 7:30 pm for a lobster dinner and mariachi show or opt for the three-hour snorkeling tour including lunch. ⊠ *Hotel Tesoro Los Cabos, Blvd. Marina, Marina San Lucas* 🕾 *624/143–8060, 866/460–4105 in U.S.* ⊕ *www.caborey.com* 🖭 *Day snorkeling tour $85; dinner show $129.*

Oceanus

TOUR—SPORTS | The double-decker party boat *Oceanus* has snorkel cruises from 10:30 am to 2 pm and a sunset dinner cruise that leaves at 5 pm (6 pm in summer) from the main dock in Cabo San Lucas. You can rent the *Oceanus* for birthdays, weddings, and other special occasions. Deep discounts can be found when booking online. ⊠ *Blvd. Marina, Marina San Lucas* 🕾 *624/143–1059, 624/143–3929* ⊕ *www.oceanusloscabos. com.mx* 🖭 *From $65.*

Pisces Luxury Yachts

BOATING | Pisces Luxury Yachts has charters starting at $750 for two-hour sunset excursions on their smallest 40-foot yacht, *Álbatros*, which holds up to eight passengers . The all-inclusive rate runs about $220,000 for six nights on the 163-foot mega yacht, *Azteca II*. Photos and descriptions of the 12 yachts in their luxury fleet are available on their website. ⊠ *Cabo Maritime Center, Blvd. Marina, Suite 1-D, Marina San Lucas* ☎ *624/143–1288, 877/286–7938 in the U.S.* ⊕ *www.piscesyachts.com.*

FLIGHTSEEING

Cabo Sky Tours

TOUR—SPORTS | Cabo Sky Tours offers exciting aerial tours over Land's End, sand dunes, and local beaches in gas-powered hang gliders. ⊠ *Camino Viejo a San José, El Medano Ejidal, Cabo San Lucas* ☎ *624/144–1294 office, 624/150–1000 cell* ⊕ *www.caboskytours.com* ⊠ *From $100.*

Calafia Whales

TOUR—SPORTS | One of the most spectacular ways to view Baja is from the air. Calafia Whales is a private charter company that offers one very special small-plane flight to Magdalena Bay where gray whales calve during winter months. The tours include the flight, a boat tour among the whales, and lunch. Available mid-January to late March only. ⊠ *Calle Adolfo López Mateos Manzana 02, Cabo San Lucas* ☎ *624/143–1795, 624/144-4250* ⊕ *www.tourballenas.com* ⊠ *$650 per person.*

FOUR-WHEELING

Riding an ATV across the desert is a thrill, but it is one of the more dangerous things you can do in this area. As fun as these tours may be, it is worth thinking about the destruction these vehicles cause to the fragile desert terrain. Additionally, many of the companies do not have insurance and will make you sign explicit release-of-liability forms before going. They do issue helmets, goggles, and handkerchiefs to protect you from the sand and dust.

When ATV trips are properly conducted, they can be safe and fun. The most popular trip passes first through Cabo San Lucas, continues through desert cactus fields, and arrives at a big play area of large sand dunes with open expanses and specially carved trails. You can reach frighteningly high speeds as you descend the tall dunes. Navigating the narrow trails in the cactus fields is exciting but not for the fainthearted or steering-impaired. Another favorite trek travels past interesting rock formations, little creeks, and the beach on the way to a small mountain village called **La Candelaria.**

A three-hour trip costs about $120 for a single or $140 for a double (two people sharing an ATV) and includes boxed lunches and drinks. Trips to La Candelaria include lunch and cost about $120 for a single and $150 for a double. Wear tennis shoes, clothes you don't mind getting dirty, and a long-sleeve shirt or sweatshirt for afternoon tours in winter.

Amigos Cabo's Moto Rent

TOUR—SPORTS | Amigos Cabo's Moto Rent offers a desert tour and a beach tour at Playa Migriño on the Pacific, along with Candelaria tours and horseback riding experiences. Transportation is included. ⊠ *Hwy 19, Km 106, Migriño, Cabo San Lucas* ☎ *624/143–0808, 624/144–4161* ⊕ *www.amigosactivities.com* ⊠ *ATV tours, $130 per person or $160 per couple.*

Wide Open Cabo

FOUR-WHEELING | Wide Open takes off-roading to new levels, putting you behind the wheel of a high-performance Baja Challenge race car capable of speeds up to 90 miles an hour. To put that into perspective, these cars have survived the Baja 1000, the toughest off-road race on the planet, 121 times since 2000; and indeed, Wide Open does offer opportunities to enter actual races (including the Baja 1000) with their cars and pit crews. First-timers are advised to start a little slower, however

Horseback riding along stretches of desolate Los Cabos beaches is a treat not to be missed.

(although not by much), with one of three single-day options: three-hour race adventures at their five-mile off-road track overlooking the Pacific Ocean (nine laps guaranteed); five-hour trips to the track with up to 16 laps, lunch included; and nine-hour lunch runs from Cabo San Lucas to Todos Santos and back, with lunch at El Faro Beach Club (120 miles plus of total driving). Cars are rigged for tandem seating, so take turns driving with a friend. ⊠ *Plaza Bonita, Blvd. Paseo de la Marina, Marina San Lucas* ☎ *624/105-0500* ⊕ *www.wideopenbaja. com* ☞ *From $715.*

GOLF

Greens fee prices quoted include off- and high-season rates and are subject to frequent change.

Cabo San Lucas Country Club

GOLF | Don't let the name fool you: Cabo San Lucas Country Club has long been popular due to its public accessibility; plus, it's the only course in the area to feature Land's End views. Designed by Pete Dye's late brother Roy (and finished by *his* son Matt), this was one of the first 18-hole golf layouts ever completed in Los Cabos. The latest renovation by acclaimed Mexican course designer Agustín Pizá in 2018 resulted in changes on the back-nine, but the double-dogleg par-5 7th is the same, and, at 610-yards, remains one of the longest holes in México. The driving range is open at night, which has made it a big hit with locals, who often stop by with friends to hit buckets of balls and share buckets of beer. ⊠ *Hwy. 1, Km 3.7, Cabo San Lucas* ☎ *624/143–4653* ⊕ *www.cabocountry. com* ⊠ *$205* ⚐ *18 holes, 6852 yards, par 71* ☞ *Pro shop, golf academy, lighted driving range, putting green, golf carts, rental clubs, restaurant.*

Quivira Golf Club

GOLF | Pueblo Bonito's four Cabo San Lucas–based properties have plenty to offer in the way of amenities, but the best may be tee time access at this 7,085-yard Jack Nicklaus designed masterpiece. The course meanders through desert foothills and windswept dunes, and skirts cliffs above crashing Pacific Ocean waves before finishing at the best steak house in town. The three on-site comfort food stations are pretty good, too, but the focus here is on amazing golf, and even more amazing scenery. El Faro Viejo, the picturesque lighthouse which is the oldest structure in Cabo San Lucas, is shown off to great advantage from the seventh tee, and players occasionally spot roadrunners and breaching whales during winter months. ⊠ *Paraiso Escondido, Cabo San Lucas* ✛ *Next to Pueblo Bonito Pacifica* ☎ *800/990–8250 in the U.S.* ⊕ *quiviraloscabos.com/golf* ⅄ *18 holes, 7065 yards, par 72* ☞ *Greens fees from $275.*

Rancho San Lucas Golf Course

GOLF | This 7,210-yard, Greg Norman–designed course opened to acclaim in 2020 as part of the 834-acre resort and residential development at Rancho San Lucas. The most spectacular hole is the 161-yard, par-3 17th, which features an island green that will conjure images of TPC Sawgrass in Florida. The course impresses with pristine fairways, Pacific Ocean views, windswept dunes, and British links–style bunkering. Comfort-food stations are strategically placed, ensuring players don't have to take too many swings between refreshing food and drinks. The course is only open to guests at Solmar Group Resorts, a list that includes Grand Solmar properties at Land's End and Rancho San Lucas, as well as Playa Grande and The Ridge at Playa Grande. ⊠ *Carretera Todos Santos (Hwy 19), Km 120, Cabo San Lucas* ☎ *624/145–7575* ⊕ *www.ranchosanlucas.com* ⅄ *18 holes, 7210 yards, Par 72* ☞ *Greens fees from $194.*

GUIDED TOURS

Cabo Adventures

TOUR—SPORTS | With a wide variety of unusual activities Cabo Adventures is a unique adventure operator. Along with its popular Cabo Dolphins program are the four-hour Desert Safaris, located in a private ranch by the Pacific Ocean where you can commune with camels, of all things! They also offer ziplining, mountain biking, whale shark tours, and guided Jet Ski rides. ⊠ *Blvd. Paseo de la Marina, Marina San Lucas* ☎ *624/173–9500, 888/526–2238* ⊕ *www.cabo-adventures.com* ✉ *From $89 per person.*

KAYAKING

In Cabo San Lucas, Playa El Médano is the best beach for kayaking. A number of companies located along El Médano offer kayak rentals, and there are guided tours that go out to Lover's Beach to view El Arco, and around the Land's End Rocks. Rates are generally uniform from one operator to another.

Cabo Expeditions

KAYAKING | Tandem kayak to Land's End and back, with stops for snorkeling and a visit to Lover's Beach. ⊠ *Blvd. Marina s/n, Plaza de la Danza Local 6, Marina San Lucas* ☎ *624/143-2700* ⊕ *www.caboexpeditions.com.mx* ☞ *$75.*

Tio Sports

KAYAKING | Tio Sports was one of the original water-sports companies on El Médano Beach more than 30 years ago, and is still a major operator with a sports palapa located on the beach at the ME Cabo Resort, plus stands and offices throughout Los Cabos. It provides aquatic tours, kayak rentals, stand-up paddleboards, and packages that include scuba and snorkeling. ⊠ *Playa El Médano, Marina San Lucas* ☎ *624/143–3399* ⊕ *www.tiosports.com* ✉ *From $25.*

SAILING

Cabo San Lucas has very good sailing winds once boats clear the protected bay. But since most sailboat tours focus on sightseeing around Land's End (where they motor without sails), it's a good idea to inquire in advance if the tour includes full-fledged sailing beyond this area. On private tours, this is not an issue, and the captain will sail as much as guests desire, weather permitting.

Cabo Sailing

SAILING | Forget the party-boat scene. The best introduction to the coastal geography and laid-back lifestyle of Cabo San Lucas is via private charters with Cabo Sailing. The company has a superb collection of boats, including both 38-foot and 42-foot Hunter sailboats perfect for group outings, family snorkeling expeditions, or romantic sunset sails for two complete with champagne. Cabo Sailing's focus is on service and upscale amenities, plus air-conditioned cabins and premium bar selections aboard their pair of luxurious 46-foot fishing boats. Whale-watching makes the trip extra special between mid-December and mid-March. Round-trip van transportation from your resort is an optional upgrade for an extra $90. ⊠ *Plaza Nautica, Blvd. Marina, Local C-5, Marina San Lucas* ⊹ *Next to Plaza de la Danza* ☎ *624/143–8485, 800/209–1669 in the U.S.* ⊕ *www.cabosailing.com.*

Cabo Sails

SAILING | Sailor types are welcome to help sail one of Cabo Sails' eight sailboats— ranging in size from 28 feet to 44 feet— but most visitors are content to lay back on towel-wrapped cushions and enjoy fresh sea breezes, cocktails, and gorgeous Land's End scenery. A catamaran and trimaran offer the smoothest rides, and like all vessels are ringed with lifeline safety netting, a family-friendly feature that alleviates worry for parents traveling with small children. The staff's attention to detail is impressive in all areas. Dog-sized life preservers are offered for those traveling with pets, bouquets of roses or birthday cakes are optional for special occasions, and in a long-standing commitment to eco-friendly measures, no plastics are used aboard any of the boats (the 44-foot *Espíritu Santi* even uses solar power to motor in and out of the marina). ⊠ *Plaza Gali, Blvd. Paseo de la Marina, Marina San Lucas* ⊹ *Across from Manta Scuba Diving* ☎ *624/355–6386, 800/243–4206 in the U.S.* ⊕ *www.cabosails.com* ☞ *Private boat tours from $400.*

SCUBA DIVING

Generally, diving costs about $70 for one tank and $95 for two, including transportation. Equipment rental, dives in the Corridor, and night dives typically cost extra. Full-day trips to Gordo Banks and Cabo Pulmo cost about $220, including transportation, food, equipment, and two tanks. Most operators offer two- to four-day package deals.

Most dive shops have courses for noncertified divers; some may be offered through your hotel. Newly certified divers may go on local dives no more than 30 to 40 feet deep. Divers must show their C-card (diver certification card) before going on dives with reputable shops. Many operators offer widely recognized Professional Association of Diving Instructors (PADI) certification courses, which usually take place in training pools for the first couple of lessons.

At sites in **Bahía San Lucas** near El Arco, you're likely to see colorful tropical fish traveling confidently in large schools. Yellow angelfish, green and blue parrot fish, red snappers, perfectly camouflaged stonefish, and long slender needlefish share these waters. Divers regularly see stingrays, manta rays, and moray eels. The only problem with this location is the amount of boat traffic. The sound of motors penetrates deep into the water and can slightly mar the experience. **Neptune's Fingers** (60–120 feet) is a long rock formation with abundant fish. About 150 feet off Playa del Amor, **Pelican Rock** (25–100 feet) is a calm protected spot where you can look down on Sand Falls (underwater cascades that drop into a 1,200 foot canyon) discovered by none other than Jacques Cousteau. **The Point** (15–80 feet) is a good spot for beginners who aren't ready to get too deep.

OPERATORS
Manta Scuba Diving

SCUBA DIVING | This centrally located PADI 5-star outfit makes trips locally in the Corridor, as well as to Cabo Pulmo,

Mutual curiosity between a scuba diver and a gentle whale shark (*Rhincodon typus*)

Gordo Banks, and East Cape. ⊠ *Plaza Gali, Blvd. Marina 7D Local 37 Int., Marina San Lucas* ☎ *624/144-3871* ⊕ *www.caboscuba.com* ✉ *Two-tank dives from $125; equipment rental $35.*

Solmar V

SCUBA DIVING | Find luxury on the über-comfortable live-aboard dive boat *Solmar V*, which takes nine-day remote diving trips to the Revillagigedo Archipelago (November–June) for spotting giant mantas, humpback whales, dolphins, tuna, and shark. They also have trips to Isla Guadalupe off the northwest coast of Baja California (August–October) for great-white-shark cage diving. Air is surface supplied so you don't need to be a certified diver to enjoy the Guadalupe trip. Twelve cabins with private baths serve a maximum of 20 passengers. This is one of Cabo's top diving experiences, so book well in advance. A second boat, *Vortex*, can accommodate up to 14 divers in seven cabins for trips to the same two destinations, and the smaller *Mobula* offers half- and full-day snorkeling and free diving encounters with sharks and mobulas off the coast of Cabo San Lucas. ⊠ *Cabo San Lucas* ☎ *626/678-0919 in the U.S., 624/144-4482 in Cabo San Lucas* ⊕ *www.solmarv.com* ✉ *$3,095–$4,299 for Solmar V; $5,000–$10,000 for Vortex; from $175 for Mobula.*

SNORKELING

Many of the best dive spots are also good for snorkeling. Prime areas include the waters surrounding **Playa del Amor, Bahía Santa María, Bahía Chileno**, and **Cabo Pulmo** on the East Cape. Nearly all scuba operators also offer snorkel rentals and trips. Equipment rentals generally cost $10 per hour ($20 for the day). Two-hour guided trips to Playa del Amor are about $75; day trips to Cabo Pulmo cost about $150. Most of the snorkeling and excursion boats are based in the Cabo San Lucas harbor and the best place to make reservations is along the marina boardwalk, or along El Médano Beach.

If you're willing to plan ahead, booking online will often bring you significant discounts on these tours.

Pez Gato

SNORKELING | The Pez Gato catamaran and trimaran fleet boast several smooth-sailing tour options, highlighted by a snorkeling trip to beautiful Bahía Santa María with lunch included aboard the 45-foot catamaran *Pez Gato I*. They also offer in-season whale-watching, party cruises aboard the 46-foot *Pez Gato III*, romantic jazz and wine-themed sunset sails aboard the 65-foot *Tropicat*, and Mexican theme dinner cruises aboard the 65-foot *Cabo Mar*. ⊠ *Main Dock Gate 4, Cabo San Lucas Marina, Marina San Lucas* ☎ *624/143–3797, 619/446–6339* ⊕ *www.pezgato.com* ⊠ *Snorkeling trip $92 per person.*

SPAS

Armonia Spa at Pueblo Bonito Pacifica

SPA/BEAUTY | This resort complex on the Pacific side of Cabo is an adults-only property, filled with feng shui design, immaculately kept cactus gardens, and water, water, everywhere. Treatments at the Armonia Spa run the gamut from crystal Reiki healing to a yogurt-and-violets exfoliation, and even spa treatments for kids at their neighboring sister property, Pueblo Bonito Sunset Beach. ⊠ *Pueblo Bonita Pacifica Golf and Spa Resort, Predio Paraiso Escondido, Cabo San Lucas* ☎ *624/142–9696* ⊕ *www.pueblobonitopacifica.com* ⊠ *Body treatments: $130–$330. Facials: $90–$275. Hair: $25–$110. Mani/Pedi: $35–$62.*

Luna y Mar at Waldorf Astoria Spa

SPA/BEAUTY | "Moon and Sea" at Waldorf Astoria Spa promises a revitalizing escape with treatments based around the themes of moon, sea, and Mexican healing. The 10 treatment rooms in this body-melting spa, easily one of the best in the region, offer guests passage to the ultimate in relaxation. Cascading pools create a soothing soundtrack to the kneading of top technicians. Beyond body and skin treatments, the facility has a hair salon, fitness center, and tennis courts. ⊠ *Waldorf Astoria Los Cabos Pedregal, Camino del Mar 1, Pedregal* ☎ *624/163–4300* ⊕ *www.waldorfastoria-loscabospedregal.com* ⊠ *Body treatments: $145–$360. Facials: $175–$240.*

Playa Grande Spa by Solmar

SPA/BEAUTY | Playa Grande Spa by Solmar features a seawater pool and hydrotherapy circuit, traditional Temazcal rituals, and a variety of other treatments to ease stress for both body and mind. Pampering options include anti-aging facials, manicures, pedicures, and hands-on body therapies. Their standout "Four Hands Massage" includes a massage from two therapists working at the same time. ⊠ *Playa Grande Resort, Av. Playa Grande 1, Playa Solmar, Cabo San Lucas* ☎ *624/145–7575* ⊕ *playagranderesort.solmar.com* ⊠ *Body treatments: $175–$250. Facials: $130–$175. Hair: $30–$190. Mani/Pedi: $30–$60. Waxing: $20–$60* ☞ *Body treatments: $175–$250. Facials: $130–$175. Hair: $30–$190. Mani/Pedi: $30–$60. Waxing: $20–$60.*

SPORTFISHING

The waters off Los Cabos are home to more than 800 species of fish—a good number of which bite all year-round. It's easy to arrange charters online, through hotels, and directly with sportfishing companies along the docks at Marina Cabo San Lucas. (Rather than book through an independent agent roaming the marina, it's best to reserve through a reputable company in an actual office.) Ships depart from sportfishing docks at the south end of the marina, near the Puerto Paraíso Mall, or from the docks at Hotel Tesoro Los Cabos. It's important to get specific directions, since it's hard to find your spot before departing at 6:30 a.m.

Prices range from $250 or $350 a day for a *panga* (small skiff) to $600 to $2,700 a day for a larger cruiser with a bathroom, a sunbathing deck, and AC. The sky's the

Continued on page 97

SPORTFISHING

By Larry Dunmire

Cabo San Lucas is called both the Marlin Mecca and Marlin Capital of the World for good reason. Thanks to the warm waters of the Sea of Cortez, the tip of the Baja Peninsula has one of the world's largest concentrations of billfish. And, no matter what time of year you visit, there's a great chance—some locals say a 90% one—you'll make a catch, too.

More than 800 species of fish swim off Los Cabos, but anglers pursue only about half a dozen types. The most sought-after are the húge blue or black marlin, which have been known to fight for hours. The largest of these fish—the so-called granders—weigh in at 1,000 pounds or more. The more numerous, though smaller (up to 200 pounds), striped marlin are also popular catches.

Those interested in putting the catch-of-the-day on their table aim for the iridescent green and yellow dorado (also called mahi-mahi), tuna, yellowtail, and wahoo (also known as ono)—the latter a relative of the barracuda that can speed along at up to 50 mph. Also gaining popularity is light-tackle fly-fishing for roosterfish, jack crevalle, and pargo from small boats near the shore.

Something's always biting, but the greatest diversity of species inhabit Cabo's waters from June through November, when sea temperatures climb into the high 80s.

(above) A billfish catch in progress

WHAT TO EXPECT

You don't need to be experienced or physically strong to sportfish. Your boat's captain and crew will happily help you along, guiding you on how to properly handle the equipment.

Some of the larger boats have the so-called fighting chairs, which resemble a dentist's chair, firmly mounted to the deck. These rotate smoothly allowing you to follow the movement of a hooked fish and giving you the support you need to fight with a large black or blue marlin for an extended period of time.

Experienced fishermen sometimes forego chairs for the stand-up technique using a padded harness/fighting belt that has a heavy-duty plastic-and-metal rod holder connected to it. Though physically demanding—especially on the arms and lower back—this technique often speeds up the fight and is impressive to watch.

FISHING TWO WAYS

Most of Cabo's boats are equipped for the more traditional heavy-duty sportfishing using large, often cumbersome rods and reels and beautiful, colorful plastic lures with hooks. A modified form of fly-fishing is gaining popularity. This requires a finessed fly-casting technique and spot-on timing between crew and the fisherman. It utilizes ultra-lightweight rods and reels, relatively miniscule line, and a technique known as bait and switch.

You attract fish as near to the back of a boat as possible with hook-less lures. As the crew pulls in the lures, you cast your fly (with hooks) to the marlin. Fights with the lighter equipment—and with circle hooks rather than regular ones—are usually less harmful, enabling more fish to be released.

(top) Sportfishing in Los Cabos—one man's catch

CONSERVATION IN CABO

You're strongly encouraged to use the less-harmful circle hooks (shaped like an "O"), as opposed to J-hooks, which do terrible internal damage. It's now common to release all billfish, as well as any dorado, wahoo, or tuna that you don't plan to eat. Folks here frown on trophy fishing unless it takes place during an official tournament. Instead, quickly take your photos with the fish, then release it.

The Cabo Sportfishing Association has a fleet-wide agreement that no more than one marlin per boat be taken per day. Usually all are released, denoted by the "T" flags flown from a boat's bridge as it enters the marina.

The few marlin that are brought in are hoisted and weighed, photographed, and then put to good use—taken to be smoked or given to needy locals. You can ask the crew to fillet the tastier species right on your boat, and you can usually arrange for the fish to be smoked or vacuum-packed and frozen to take home. Many restaurants, especially those found marina-side in Cabo San Lucas, will gladly prepare your catch any way you like. You hook it, they cook it.

CHARTERING A BOAT

You can arrange charters at hotels—through a concierge or a charter desk—at Los Cabos tackle shops, or directly through charter companies. It's also possible to make arrangements online before you arrive. Indeed, it's good to do this up to three months in advance for the busiest months of October and November. ■ TIP ➜ **Don't arrange charters through time-share companies. They aren't always reliable and sometimes work with boats that aren't that well equipped.**

Rates usually include a captain and crew, tackle, bait, fishing licenses, and soft drinks. You often need to bring your own lunch; if it is included, it usually costs extra, as do alcoholic drinks. Unless you're quoted an all-inclusive charter price, confirm what is and isn't included. Also, a tip of 15% of the cost of the charter will be appreciated. Note, too, that some charter companies will try to help solo anglers hook up with a group to share a boat.

A walk along the perimeter of the Marina Cabo San Lucas demonstrates that Cabo really is all about fishing. Indeed, this is where most vendors are based and where most yachts set sail. (Departures are generally predawn—between 6 and 6:30 am—so it's not a bad idea to locate your dock and boat ahead of time, in the light of day.)

It seems as if every yacht tied to the docks is a sport fisher, and you'll see different colored flags flying from the boats' outriggers. These designate the numbers and types of fish caught during the previous day of fishing as well as the number of marlin released. The blue flags are for marlin, yellow for dorado, white for wahoo, and red for tuna. Each red and white "T"-flag means a billfish was tagged and released.

(top) A cruiser out to sea

The Original Cabeños

The indigenous inhabitants of Cabo San Lucas were the Pericú, hunter-gatherers whose territory included much of the present day Los Cabos municipality, as well as offshore islands like Cerralvo, Espíritu Santo, Partida, and San José.

Although the Pericú have been culturally extinct since the late 18th century, they were much in the news earlier this century when it was discovered they shared a genetic makeup remarkably similar to that of Australian aborigines.

Based on this discovery and mounting evidence, it is now thought that the Pericú migrated from Melanesia some 15,000 years ago, a separate and earlier migration than was previously thought (that they crossed the Bering Strait at the end of the last ice age, when much of the Americas became populated).

In 1992 a major excavation on the site of what would become Villa del Palmar Resort and Spa on Playa El Médano provided compelling evidence that the Pericú used the same primitive tools for the entirety of their existence. They were remarkable fishermen, nonetheless, a fact remarked on by all the early European visitors to the region.

limit with the larger private yachts (think 80 feet); it's not unheard of for such vessels to cost $6,000 or $10,000 a day. No matter what you pay, rates should include a captain and crew, tackle, bait, drinks, and sometimes lunch. If you plan to spend a full day at sea, it's best to purchase an all-inclusive package rather than a bare-bones trip lacking in services. Factor in the cost of a fishing license (about $18), required for all passengers over 18 years of age. Fishing licenses can be purchased for about half the price through the CONAPESCA website (⊕ www.conapescasandiego.org).

Minerva's Baja Tackle

FISHING | Renowned tackle store Minerva's Baja Tackle and Sportfishing Charters has been around for more than 40 years and has its own small fleet with two sportfishing charter boats from 31 feet to 33 feet. ✉ Madero between Blvd. Marina and Guerrero, Centro ☎ 624/143–1282, 888/480–7826 from the U.S. ⊕ www.minervas.com ⛴ From $696 bare boat; $800 all-inclusive.

★ Picante Fleet

FISHING | One of the top sportfishing fleets, Picante Fleet offers a wide selection of more than a dozen well-equipped boats, from top-of-the-line, 31-foot sport fishers to a 110-foot luxury yacht. If you prefer smaller boats, there's the Picantito fleet, with a trio of 24-foot Shamrock walk-around boats. These are primarily used for fishing close to shore. Picante offers trips and boats that vary in size and price. ✉ Puerto Paraíso Mall Local 39-A, near WTF Burger Bar, Marina San Lucas ☎ 624/143–2474, 714/442–0644 in U.S. ⊕ www.picantesportfishing.com ⛴ From $1,020 for 8 hrs.

★ Pisces Sportfishing Fleet

FISHING | Some of Cabo's top hotels use the extensive range of yachts from Pisces Sportfishing Fleet. The fleet includes the usual 31-foot Bertrams, but also has a sizable fleet of 50- to 70-foot Viking and Riviera yachts with tuna towers, air-conditioning, and multiple staterooms. Pisces also has luxury yachts up to 163 feet in length. Chartering a 31-foot Bertram is all-inclusive for up to six people, and trips last for around eight hours. ⊠ *Cabo Maritime Center, Blvd. Marina, Suite 1-D, Marina San Lucas* ☎ *624/143–1288, 877/286–7938 toll-free in U.S.* ⊕ *www.piscessportfishing.com* ☎ *From $250 for a 22-foot panga; Bertram charter $695, all-inclusive.*

WHALE-WATCHING

Long before snowbirds discovered the joys of wintering in Los Cabos, the world's largest creatures were migrating annually from their arctic summer feeding grounds to warm-water winter breeding grounds in coves and inlets around Baja California Sur. These are the longest mammalian migrations ever tracked, with the record held by a gray whale dubbed Varvara, who logged over 14,000 miles round-trip from Sakhalin Island, Russia to Cabo San Lucas in 2015. It's estimated that upwards of 5,000 whales make the journey to Southern Baja each year, with gray whales heading primarily to lagoons in San Ignacio, Ojo de Liebre, and Magdalena Bay on the Pacific Coast, 175 miles or more north of Cabo San Lucas.

Grays *are* commonly seen in Los Cabos, but the focus of local tours is on humpbacks; not only because of their large numbers, but also their spectacular breaches. They lift nearly their entire bodies—all 30 tons or so—out of the water for epic splashdowns, and are known for photogenic behaviors such as spyhopping (lifting their giant heads to take a gander at the surroundings) and lobtailing (a hard slap of the fluke on the surface of the water).

Other species are less prevalent, but orcas, sperm whales, fins, pilot whales, and even blue whales (the largest creature to ever exist on Earth) are sometimes spotted. Whale-watching season officially begins in Los Cabos on December 15 and ends on April 15. The best tours include hydrophones, so in addition to seeing whales you can also hear their haunting "songs."

To watch whales from the shore, go to the beach at the Solmar Suites, The Grand Solmar, Sandos Finisterra, or any Corridor hotel, or the lookout points along the Corridor highway. *Virtually all the companies listed in "Boating" offer whale-watching tours (about $80–$100 depending on size of boat and length of tour) from Cabo San Lucas.*

Cabo Expeditions

WHALE-WATCHING | Like many Cabo tour operators, Cabo Expeditions offers snorkeling and in-season whale-watching tours, the latter in Zodiac high-speed inflatable boats. ⊠ *Blvd. Marina S/N, Plaza de la Danza Local 6, Marina San Lucas* ☎ *624/143–2700* ⊕ *www.cabo-expeditions.com.mx* ☎ *Snorkeling $77, whale-watching $83.*

Whale Watch Cabo

WHALE-WATCHING | With a sustainable, small-group ethos and dedicated focus on whale-watching, Whale Watch Cabo offers seasonal tours from Cabo San Lucas, as well as two-day gray whale adventure excursions by van to Magdalena Bay. ⊠ *Plaza Bonita, Blvd. Paseo de la Marina 17, Marina San Lucas* ☎ *624/105–9336* ⊕ *www.whalewatchcabo.com.*

Chapter 4

THE CORRIDOR

Updated by
Luis Domínguez

👁 **Sights**   🍴 **Restaurants**   💼 **Hotels**   🛍 **Shopping**   🍸 **Nightlife**

★★☆☆☆   ★★★★★   ★★★★★   ★★★☆☆   ★★★☆☆

NEIGHBORHOOD SNAPSHOT

TOP EXPERIENCES

■ **Luxury Resorts:** A few of the most exclusive resorts in Mexico are located here, including Esperanza, Montage, and Las Ventanas al Paraiso. You may be tempted not to leave the property.

■ **Snorkeling:** For an unforgettable experience that's just like swimming in an aquarium, submerge yourself into the water of Chileno Bay. You'll spot fish close to the shore, even while standing.

■ **Fine Dining:** The Corridor is home to some of the most spectacular restaurants in the Baja Península, where you can enjoy sophisticated dishes prepared by celebrity chefs in stunning outdoor settings.

■ **Golf:** The number of first-class golf courses may surprise you. Designed by the best, with lush fairways, the courses suit all types of putters.

■ **Spa Time:** Indulge yourself with pampering massages and treatments at one of the area's dizzying array of upscale resort spas.

GETTING HERE

The easiest way to arrive from the airport (SJD) is to take a shuttle, which costs about $125 for a private ride for up to six people. Taxi prices will always be higher and will depend on your negotiation skills. Renting a car is a good (and cheaper) option, as it will give you freedom to explore the region.

The Corridor runs along the four-lane Carretera Transpeninsular (Highway 1), which has more-or-less well-marked turnoffs for hotels. Be alert: signage as a rule appears at the very last minute. Drivers tend to speed along most of the highway, so drive with caution.

PLANNING YOUR TIME

The Corridor is quietest between June and mid-November. For more excitement, visit during high season between December and May, when snowbirds flock south and whale watching tours take place. Save a day to venture outside the resort-heavy area if you desire authentic, local experiences.

QUICK BITES

■ **Cream Café.** Stop into this European-style café and bakery for a quick coffee, pastry, or a slice of pizza. It's the go-to place for brunch outside of the big-resort restaurants. ⊠ *The Shoppes at Palmilla, Carretera Transpeninsular, Km. 19.5, The Corridor* ⊕ *www. creamcafeloscabos.com*

■ **Chin's.** Take a break from Mexican cuisine with unpretentious Chinese food that's found its way to the desert heart of the Corridor. ⊠ *The Shoppes at Palmilla, Carretera Transpeninsular, Km. 19.5, The Corridor* ⊕ *www.chinscabo.com*

■ **La Carreta.** For authentic Mexican food visit this spot serving traditional dishes from Oaxaca. Try the enchiladas, the memelas, or the amazing guacamole with *chapulines* (grasshoppers). ⊠ *Koral Center, Carretera Transpeninsular, Km. 7.5, The Corridor* ⊕ *lacarretamx. com*

■ **Ufficio.** Refuel with a coffee and pizza of Neapolitan roots at the Koral Center food hall. Order a takeaway tiramisu and choose your coffee beans for a premium espresso. ⊠ *Koral Center, Carretera Transpeninsular, Km. 7.5, The Corridor* ⊕ *www.pandibacco.com/ufficio*

Carretera Transpeninsular dips into *arroyos* (riverbeds) and climbs onto a floodplain studded with boulders and cacti between San José del Cabo and Cabo San Lucas. This stretch of desert terrain connecting Los Cabos' sister cities, known as the Corridor, has long been the haunt of the rich and famous. In the 1950s a few fishing lodges and remote resorts with private airstrips attracted adventurers and celebrities. As the fastest developing area in Los Cabos, today the region has gated communities, resorts lining beautiful beaches, posh hotels, and championship golf courses.

Although it doesn't have the nightlife of Cabo San Lucas or local flavor of San José del Cabo, the Corridor hits a sweet spot for travelers whose top priority is a luxurious, private resort with access to top-notch restaurants, beaches, and activities. In fact, the Corridor is arguably the most action-packed location in Los Cabos. The stretch of land between the Sea of Cortez and Baja desert packs in world-famous golf courses, the biggest adventure park in the area, plus snorkeling, diving, whale-watching, sportfishing, and turtle releases along the beaches of the area's lavish hotels.

Sometimes referred to as the Tourist Corridor, the area primarily caters to out-of-towners. Travelers looking for a more profound Mexico experience will need a car (or an Uber or taxi) to travel to the sights and hopping bars of Cabo San Lucas or the authentic, colorful adobe dwellings you'll find in parts of San José del Cabo. But if you're willing to drive, or if you're content to stay put at a resort area that has plenty of its own entertainment and scenery, there is no better place than the Corridor.

🏖 Beaches

The Corridor's coastline edges the Sea of Cortez, with long, secluded stretches of sand, tranquil bays, golf fairways, and huge resorts. Only a few areas are safe for swimming, but several hotels have

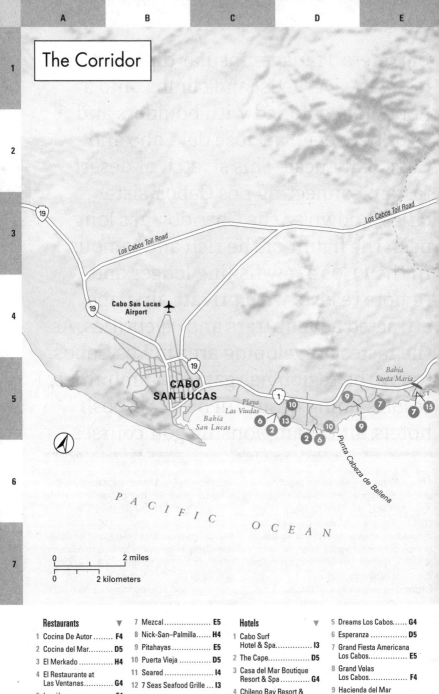

The Corridor

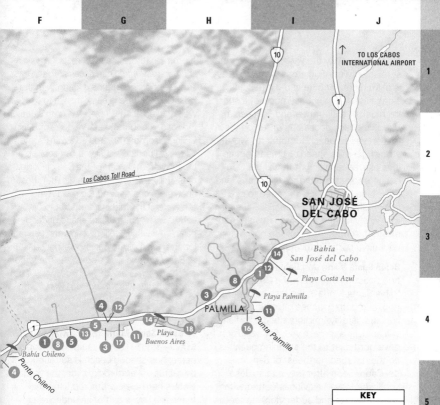

F   **G**   **H**   **I**   **J**

TO LOS CABOS
INTERNATIONAL AIRPORT

Los Cabos Toll Road

**SAN JOSÉ
DEL CABO**

*Bahía
San José del Cabo*

Playa Costa Azul

Playa Palmilla

PALMILLA

*Playa
Buenos Aires*

Punta Palmilla

Bahía Chileno

Punta Chileno

KEY

- Restaurants
- Hotels

man-made rocky breakwaters that create semisafe swimming areas when the sea is calm. Look for blue-and-white signs along Highway 1 with symbols of a snorkel mask or a swimmer and "*acceso a playa*" ("beach access") written on them to alert you to beach turnoffs. It's worth studying a map ahead of time to get an idea of where your turnoff will be. Don't hesitate to ask around for directions, and don't lose hope if you still need to circle back around once or twice. Facilities are extremely limited and lifeguards are nonexistent, though many of the beaches now have portable toilets.

Bahía Santa María and **Bahía Chileno** are two beautiful strands in the Corridor. Bahía Santa María is the less busy of the two, and both beaches offer fun snorkeling and safe swimming; the docile fish will actually approach you. For seclusion, drive northeast to the stunning beaches on the dirt road northeast of San José del Cabo. Soon after leaving San José you'll see Playa Las Viudas dotted with shade palapas and surfers looking for the next big break. Don't be put off by all of the private homes or "no trespassing" signs—beaches are plentiful and public access is clearly marked. The dirt road from the highway is well maintained and fine for passenger cars (despite dire-sounding warnings from locals who will tell you that you must have a four-wheel-drive vehicle)—but the dirt roads are best avoided if it's raining.

★ **Bahía Chileno** (*Chileno Bay*)
BEACH—SIGHT | FAMILY | A calm enclave—with golf courses, residences, and Chileno Bay Resort—is roughly midway between San José and Cabo San Lucas. Consistently ranked one of the cleanest beaches in Mexico, Chileno has been awarded "Blue Flag" certification, meaning 32 criteria for safety, services, water quality, and other standards have been met. The beach skirts a small, crescent-shaped cove with aquamarine waters and an outside reef that are perfect for snorkeling and

swimming (there are even restrooms, showers, and handicap access). To the east are tide pools great for exploring with the kids. Getting here is easy, thanks to the well-marked access ramps on both sides of the road. Along the western edge of Bahía Chileno, some 200 yards away, are some good-size boulders that you can scramble up. In winter this part of the Sea of Cortez gets chilly—refreshing for a dip, but most snorkelers don't spend too much time in the water. On weekends get to the bay early if you want to claim shade under a palapa. **Amenities:** toilets; showers; parking lot. **Best for:** swimming; snorkeling; sunset. ⊠ *Bahía Chileno, The Corridor* ⊹ *The turnoff for the beach is at Km 14.5 on Hwy. 1. Look for the signs whether driving west from San José or at Km 16 when driving east from Cabo San Lucas.*

★ **Bahía Santa María** (*Santa Maria Beach*)
BEACH—SIGHT | FAMILY | This wide, sloping, horseshoe-shaped beach is surrounded by cactus-covered rocky cliffs; the placid waters here are a protected fish sanctuary. The bay is part of an underwater reserve and is a great place to snorkel: brightly colored fish swarm through chunks of white coral and golden sea fans. Unfortunately, this little slice of paradise has limited palapas for shade, so arrive early or bring a beach umbrella. In high season, from November to May, there's usually someone renting snorkeling gear or selling sarongs, straw hats, and soft drinks. It's best to bring your own supplies, though, including lots of drinking water, snacks, and sunscreen. Snorkel and booze-cruise boats from Cabo San Lucas visit the bay in midmorning through about 1 pm. Arrive midafternoon if you want to get that total Robinson Crusoe feel. The parking lot is a quarter mile or so off the highway and is sometimes guarded; be sure to tip the guard. The bay is roughly 19 km (12 miles) west of San José and 13 km (8 miles) east of Cabo San Lucas. Heading east, look for the sign saying "playa santa maría." **Amenities:** toilets; free parking; showers; lifeguards. **Best for:**

Boat tours from Cabo San Lucas often stop at Bahía Santa María for snorkeling.

snorkeling; swimming; surfing; walking. ☒ *The Corridor ⊹ 19 km (12 miles) west of San José del Cabo, 13 km (8 miles) east of Cabo San Lucas.*

Playa Buenos Aires

BEACH—SIGHT | This wide, lengthy, and accessible stretch of beach is one of the longest along the Cabo Corridor, but is rapidly developing with new resorts. Reef breaks for surfers can be good, but the beach is also known for its riptides, making it unswimmable. It's a great beach for long, quiet runs or walks, and it's not uncommon to find locals with horses to rent for a beachside ride. Whales can easily be spotted from the beach from January through March. The small, man-made "Tequila Cove" between Hilton and Paradisus has calm waters, excellent for swimming. Here you'll find a tiny shack renting bodyboards and other water-sports equipment. **Amenities:** toilets; water sports; free parking. **Best for:** surfers; walking. ⊹ *Near the Secrets Marquis Hotel Los Cabos/Hilton and stretching down to Meliá Cabo Real.*

Playa Costa Azul

BEACH—SIGHT | Cabo's best surfing beach runs 3 km (2 miles) south from San José's hotel zone along Highway 1. The Zipper and La Roca breaks are world famous. Playa Costa Azul connects to neighboring **Playa Acapulquito** in front of the Cabo Surf Hotel. Surfers gather at both beaches year-round, but most come in summer, when hurricanes and tropical storms create the year's largest waves, and when the ocean is at its warmest. This condo-lined beach is popular with joggers and walkers, but swimming isn't advised. When getting in and out of the water in front of Cabo Surf Hotel (where surf lessons take place), watch out for the sea urchins that cling to the shallow rocks. Beginner surfers should ask locals to point out the mound of hidden rocks near the break closest to the cliffs; this means it's much safer to take "rights" than "lefts" at this break. Although not overly common, jellyfish can also be a problem here. The turnoff to this beach is sudden and only available to drivers coming from Cabo

San Lucas (not from San José del Cabo). It's on the beach side of the highway, at Zipper's restaurant, which is on the sand by the surf breaks. If coming from San José del Cabo, you have to exit at Costa Azul Surf Shop and drive under the highway to the parking area. Food and drinks are available at Zipper's restaurant or at 7 Seas restaurant. Surfboards can be rented at Costa Azul Surf Shop or at Cabo Surf Hotel. **Amenities:** toilets; food and drink; free parking. **Best for:** surfing; walking; sunset. ⊕ *Just over 1 km (½ mi) southwest of San José del Cabo.*

Playa Las Viudas (*Widow's Beach*)
BEACH—SIGHT | Just west of Santa María Bay, this small public beach is often referred to as Twin Dolphin Beach after the Twin Dolphin Hotel, a longtime landmark that was demolished in mid-2007 to make room for Chileno Bay Club. The reef makes it a great place for snorkeling (bring your own gear), but it is open to the ocean and all the inherent dangers that entails, so swimming is not recommended. Low tides reveal great tidal pools filled with anemone, starfish, and other sea creatures (please leave these creatures in the sea). Rock outcroppings create private areas and natural tabletops in the sand for beach picnics. The waters are also popular for kayaking and paddleboarding. **Amenities:** toilets; showers; free parking. **Best for:** snorkeling; walking; sunrise. ✉ *Hwy. 1, Km 12, Santa Maria Bay* ⊕ *Turnoff sign after El Tule bridge.*

Playa Palmilla
BEACH—SIGHT | **FAMILY** | Check out the impressive multimillion-dollar villas on the road to Playa Palmilla, the best swimming beach near San José. Turn off the highway as if you're going to the One&OnlyPalmilla and then cross over the highway on an overpass. Continue about half a mile. The entrance is from the side road through the ritzy Palmilla development; take a left before you reach the guardhouse of the One&Only hotel. There are signs, but they're not exactly large. The beach is protected by a rocky point and the water is almost always calm; Punta Palmilla, farther out, is popular with surfers during huge swells (20 feet or more). A few thatched-roof palapas on the sand provide shade; there are trash cans but no restrooms. Guards patrol the exclusive section known as Pelican Beach fronting the hotel, discouraging nonguests from entering—although the public legally has access to cross the beach in front of the resort property. Guests of One&Only have access to beachfront cabañas, surf instruction, beach equipment, toilets, and a restaurant. **Amenities:** toilets; showers; lifeguards; free parking. **Best for:** walking; swimming; snorkeling. ✉ *Entrance on Hwy. 1, at Km 27* ⊕ *8 km (5 mi) southwest of San José del Cabo.*

🍴 Restaurants

Dining along the Corridor between San José del Cabo and Cabo San Lucas used to be restricted to the ever-improving hotel restaurants. But with the addition of the Tiendas de Palmilla shopping center, just across from the One&Only Palmilla resort, top-notch eateries are establishing a new dining energy along this stretch of highway, giving drivers along the Corridor a tasty reason to slow down, and maybe even stop.

Cocina De Autor
$$$$ | **CONTEMPORARY** | Led by two-Michelin-starred chef Sidney Schutte, the signature restaurant at Grand Velas is turning heads for its 10-course tasting menu that's as impressive on presentation as it is on taste. Each bite is a mini-explosion in your mouth—not to be confused with molecular gastronomy (according to the chef himself). **Known for:** 10-course tasting menu; European techniques; reservations required. [$] *Average main: $170* ✉ *Grand Velas, Carretera Transpeninsular, Km 17.3, The Corridor* ☎ *624/104–9826* 🌐 *www.loscabos.grandvelas.com* 🕐 *No breakfast or lunch.*

★ Cocina del Mar

$$$$ | SEAFOOD | Argentinean chef Guillermo Gomez delivers an elevated culinary experience at Cocina del Mar, the elegant restaurant in the exquisite Esperanza Resort. Using daily market ingredients and focusing on simple seafood, Gomez presents inventive dishes such as lobster macaroni, grilled Kumiai oysters, or the impressive seared totuaba. **Known for:** romantic location on the cliff; delicious banana soufflé; whole fish encased in salt and herbs. $ Average main: $50 ⊠ Esperanza Resort, Carretera Transpeninsular, Km. 7, The Corridor ☎ 624/145–6400 ⊕ aubergeresorts.com/esperanza.

El Merkado

$ | MODERN MEXICAN | FAMILY | At this glorified food court, more than 20 culinary offerings are at your disposal, ranging from Mexican and Greek to Spanish and Italian. Savor wine, cheese, or tapas while the little ones dig into gourmet hot dogs, creamy gelato, or treats from the candy shop. **Known for:** multitude of choices; reasonable prices; great sushi. $ Average main: $8 ⊠ Koral Center, Blvd. Cerro Colorado, Carretera Transpeninsular, Km 24.5, The Corridor ☎ 624/137–9834 ⊕ facebook.com/elmerkadocabo.

El Restaurante at Las Ventanas

$$$$ | MEXICAN | It's well known that Las Ventanas is one of the best hotels in Mexico, and the on-site dining likewise does not disappoint. A diverse Mexican menu pays homage to the country's culinary traditions, with a focus on family recipes. **Known for:** gourmet tacos; traditional Mexican dishes from around the country; nightly live music. $ Average main: $50 ⊠ Carretera Transpeninsular, Km 19.5, The Corridor ☎ 624/144–2800 ⊕ www.rosewoodhotels.com/en/lasventanas.

Lumière

$$$$ | FRENCH FUSION | For refined dining in an intimate atmosphere, head to this modern French restaurant that serves refreshingly original dishes created by Mexican chef Alvaro Zepeda. The setting is sophisticated without excess, while the cuisine is bold and authentic. **Known for:** extraordinary seven-course tasting menu; delicious seared scallops; organic, local ingredients. $ Average main: $35 ⊠ Carretera Transpeninsular, Km. 18.4, The Corridor ☎ 624/163–0100 ⊕ www.leblancsparesorts.com/los-cabos.

Manta

$$$ | MEXICAN FUSION | Dine with übercool people at Manta, The Cape's culinary centerpiece by chef Enrique Olvera. Sip a cocktail in the sunken lounge bar, and move on over to the terrace with views of El Arco and surfers in action. **Known for:** globally inspired Mexican cuisine; remarkable sunset views of El Arco; local ingredients from Baja Califonia Sur. $ Average main: $30 ⊠ The Cape, Carretera Transpeninsular, Km 5, Misiones del Cabo, The Corridor ☎ 624/163–0010 ⊕ www.mantarestaurant.com ☯ No breakfast or lunch.

Mezcal

$$$$ | MEXICAN | You'll be hard-pressed to find a better Mexican restaurant in the area than this stylish establishment. Modern gastronomic techniques and sophisticated dishes highlight organic ingredients from local farmers. **Known for:** octopus tempura taco; signature mezcal and tequila tastings; first-class vegan menu. $ Average main: $70 ⊠ Montage Los Cabos, Carretera Transpeninsular, Km. 12.5, The Corridor ☎ 624/163–2000, 800/772–2226 from US ⊕ montagehotels.com/loscabos.

4

The Corridor

Did You Know?

Fascinating rock formations abound along the beaches of Los Cabos. Seismologists say that about 30 million years ago, a major seismic event tore a long finger of land—now called Baja California Peninsula— away from mainland Mexico.

Nick-San–Palmilla

$$ | SUSHI | For fresh, inventive sushi, there's no question that the Nick-San franchise corners the market, and this outpost in the Tiendas de Palmilla shopping mall wins the prize. Pair wine or sake with each of your selections, perhaps the lobster roll (with cilantro, mango, mustard, and curry oil), lobster *sambal* (marinated in sake with soy, ginger, and garlic), or tuna tostadas served on rice crackers with avocado. **Known for:** great lobster roll and ahi tostada; sushi with a Mexican twist; sashimi with chili pepper sauce. $ *Average main: $18* ⊠ *The Shoppes at Palmilla, Hwy. 1, Km 27.5, The Corridor* ☎ *624/144–6262* ⊕ *www.nicksan.com.*

Pitahayas

$$$ | ASIAN FUSION | Set under a soaring palapa overlooking the rollicking surf, this restaurant above the beach in the Hacienda del Mar Los Cabos blends Asian and Polynesian ingredients with local products for a menu that showcases well-executed Pacific Rim fusion. Seafood-heavy dishes are the specialty. **Known for:** Mexican-Asian fusion; outstanding wine cellar; delicious totoaba fish. $ *Average main: $30* ⊠ *Hacienda del Mar Los Cabos, Carretera Transpeninsular, Km. 10, The Corridor* ☎ *624/145–8010 Ext.24291* ⊕ *www.pitahayas.com.*

Puerta Vieja

$$$ | INTERNATIONAL | Puerta Vieja translates into "Old Door," and the beautiful door you enter through, imported from India, is indeed over 160 years old. Though Puerta Vieja serves lunch, we suggest dinner at sunset, when the view of El Arco is the most impressive. **Known for:** tasty lobster chowder; savory chocolate cheesecake; reasonably priced seafood and steak. $ *Average main: $30* ⊠ *Carretera Transpeninsular, Km 6.3, The Corridor* ☎ *624/104–3252, 624/104–3252* ⊕ *www.puertavieja.com.*

★ Seared

$$$$ | STEAKHOUSE | Opened by three-Michelin-starred chef Jean-Georges Vongerichten, this signature restaurant at One&Only Palmilla is one of the priciest spots in Los Cabos, but it's also one of the best. Boasting hand-selected cuts of steak and freshly caught Pacific seafood, the menu showcases everything from Wagyu to Kobe beef. **Known for:** fine cuts of beef; elaborate wine list; remarkable appetizers. $ *Average main: $100* ⊠ *One&Only Palmilla, Carretera Transpeninsular, Km 7.5, The Corridor* ☎ *624/146–7000* ⊕ *www.oneandonlyresorts.com.*

7 Seas Seafood Grille

$$$ | ECLECTIC | It's quite soothing to sit in this restaurant at Cabo Surf Hotel, at the ocean's edge under the shade of a palapa while watching the surfers. For breakfast munch on their *machaca con huevos* (eggs scrambled with shredded beef) washed down with a fresh-fruit smoothie. **Known for:** gluten-free and vegetarian options; inventive seafood cuisine with eclectic style; regional organic vegetables. $ *Average main: $30* ⊠ *Cabo Surf Hotel, Carretera Transpeninsular, Km 28, at Acapulquito Beach, The Corridor* ☎ *624/142–2666* ⊕ *www.7seasrestaurant.com.*

Sunset Mona Lisa

$$$$ | ITALIAN | Stunning views of El Arco from cocktail tables along the cliffs make this restaurant just outside Cabo San Lucas the best place to toast the sunset. If the breeze is still, stay outside and enjoy dining alfresco; if not, move into the candlelit dining room under a palapa. **Known for:** champagne bar with fire pits; sunset views of El Arco; homemade pastas. $ *Average main: $60* ⊠ *Carretera Transpeninsular, Km 5.5, The Corridor* ☎ *624/145–8160* ⊕ *www.sunsetmonalisa.com.*

Zipper's

$$ | **AMERICAN** | **FAMILY** | Popular with the surfing crowd, this palapa-covered joint is right on Cabo Azul beach, just south of San José del Cabo. Though their burger is the reason to come, the aroma of grilling lobster and tacos, and a sound track of surf tunes are why many return. **Known for:** fried fish and large portions; live bands playing rock classics; incredible burger. [$] *Average main: $12* ✉ *Carretera Transpeninsular, Km 28.5, The Corridor* ☎ *624/172–6162* 🌐 *facebook.com/zippersbargrill.*

Hotels

Even before the Corridor had an official name or even a paved road, the few hotels here were ritzy and elite; one even had its own private airstrip. As the saying goes, the more things change, the more they stay the same—developers have deliberately kept this area high-end and private. The Corridor is the most valuable strip of real estate in the region, with guard-gated exclusivity, golf courses, luxury developments, and unsurpassed views of the Sea of Cortez.

★ **Cabo Surf Hotel & Spa**

$$ | **HOTEL** | **FAMILY** | Professional and amateur surfers alike claim the prime ocean-view rooms in this small hotel on the cliffs above Playa Costa Azul that has successfully blended surfing and pampering into one property. **Pros:** blends surfing and pampering; hotel guests receive discount on surf lessons and rental; free yoga on weekends. **Cons:** traffic from the highway can be noisy; usually full, as wedding parties tend to book the entire hotel; service charge added per night. [$] *Rooms from: $295* ✉ *Carretera Transpeninsular, Km 28, The Corridor* ☎ *624/142–2676, 858/964–5117 in U.S.* 🌐 *www.cabosurfhotel.com* 🛏 *36 rooms* 🍴 *No meals.*

The Cape

$$$$ | **RESORT** | Of all the draws of this Thompson Hotel—from the architectural masterpiece by Javier Sanchez to the breathtaking views of El Arco—perhaps the greatest appeal is the integration of nature, such as the spa set in natural rock formation or the boulders, cacti, and native plants that dot the grounds where two black buildings house sleek, modern rooms. **Pros:** great surf spot out front ; unbelievable view of the arch; beautifully designed. **Cons:** not ideal for children; pool area can get loud on weekends; rocky beach. [$] *Rooms from: $599* ✉ *Carretera Transpeninsular, Km 5, The Corridor* ☎ *624/163–0000, 844/778–4322 from US* 🌐 *www.thompsonhotels.com* 🛏 *161 rooms* 🍴 *No meals.*

Casa del Mar Boutique Resort & Spa

$$ | **HOTEL** | Operating as both condos and a resort, this hacienda-style gated community has guest rooms with white marble floors, dark beamed ceilings, and teak furnishings along with views of the sea and a beautiful white-sand beach. **Pros:** generous complimentary perks; great breakfast buffet and poolside service; intimate and peaceful atmosphere. **Cons:** hotel's 50 rooms are surrounded by 220 timeshare condos; undertow at beach; pushy timeshare pitch. [$] *Rooms from: $250* ✉ *Carretera Transpeninsular, Km 19.5, The Corridor* ☎ *624/279–0016* 🌐 *casadelmarboutique.com* 🛏 *50 rooms* 🍴 *No meals.*

Chileno Bay Resort & Residences

$$$$ | **RESORT** | **FAMILY** | Set on the protected cove of Chileno Bay, one of the best spots for snorkeling and swimming in Los Cabos, this 60-room hotel hits the mark with families seeking personalized, informal service. **Pros:** ideal for families; pristine beaches with tranquil waters; infinity pool and oceanfront hot tubs. **Cons:** beach can get crowded with nonguests; construction along Corridor; no meal plans. [$] *Rooms from: $430* ✉ *Carretera Transpeninsular, Km. 15, The*

The Esperanza resort boasts two secluded white-sand beaches.

Corridor ☎ 884/207–9354 US Toll Free, 624/104–9600 🌐 aubergeresorts.com/chilenobay 🛏 60 rooms 🍴 No meals.

Dreams Los Cabos

$$$$ | RESORT | FAMILY | This casual, unfussy resort is touted as a romantic getaway, but with an average of five weddings a week, it's more a destination for families and wedding parties with guests of all ages in attendance. **Pros:** Explorer's Club for kids; golf concierge; plenty to entertain. **Cons:** resort can sometimes feel overrun with children; food is abundant but cuisine is only average; nonswimmable beach. [$] *Rooms from: $400 ✉ Carretera Transpeninsular, Km. 18.5, The Corridor ☎ 866/237–3267, 624/145–7600 🌐 www.dreamsresorts.com 🛏 255 rooms 🍴 All-inclusive.*

★ Esperanza

$$$$ | RESORT | One of the most exquisite resorts in Los Cabos, focused on privacy and impeccable service, and home to one of the best spas in the region, Esperanza is true luxury. **Pros:** most private property in Los Cabos; two secluded white-sand beaches; casitas have ocean views and renovated interiors. **Cons:** the high cost of incidentals can get exhausting; wind can be fierce on the rocky cliffs; nonswimmable beach. [$] *Rooms from: $935 ✉ Carretera Transpeninsular, Km. 7, Punta Ballena, The Corridor ☎ 624/145–6400, 866/311–2226 in U.S. 🌐 aubergeresorts.com/esperanza 🛏 123 villas 🍴 Free breakfast.*

Grand Fiesta Americana Los Cabos

$$$$ | RESORT | FAMILY | The dramatic lobby of this all-inclusive resort is eight stories above the beach, and every room looks out onto the Sea of Cortez. **Pros:** every room has an ocean view; discounts to the spa and golf course; complimentary minibar and free Kids' Club. **Cons:** rocky beach; service is notoriously spotty; slow elevators. [$] *Rooms from: $450 ✉ Cabo del Sol, Carretera Transpeninsular, Km 10.3, The Corridor ☎ 624/145–6200 🌐 grandfiestamericana.com ⛳ Jack Nicklaus Ocean Golf Course at Cabo del Sol 🛏 527 🍴 All-inclusive.*

★ Grand Velas Los Cabos

$$$$ | RESORT | FAMILY | With a curved, half-moon layout that ensures ocean views for all rooms, this luxury resort does not cut the usual "all inclusive" corners: instead the Grand Velas offers an excess of everything, from its spacious rooms (1,180-square-feet), each with an outdoor Jacuzzi, minibar, walk-in closet, and views of the ocean and three pools, to top-notch dining options, premium drinks, and excellent service. **Pros:** coolest Kids-and-Teens' clubs in Cabo; two-Michelin-star chef at Cocina de Autor; tequila and mezcal tasting room. **Cons:** restaurants require reservations; rocky beach; extra charge for hydrotherapy treatments. $ *Rooms from: $1,100* ✉ *Carretera Transpeninsular, Km 17.3, The Corridor* ☎ *624/104–9800, 888/505–8406 Reservations* ⊕ *loscabos.grandvelas.com* ⊷ *304 rooms* ○|*All-inclusive.*

Hacienda del Mar Los Cabos

$$ | RESORT | FAMILY | Small domes and barrel tile roofs top eight buildings at this lovely, hacienda-style resort in the Cabo Del Sol development. **Pros:** rooms are serene and quiet; access to amazing golf courses; great for families with kids. **Cons:** beach is not usually good for swimming; thin walls; Wi-Fi not included. $ *Rooms from: $220* ✉ *Carretera Transpeninsular, Km. 10, The Corridor* ☎ *624/145–6186, 855/652–7362 in U.S.* ⊕ *www.haciendadelmar.com.mx* ⊷ *234 suites* ○|*No meals.*

Hacienda Encantada Resort & Residences

$$ | RESORT | FAMILY | Despite the enormous size of this timeshare-resort hybrid, there are only 222 rooms, meaning guests are treated to 1,400-square-foot hacienda-style suites. **Pros:** outstanding views; excellent taco bar; all-inclusive package includes dining at marina restaurants. **Cons:** beach not swimmable; extra charge for premium alcohol, certain menu items, and room service; noisy golf carts putt around the property. $ *Rooms from: $200* ✉ *Carretera Transpeninsular, Km 7.3, The Corridor* ☎ *624/163–5555, 844/289–6318 toll free in U.S.* ⊕ *www.haciendaencantada.com* ⊷ *222 rooms* ○|*All-inclusive.*

Hilton Los Cabos

$$$ | RESORT | FAMILY | Rooms are spacious at this hacienda-style Hilton built on one of the Corridor's few swim-friendly beaches. **Pros:** 24-hour gym; 20% discount on greens fees; great cocktail bar. **Cons:** spa services are not up to par with the rest of the resort; obstructed ocean views from some rooms; one side of the pool is reserved for Vista Club members. $ *Rooms from: $350* ✉ *Carretera Transpeninsular, Km. 19.5, The Corridor* ☎ *877/354–1399* ⊕ *www.hiltonloscabos.com* ⊷ *375 rooms* ○|*No meals.*

★ Las Ventanas al Paraíso

$$$$ | RESORT | From the moment your private butler greets you with a foamy margarita and escorts you to the spa for a welcome massage, you know you're in for some serious pampering and a special experience. **Pros:** exceptional service; stellar dining and wine/tequila selection; experiences include whale safaris, magic show dinners, and more. **Cons:** there can be a four- to eight-night minimum depending on the season and holiday; 35% tax and gratuity added to every bill; dangerous riptides. $ *Rooms from: $1,200* ✉ *Hwy. 1, Km 19.5, The Corridor* ☎ *624/144–2800, 833/224–1926 in U.S.* ⊕ *www.lasventanas.com* ⊷ *83 rooms* ○|*No meals.*

★ Le Blanc Spa Resort Los Cabos

$$$$ | ALL-INCLUSIVE | One of the truly all-inclusive luxury resorts in the area, Le Blanc distinguishes itself by being adults-only and providing outstanding dining and wellness options. **Pros:** adults only; personalized butler service; a la carte and buffet dining options included. **Cons:** far from Cabo and from San José; vibe isn't exactly Mexican; nonswimmable beach. $ *Rooms from: $623* ✉ *Carretera Transpeninsular, Km. 18, The Corridor* ☎ *624/163–0100* ⊕ *www.leblancsparesorts.com/los-cabos/* ⊷ *369 rooms* ○|*All-inclusive.*

One&Only Palmilla is a stunning seaside resort.

Marquis Los Cabos

$$$$ | **RESORT** | Stunning architecture, a propertywide art collection of unique pieces, noticeable attention to detail, and loads of luxurious touches make the Marquis a standout. **Pros:** tranquillity prevails for complete escape; exceptional full-service spa; six on-site restaurants. **Cons:** busy wedding venue; surf is unswimmable; limited hours in some restaurants. $ *Rooms from: $548* ✉ *Carretera Transpeninsular, Km 21.5, The Corridor* ☎ *624/144–2000, 877/238–9399* ⊕ *www.marquisloscabos.com* ⇴ *235 rooms* ❍❙ *All-inclusive.*

★ Montage Los Cabos

$$$$ | **RESORT** | **FAMILY** | Set in a beautiful natural location that blends perfectly with its design, Montage is an idyllic desert-beach retreat that pampers with lavish luxury; plus, there's a touch of local authenticity missed in other properties in the area. **Pros:** semiprivate beach; fitness lessons and water sports equipment included; unlike other Corridor beaches, you can actually swim here. **Cons:** far from Cabo and from San José; luxury comes at a price; no adults-only section. $ *Rooms from: $895* ✉ *Carretera Transpeninsular, Km. 12.5, The Corridor* ☎ *624/163–2000, 800/772–2226* ⊕ *www.montagehotels. com/loscabos* ⇴ *125* ❍❙ *No meals.*

★ One&Only Palmilla

$$$$ | **RESORT** | Built in 1956 by the son of the then-president of Mexico, the One&Only was the first resort in Los Cabos area, and it retains an old-world atmosphere and elegance, superior attention to detail and service, and its position as one of the most exclusive luxury resorts in the region. **Pros:** flawless service and amenities; complimentary tequila and snacks delivered daily by personal butler; notable dining options. **Cons:** prices are high; often boisterous groups mar the otherwise genteel atmosphere; far from both San José and Cabo San Lucas. $ *Rooms from: $1,100* ✉ *Carretera Transpeninsular, Km 27.5, The Corridor* ☎ *624/146–7000, 888/691–8081 in U.S.* ⊕ *www.oneandonlyresorts.com* ⚑ *Jack Nicklaus–designed 18-hole course* ⇴ *176 rooms* ❍❙ *No meals.*

Paradisus Los Cabos

$$ | RESORT | This beachside all-inclusive has fabulous rooms decorated in beachy tones of turquoise and gold, with private terraces overlooking the ocean or gardens as well as swim-up rooms, part of the Royal Service section open to adults only. **Pros:** near golf courses; decent rates; swimmable beach with man-made cove. **Cons:** Gastro Bar not part of all-inclusive plan; slippery pool area; loud music at pool carries into some rooms. $ *Rooms from: $250* ⊠ *Carretera Transpeninsular, Km. 19.5, The Corridor* ☎ *624/144–0000* ⊕ *www.melia.com* ⇌ *350 rooms* ❍ *All-inclusive.*

Westin Resort & Spa, Los Cabos

$$ | RESORT | FAMILY | Built by prominent Mexican artist Javier Sordo Madaleno, the colorful design and architecture reflecting the famous Arco (arch) makes this Westin more memorable than some of the others in the Corridor. **Pros:** good children's center; great gym with yoga and Pilates classes; multiple pools including an adults-only option. **Cons:** it's a trek from the parking lot and lobby to the rooms and pools; lots of groups; nonswimmable beach. $ *Rooms from: $239* ⊠ *Carretera Transpeninsular, Km 22.5, The Corridor* ☎ *624/142–9000, 888/625–5144 in U.S.* ⊕ *marriott.com* ⇌ *223 rooms* ❍ *No meals.*

▼ Nightlife

Nightlife along Carretera Transpeninsular (Highway 1) between San José del Cabo and Cabos San Lucas historically consists of hotel bars in big resorts, most of which are frequented only by their guests. A few stand-alone places have sprung up in recent years, including the chic Privé nightclub. A taxi or car is the best way to reach these places. Because walking home is generally not an option unless you're staying in-house or next door, nightlife ends early out here, with most bars turning off the lights around 10 or 11 pm. Head to Cabo San Lucas if you want to party later.

Surfing in Style

One&Only Palmilla offers guests a range of five-star surf tours with the acclaimed company Tropic Surf—the pioneer in "luxury surfing." Regardless of age or ability, guests can paddle into Cabo's best breaks in style, all with an emphasis on service, luxury, water safety, and improvement.

BARS

Azul

BARS/PUBS | As far as posh hotel bars go, it's hard to top the Hilton Los Cabos' Azul, whose terrace overlooks the Sea of Cortez. There's nothing raucous here, just intimate conversation over margaritas and other agave-based spirit cocktails. Mexican *antojitos* (small appetizers) and raw snacks provide the perfect complement. ⊠ *Hilton Los Cabos, Carretera Transpeninsular, Km. 19.5, The Corridor* ☎ *624/145–6500, 877/354–1399* ⊕ *www. hiltonloscabos.com.*

Latitude 22+ Roadhouse

BARS/PUBS | This noisy, friendly roadhouse always attracts gringos looking to down a shot of tequila, sip cold beer, and mingle with old or new friends. The menu features good, dependable, and mostly American fare. From October to June they host live music, ranging in style from pop to blues to country. ⊠ *Carretera Transpeninsular, Km. 4.5, The Corridor* ☎ *624/143–1516* ⊕ *www.latno2baddays. com* ☼ *Closed Sun.* ☞ *Closed Tues.*

The Lounge Bar

BARS/PUBS | The name sounds rather utilitarian, but the dim lighting and intimate setting here are anything but. Enjoy stunning views of El Arco—you are, after all, on the Cabo San Lucas end of the Corridor—at Esperanza's elegant bar and lounge on lush couches. Linger over quiet drinks or smoke a cigar as you listen to the sounds of the ocean. ⊠ *Esperanza Resort, Carretera Transpeninsular, Km. 7, Manzana 10, Punta Ballena, The Corridor* ☏ *624/145–6400* ⊕ *aubergeresorts.com/esperanza.*

★ The Rooftop

PIANO BARS/LOUNGES | For drinks with a view of El Arco, head to The Rooftop bar and lounge at The Cape hotel. The sleek setting boasts a beer garden, handcrafted cocktails, and live music at sunset. If it gets too breezy, move to their Glass Box boutique hotel bar specializing in tequilas and mezcals. ⊠ *The Cape , Carretera Transpeninsular, Km 5, The Corridor* ☏ *624/163–0000* ⊕ *www.thompsonhotels.com.*

Sunset Point

TAPAS BARS | This casual wine-and-pizza lounge is a colorful rooftop hot spot that shares the same stunning view of famous Los Cabos Arch as its downstairs counterpart, Sunset de Mona Lisa. With a selection of more than 140 wines and champagnes, complemented by free tapas daily 5–6 pm, this is the place to watch the sun set over light bites and cocktails. ⊠ *Mona Lisa Sunset Restaurant, Carretera Transpeninsular, Km. 6.5, The Corridor* ☏ *624/145–8160* ⊕ *www.sunsetmonalisa.com.*

Zipper's

BARS/PUBS | Named for the nearby surf break, beachfront Zipper's attracts a mixed crowd of surfers and nonsurfers alike. A good selection of beer, as well as ribs and burgers, is always on hand, with live music weekdays and Sunday. ⊠ *Carretera Transpeninsular, Km 28.5, The Corridor* ☏ *624/172–6162* ⊕ *facebook.com/zippersbargrill.*

🛍 Shopping

There are shopping options along the Corridor—the stretch of land between San José del Cabo to the east and Cabo San Lucas to the west—but the shops cater more to resort guests and American expats than to travelers looking to experience Los Cabos. The closest thing you'll find to a shopping mall here is Las Tiendas de Palmilla, across from Palmilla Resort, with fewer than a dozen shops, galleries, and restaurants. Unless you're in search of something specific at one of the shops on the Corridor, you'll have much more fun shopping in San José del Cabo, Cabo San Lucas, or Todos Santos.

MALLS

★ Koral Center (*El Merkado*)

SHOPPING CENTERS/MALLS | FAMILY | Conveniently located in the Corridor, the Koral Center houses stores, medical facilities, a day spa, and El Merkado—a gourmet food court that converges 20 culinary offerings and the latest in Mexican gastronomy. You'll find everything from tacos and tapas to sushi and an organic market selling local products. ⊠ *Blvd. Cerro Colorado, Carretera Transpeninsular, Km. 24.5, The Corridor* ☏ *624/122–3840* ⊕ *www.koralcenter.com.*

Las Tiendas de Palmilla

SHOPPING CENTERS/MALLS | FAMILY | Las Tiendas de Palmilla is across from the posh Palmilla Resort. There is a smattering of shops and galleries, a couple of restaurants, a coffee shop, a nice terrace with a peaceful fountain, and a view of the Palmilla development with the Sea of Cortez beyond. **Antigua de México** is a branch of the famous Tlaquepaque store, and shoppers will discover distinctive furniture and bedding supplies, and many Mexican-flavor interior-decorating items. **Pez Gordo Art Gallery** is artist Dana Leib's second location, and offers her pieces, as well as those by other artists. If you need to fuel up during your time here, there's an outpost of popular **Nick-San**, and **Cream Cafe.** ✉ *Carretera Transpeninsular, Km 27.5, The Corridor* ☎ *624/144–6999* ⊕ *theshoppesatpalmilla.com.*

GROCERY STORES

California Ranch Market

OUTDOOR/FLEA/GREEN MARKETS | At this farmers' market in the middle of the Corridor, you can find organic food, plus kosher and imported products. You can also enjoy a fresh, healthy meal at their next-door sister restaurant Baja Fresh Kitchen. ✉ *Carretera Transpeninsular, Km. 27.5, The Corridor* ☎ *624/129–9996* ⊕ *www.californiaranchmarket.com.*

🏃 Activities

Although there's plenty of snorkeling, diving, and surfing to be done at beaches along the Corridor, most of the tours—including popular ones from Surf in Cabo and Costa Azul Surf Shop—depart from Cabo San Lucas or San José del Cabo. Thanks to the plentiful luxury resorts in the area, spas and golf are also top activities. The Wild Canyon adventure park, too, has grown in popularity.

DIVING

The Corridor has several popular diving sites. **Bahía Santa Maria** (20–60 feet) has water clear enough to see hard and soft corals, octopuses, eels, and many tropical fish. **Chileno Reef** (10–80 feet) is a protected finger reef 1 km (½ mile) from Chileno Bay, with many invertebrates, including starfish, flower urchins, and hydroids. The **Blowhole** (60–100 feet) is known for diverse terrain—massive boulders, rugged tunnels, shallow caverns, and deep rock cuts—which house manta rays, sea turtles, and large schools of amberjacks and grouper.

GOLF

Cabo del Sol Golf

GOLF | Home to two outstanding 18-hole courses set between the mountains and the ocean, Cabo del Sol has been the region's standard-bearer since 1994. The Cove Club Golf Course designed by Jack Nicklaus has consistently been considered among the best in the world. The Desert Course, designed by Tom Weiskopf, offers amazing ocean views from every hole. Clinics and one-on-one lessons are available upon request. ✉ *Carretera Transpeninsular, Km. 10.3, The Corridor* ☎ *800/543–9076, 866/231–4677 from US* ⊕ *cabodelsol.com/golf* 🏌 *Green fee $350, two–four players* ⛳ *Cove Club Course 7091 yards, 18 holes, par 72; Desert Course 7049 yards, 18 holes, par 72.*

Cabo Real Golf Course

GOLF | This visually attractive layout features spectacular views of the mountains and sea, as well as a challenging test. Designed by Robert Trent Jones Jr., Cabo Real has straight and narrow fairways, difficult slopes, and strategically placed bunkers. A recent reversal of the club's nines have completely refashioned the course's design, which now starts with stunning ocean views and moves through the desert and into rugged mountain peaks. Recovering from mistakes here can be quite difficult. Greens fee includes cart (walking is not permitted), water, and towel. Balls are not included. ✉ *Carretera Transpeninsular Km. 19.5, San José del Cabo* ☎ *624/173–9400, 877/795–8727* ⊕ *www.questrogolf.com* 🏌 *$245; $125 after 1:30 pm* 🏌 *18 holes, 6848 yards, par 71.*

★ One&Only Palmilla Golf Course

GOLF | At the first course crafted by Jack Nicklaus, you will encounter 27 holes of some of the best resort golf that Mexico has to offer. The Mountain and Arroyo Nines came first, with the Ocean Nine finished later. Generous target-style fairways wind their way through rugged mountainous desert terrain that is beautifully landscaped. The Ocean Nine drops 600 feet in elevation as you visit the edge of the Sea of Cortez, while the Mountain and Arroyo Nines are positioned higher and farther back from the water. Many will remark that the stretch of 6 to 8 holes on the Arroyo Course is one of the best anywhere, while the 3rd through 5th holes really get your attention on the Mountain Course. No matter the combination of Nines, you won't feel cheated; the conditioning is excellent though expensive. Five sets of tees on every hole accommodate various skill levels. ✉ *Carretera Transpeninsular, Km 7.5, San José del Cabo* ☎ *624/144–5250* ⊕ *www. palmillagc.com* ✆ *$145–$170* ⚑ *27 holes. Mountain Nine, 3602 yards; Ocean Nine, 3527 yards; Arroyo Nine, 3337 yards. All nines are par 36.*

GUIDED TOURS
Wild Canyon Adventures

FOUR-WHEELING | FAMILY | It's all in the name at this outdoor adventure company that offers ziplining, camel rides, bungee jumping, ATV tours, a giant swing, and a glass-bottom gondola—all of which enter vast El Tule Canyon. ATV tours (and brave hikers) can cross Los Cabos Canyon Bridge, the longest wooden pedestrian bridge in the world, measuring 1,082 feet long. Free transportation is offered from your hotel, but be sure to time your activities properly since the shuttle only runs every 3½ hours. ✉ *El Tule Bridge, The Corridor* ☎ *624/144–4433, 866/230–5253* ⊕ *www.wildcanyon.com.mx* ✆ *Tours from $85.*

HORSEBACK RIDING
Cuadra San Francisco Equestrian Center

HORSEBACK RIDING | FAMILY | The Cuadra San Francisco Equestrian Center offers trail rides and lessons on 50 beautiful and extremely well-trained horses. Trail rides go on the beach, into the fields, or exploring the nearby canyon. Cuadra also specializes in private trail rides, photo sessions, and equestrian courses. Note that you must query them for rates, but expect to pay close to $70 per hour. ✉ *Carretera Transpeninsular, Km 19.5, San José del Cabo* ✛ *Across from Casa del Mar and Las Ventanas al Paraíso hotels* ☎ *624/144–0160* ⊕ *www.loscaboshorses.com.*

SPAS
BlancSpa

SPA/BEAUTY | While the concept of wellness permeates every square foot of Le Blanc Spa Resort, it finds its pinnacle at BlancSpa. Its outstanding facilities include 25 treatment suites, 9 indoor couples suites, 15 singles suites, and 1 Le Blanc D'Or suite. With a wide range of treatments, from a signature four-hand Pericú massage to a series of beauty services and hydrotherapy, this is a spa that never disappoints. ✉ *Carretera Transpeninsular, Km. 18, The Corridor* ☎ *624/163-0100* ⊕ *www.leblancsparesorts.com/los-cabos.*

★ One&Only Palmilla Spa

SPA/BEAUTY | Therapists lead you through a locked gate into peaceful palm-filled gardens with a bubbling hot tub and a daybed covered with plump pillows. There are 13 private treatment villas for up to two people; seven are equipped with an outdoor shower, bathtub, and thatched-roof daybed for relaxing in between or after treatments. Each treatment begins with a Floral Footbath, including the signature Secret Garden Remedy, using oil infused with herbs grown on-site. Achy athletes can opt for the surfers or golfers massage. The spa

Continued on page 125

Los Cabos' perfect waves

SURFING CABO STYLE

From the gentlest of beginner waves at Old Man's surf spot to the gnarliest winter waves at Los Cerritos, Los Cabos has surf for everyone. The tip of the Baja Peninsula has three key areas: the Pacific coast (often called "the Pacific side"), the East Cape, and the Cabo Corridor between them. This means that there are east-, west- and south-facing beaches taking waves from just about every direction.

There are also warm, crystalline seas and great surf schools. Friendly instructors make lessons fun and are more than willing to tailor them to the needs of anyone—from groms to retirees, aspiring surfers to experts. Schools also offer surf tours so you can benefit from insider knowledge of the local waves and quirky surf spots before heading out on your own.

by Larry Dunmire

LOS CABOS SURF FINDER

Surfer at a right-hand point break

Todos Santos

Punta Conejo

Punta Lobos

Playa San Pedrito

El Pescadero

El Pescade

Playa Los Cerrit

Pacific Coast

WEST CAPE

Gentle waves during summer time.

19

PACIFIC SIDE

In winter, the Pacific from Cabo San Lucas town north to Todos Santos, often roils with rough, thundering swells. Surf spots here are only for the most accomplished although Los Cerritos, home to the Costa Azul Surf Shop and school, can have gentle waves in summer. Pacific-side beaches face essentially west and slightly north. Hence, winter swells coming from these directions (thanks to Alaskan storms) make landfall head on, creating great waves.

Punta Conejo: a rocky point break north of Todos Santos; unique in that it's surfable on both north and south swells. Has good right and left breaks. *11 km (7 miles) north of Todos Santos; turn off Hwy. 19 near Km 80.*

Punta Lobos: big point breaks with south swells. *South of Todos Santos; turn off Hwy. 19 at Km 54 onto dirt road, and continue for about 2.5 km (1.5 miles).*

Surfer on the nose of his longboard on a clean wave

Perfect waves in Salsipuedes, Baja California

Playa San Pedrito: a beautiful, broad, curved, sandy beach break, surfable on both west and north swells. *From Cabo San Lucas take Hwy. 19 until Km. 58; turn right onto the dirt road after the Campo Experimental agriculture station and continue about 2 km (1.3 miles).*

El Pescadero: fast, consistent, right reef and beach breaks; watch out for painful sea urchins in shallow water! *Hwy. 19 at Km 59.*

Playa Los Cerritos: highly versatile beach—in summer, good for beginners, with gentle breaks and a safe, sandy bottom; winter waves are gnarly. Best ones are on northwest swells, though south swells aren't bad. Both left and right beach breaks. Home to Costa Azul Surf Shop; can get crowded. *Less than a km (half a mile) south of Todos Santos; Hwy. 19 at Km 66.*

CABO CORRIDOR

The 20-mile stretch of beautiful beaches and bays between the towns of Cabo San Lucas and San José del Cabo has no less than a dozen surf spots, including some that are hard to find and access. Opportunities range from the expert-only Monuments break just outside of Cabo to the beginner-friendly Old Man's spot. For experts, surfing in the Corridor is generally best in the summer and fall, when storms as far away as New Zealand and Antarctica can send south swells all the way up here.

Playa Monumentos: powerful left point break, offering great gut-wrenching waves on south and west swells. Dangerously shallow at low tide; many sea urchins. Great surf and sunset watching from bluff near parking area. *Far south end of Cabo's El Medano Beach, east of Cabo San Lucas on Hwy 1 at Km. 5.5; pull off at Misiones de Cabo, drive to gate.*

Playa El Tule: long wide beach with great right reef break in El Tule Arroyo, near highway bridge of same name. One of few places you can still camp; need 4WD to get here. *Midway btw. Cabo San Lucas and San José. East on Hwy. 1 at Km. 16.2, look for EL TULE sign, pull off road and drive toward ocean on sandy road.*

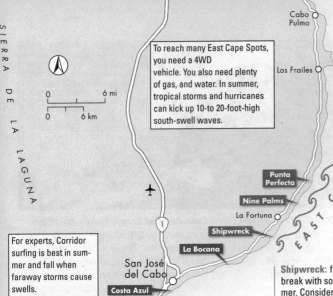

SIERRA DE LA LAGUNA

Cabo Pulmo

Los Frailes

Sea of Cortez

To reach many East Cape Spots, you need a 4WD vehicle. You also need plenty of gas, and water. In summer, tropical storms and hurricanes can kick up 10-to 20-foot-high south-swell waves.

0 — 6 mi
0 — 6 km

Punta Perfecta

Nine Palms

La Fortuna

EAST CAPE

Shipwreck

La Bocana

San José del Cabo

For experts, Corridor surfing is best in summer and fall when faraway storms cause swells.

Costa Azul

Playa El Tule

Playa Monumentos

THE CORRIDOR

Cabo San Lucas

Costa Azul: beach of choice in summer. World-famous, experts-only Zippers break often tops 12 feet. Has two other popular breaks: Acapulquito (Old Man's) in front of Cabo Surf Hotel—forgiving with a gentle surf break and good for beginners—and The Rock, a more challenging reef break to the east. The rocks are near the surface; quite shallow at low tide. There's a restaurant and a branch of the Costa Azul Surf Shop here. *Between Km. 28 and 29 on Hwy 1.*

La Bocana: freshwater estuary with a river mouth beach break (i.e., giant barrels break upon sand bars created by runoff sand deposited here after powerful summer rains). Both left and right rides. *Hwy. 1, south of Intercontinental hotel.*

EAST CAPE

North and east of San José, up the rough, unpaved East Cape Road, there are many breaks with good waves that are perpetually empty—with good reason. To get here, you need a 4WD vehicle. You also need plenty of gas, sufficient water, an umbrella, and mucho sun block. Waves here aren't for beginners, and some of the coast is on private property. Note, too, that locals (both Mexican and gringo) can be protective of their spots. East Cape beaches face south and east, and, in summer, tropical storms and hurricanes can kick up 10-, 15-, and even 20-foot-high south-swell waves—exciting for beginners to watch from the shore.

Shipwreck: fast, right reef break with south swells in summer. Considered the second-best summer surfing spot. Need 4WD to get here. *Off East Cape Rd., about 16 km (10 miles) up a rough, washboard road.*

Nine Palms: right point break with good, long waves and great shape but at least an hour's drive out. *East Cape Rd., near village of Santa Elena and a palm-tree grove.*

Punta Perfecta: right point break; can get big and hollow (i.e., "tubular") during summer's south swells. Out of the way (4WD required) and hard to find; territorial local surfers get testy when asked for directions. *East Cape Rd., near Crossroads Country Club and Vinorama.*

Los Frailes: Waves get big on a south swell. Down a long, dusty, pounding drive (need 4WD). Beautiful white sand beach and tranquil desert surroundings. *East Cape Rd.*

Stand-up paddleboarding (SUP)

LEARNING TO SURF

Surf's up: you can really ride the waves in Los Cabos.

WHAT TO EXPECT

Expect introductory classes to cover how to lie on the board, paddle properly, pop up into a surf stance, and handle riding white wash (inside waves)

GEARING UP

Both surf shops and schools offer a wide selection of lessons, gear, and boards—sometimes including "skegs," soft, stable beginners's boards with plastic fins. Novices will want to use longboards, which offer the most stability. Rash guards (form-fitting polyester vests) protect you from board chafing and sunburn. Booties, rubberized watershoes, protect your feet from rocks, coral and sea urchins.

GETTING OUT THERE

Most agree that the best place for beginners is San José del Cabo's Acapulquito Beach, home to Old Man's surf spot. It has gently breaking, "feathering" (very forgiving) waves and the region's most understanding surfers. Acapulquito Beach is also home to the Cabo Surf Hotel, with a top school. The **Mike Doyle Surf School** (⊕ *www.mikedoylesurf-school.com*) has two full-time teachers, certified by the NSSIA, the National Surf Schools and Instructor's Association (U.S.) and a great selection of more than 100 boards—short, long, "soft" boards for novices, and even a couple of SUP boards.

Costa Azul Surf Shop (⊕ *www.costa-azul. com.mx*), with branches in San José del Cabo (near Zipper's Restaurant) and south of Todos Santos, near Los Cerritos Beach, is another option for lessons. Staff here can arrange tours to breaks so far off the path that roads to them aren't always marked on maps, let alone paved. The shop's website also has good interactive surfing maps.

Costa Azul's three-hour surf excursions include two boards per person, rash guards, and surf shoes. The cost is US$180 per person.

SURF'S DOWN?

If the surf's flat, no problema! SUP, or stand-up paddleboarding, is done on flat waters using broad, long, lightweight boards that are comfortable to stand on. You paddle along, alternating sides for balance, using what resembles a single-bladed kayak paddle. SUP is easy to master, great exercise, and highly enjoyable.

Accomplished surfers have pushed the SUPing envelope, paddling their boards into the lineup (or surf zone) and right into the waves, be they small or large. The paddle is then used to steer, almost like a boat's rudder. One step at a time, though—this type of SUP is not as easy as the masters make it look!

BOARD SHAPES

Longboard: Lengthier (about 2.5–3 m/9–10.5 feet), wider, thicker, and more buoyant than the often-miniscule shortboards. Offers more flotation and speedier paddling, which makes it easier to get into waves. Great for beginners and those with relaxed surf styles. **Skill level:** Beginner to Intermediate.

Funboard: A little shorter than the longboard with a slightly more acute nose and blunt tail, the funboard combines the best attributes of the longboards with some similar characteristics of the shorter boards. Good for beginners or surfers looking for a board more maneuverable and faster than a longboard. **Skill level:** Beginner to Intermediate.

Fishboard: A stumpy, blunt-nosed, twin-finned board that features a "V" tail (giving it a "fish" like look, hence the name) and is fast and maneuverable. Good for catching small, steep slow waves and pulling tricks. At one point this was the world's best-selling surfboard. **Skill level:** Intermediate to Expert.

Shortboard: Shortboards came on the scene in the late '60s when the average board length dropped from 9'6" to 6'6" (3m to 2m) and changed wave riding forever. This short, light, high-performance board is designed for carving the wave with a high amount of maneuverability. These boards need a fast steep wave, completely different from a "longboard" break, which tends to be slower with shallower wave faces. **Skill level:** Expert.

Beginner — Expert

Funboards

Fish

Longboards

Shortboards

Shallow wave faces, easiest surfing — Steeper wave faces, difficult surfing

SURF SLANG

By Leland Baxter-Neal
and Larry Dunmire

Barrel: The area created when a wave breaks onto itself in a curl, creating a tube that's the surfer's nirvana. Also called the green room.

Barreled: becoming totally enclosed inside the wave's barrel during a ride. The ultimate "stoke!" Getting "barreled" is also sometimes known as spending time inside the "green room" or getting "tubed."

Beach break: The safest, best type for beginners. Waves break over sandy beaches. Found at Acapulquito (Old Man's), San Pedrito, and Los Cerritos.

Close out: When a wave or a section of a wave breaks all at once, rather than steadily in one direction. A frustrating situation for surfers; there's nowhere to go as the wave crashes down.

Ding: A hole, dent, crack or other damage to a board.

Drop in: To stand up and drop down in the face of a wave. Also used when one surfer cuts another off: "Hey, don't drop in on that guy!"

Duck dive: Maneuver where the surfer first pushes his or her board underwater and then dives with it, ducking under waves that have broken or are about to break. Difficult with a longboard.

Goofy foot: Having a right-foot-forward stance on the surfboard. The opposite is known as regular.

Outside: The area farther out from where waves break most regularly. Surfers line up here, and begin their paddling to catch waves.

Point break: Created as waves hit a point jutting into the ocean. With the right conditions, this can create very consistent waves and very long rides. Punta Lobos, Punta Conejo, and Monuments are examples.

Reef break: Waves break as they pass over reefs and create great (but sometimes dangerous) surf. There's always the chance of being scraped over extremely sharp coral or rocks. Found at El Tule, Shipwreck, and The Rock in Costa Azul.

Right/Left break: Terms for which direction the surfer actually travels on the wave, as seen from his or her perspective. Think of break direction in terms of when you're actually surfing the wave.

(top) A surfer rips it up in Mexico; (bottom) Baja California Sur sunset

Set: waves often come in as sets, or groups of three to seven, sometimes more, in a row.

Stick: A surfboard.

Stoked: really, totally excited—usually about the surf conditions or your fantastic wave ride.

Swells: created by wind currents blowing over the sea's surface. The harder and the longer the winds blow, the larger the waves, and the longer the swell lasts.

Turtle roll: the surfer rolls over on the surfboard, going underwater and holding the board upside down. Used by longboarders and beginners to keep from being swept back toward shore by breaking waves.

Wipeout: a nasty crash off your board, usually having the wave crash down upon you.

also boasts a yoga pavilion, juice bar, Amanda George hair salon, and a 1920s-style barber shop for men. For the ultimate in relaxation, try the Baja Deep Tissue Pindas Ritual—two hours that combine a scalp massage, hot stones, and deep pressure. ⊠ *Carretera Transpeninsular, Km 27.5, The Corridor* ☎ *624/146–7000* ⊕ *oneandonlyresorts.com/palmilla* ⊠ *Body treatments: $250–$450. Facials: $175–$250. Mani/Pedi: $55–$150. Parking: Valet (free).*

Spa Marquis

SPA/BEAUTY | With its holistic approach to wellness, this spa at Marquis Los Cabos has three categories of treatment: anima (massages), corpus (wraps), and mente (facials). The spa includes a complete hydrotherapy circuit and 10 treatment cabins with four reserved for couples. The resort's all-inclusive package doesn't include spa treatments, so be preapred for an extra fee. Treatments are also available for nonguest visitors. ⊠ *Marquis Los Cabos, Carretera Transpeninsular, Km. 21.5, The Corridor* ☎ *624/144–2000, 877/238–9399 Toll Free* ⊕ *marquisloscabos.com* ⊠ *Body treatments: $109–$235. Facials: $105–$275. Mani/Pedi: $45–$85. Waxing: $39–$85.* ☞ *Parking: Valet (free).*

SOMMA Wine Spa

SPA/BEAUTY | SOMMA is the only spa of its kind in Mexico, with only seven others throughout the world. The concept spa uses grapes from the up-and-coming Valle de Guadalupe wine region just outside Ensenada. It's an unusual experience blended with classical treatments, focusing on the calming, cosmetic, and antioxidant properties of grapes and wine, or vinotherapy. It towers high above the Sea of Cortez with 15 treatment rooms, both indoor and open-air, and offers a geothermal hot spring and more than 33 facial and body treatments from a Champagne Mud Wrap to a Le Vine Massage. ⊠ *Grand Fiesta Americana Los Cabos, Carretera Transpeninsular, Km. 10.3, Cabo del Sol,* *The Corridor* ☎ *624/145–6200 Ext. 31300* ⊕ *sommaspa.com* ⊠ *Body treatments: $80–$250. Facials: $170–$234. Mani/Pedi: $40–$60.* ☞ *Parking: Valet and self-parking.*

Spa Montage Los Cabos

SPA/BEAUTY | Extending over 40,000 square feet of state-of-the-art wellness facilities, Spa Montage is without a doubt one of the largest and best-equipped spas in Baja. A diverse array of holistic massages, facials, and beauty treatments await, including a must-try hydrotherapy circuit and a pampering, three-hour couples massage. Its outdoor, adults-only serenity pool and jetted pool area are standouts. ⊠ *Carretera Transpeninsular, Km. 12.5, The Corridor* ☎ *624/163–2000, 800/772–2226* ⊕ *montagehotels.com/loscabos.*

The Spa at Esperanza

SPA/BEAUTY | At the exclusive, 17-acre Esperanza Resort between Cabo San Lucas and San José del Cabo, the beautiful spa is reached by way of a stone path over a koi pond. At check-in you're presented with an *agua fresca*, a healthy drink made with papaya or mango, or other fruits and herbs. Treatments incorporate local ingredients, tropical fruits, and ocean-based products. Look for such pampering as the papaya-mango body polish, the grated-coconut-and-lime exfoliation, and the four-hands massage. Yoga classes are held at 7:15 and 9 each morning for $35 (free for hotel guests). Guests can also book an evening Starlight Spa experience for exclusive after-hours access. ⊠ *Esperanza Resort, Carretera Transpeninsular, Km. 7, The Corridor* ☎ *624/145–6406* ⊕ *aubergeresorts.com/esperanza* ⊠ *Body treatments: $160–$335. Facials: $160–$295. Mani/Pedi: $45–$200.* ☞ *Parking: Valet (free).*

The Spa at Las Ventanas al Paraíso

SPA/BEAUTY | Known for its innovative treatments—nopal (cactus) anticellulite and detox wrap, crystal healing massages, and raindrop therapy, the

Spa at Las Ventanas has both indoor and outdoor facilities. Some of the eight treatment rooms have private patios, and the two couples' suites come with a private butler. Healing rituals like the Holistic Twilight Ceremony are performed daily. Salt glows and massages are available in a pavilion by the sea. There are also pampering treatments for kids (Mommy and Me) and couples (Sea and Stars). ✉ *Las Ventanas al Paraíso Resort, Carretera Transpeninsular, Km 19.5, The Corridor* ☎ *624/144–0300* ⊕ *www.lasventanas. com* ✉ *Body treatments: $185–$900. Facials: $220–$410. Mani/Pedi: $45–$145.* ☞ *Parking: Valet (free).*

Spa Otomí at Westin Los Cabos

SPA/BEAUTY | Massages and wraps are the specialties provided in seven treatment rooms at the Spa Otomí. Most popular is the Otomí Signature massage, which takes guests to the peak of relaxation. The Blue Agave Candlelight massage is also a top seller. An on-site salon, barbershop, and fitness center round out the amenities. ✉ *Westin Los Cabos, Carretera Transpeninsular, Km. 22.5, The Corridor* ☎ *624/142–9000* ⊕ *mariott.com* ✉ *Body Treatments: $128–$269. Facials: $75–$155.*

SPORTFISHING

All the Corridor hotels work with fishing fleets anchored at the Cabo San Lucas marina (most vendors are stationed there) and a few with boats in Puerto Los Cabos, so any one of them can help you set up your fishing trips. Note that some hotels send customers to the company with the highest commission, so double-check recommendations and do your research. The major drawback of arranging a fishing trip from one of the Corridor hotels is the travel time involved in getting down to the water. It takes up to half an hour or more to reach the docks from Corridor hotels, and most boats depart at 6:30 am.

Gordo Banks Pangas

FISHING | The *pangas* (small fishing boats) of Gordo Banks Pangas are near some of the hottest fishing spots in the Sea of Cortez: the Outer and Inner Gordo banks. The pangas accommodate up to three. Their cruisers accommodate up to five. ✉ *La Playa near San José del Cabo, San José del Cabo* ☎ *624/142–1147, 619/488–1859 in U.S.* ⊕ *www.gordobanks.com* ✉ *Pangas from $250; cruisers from $420 per day.*

SURFING

The waves and undercurrent along the Corridor are notoriously strong, making much of the beach here unfavorable for swimming but great for surfing.

Mike Doyle Surf School

SURFING | FAMILY | The Mike Doyle Surf School is the top "surfer-friendly" location in all of Los Cabos. If you stay at the Cabo Surf Hotel where Mike Doyle is located, you can check the surf conditions from the restaurant, bar, pool, or even from your balcony. The school has more than 100 rental boards, from foam boards and short boards to longboards and stand-up paddleboards. There are five surf instructors available at the shop for lessons. ✉ *Cabo Surf Hotel, Carretera Transpeninsular, Km 28, Playa Acapulquito, The Corridor* ☎ *624/142–2676, 858/964–5117 in U.S.* ⊕ *mikedoylesurfschool.com* ✉ *Starting at $79.*

Surf in Cabo

SURFING | Surf in Cabo has provided surf and SUP lessons for all levels, tours (half- and full-day), and rentals for more than a decade. They're located at Playa Pescadito, where they organize well-rounded surfing camps, "surfaris," and "supfaris." Another bonus: they're open every day and accept credit cards. ✉ *Carretera Transpeninsular, Km 28.5, The Corridor* ✛ *Next to Zipper's* ☎ *624/117–9495* ⊕ *www.surfincabo.com* ☞ *Lessons start at $69; tours at $129.*

Chapter 5

SAN JOSÉ
DEL CABO

Updated by
Luis Domínguez

⦿ Sights	🍴 Restaurants	🛏 Hotels	🛍 Shopping	🍸 Nightlife
★★★★☆	★★★★★	★★★★★	★★★★☆	★★★☆☆

NEIGHBORHOOD SNAPSHOT

TOP EXPERIENCES

- **Gallery Hopping:** Visit the charming Art District during a Thursday Art Walk, when artists open their galleries and invite visitors to mingle, purchase art, and sample local food and drinks.

- **Farm-to-Table Dining:** There are several opportunities to dine right in the picturesque farms that produce the fresh ingredients for your organic meal.

- **Surfing:** If surfing is on your bucket list, this is the place to cross it off and simply a must when visiting San José. For something a tad easier, try paddleboarding.

- **Strolling Downtown:** Walk the quaint streets of San José's historic center, and discover its collection of centuries-old buildings, a vibrant community plaza, and food stalls full of local flavor.

- **Shopping:** Whether you're in the market for art, jewelry, or fresh produce from the stellar Farmer's Market (Mercado Organico), you'll find it here.

GETTING HERE

Since this is the closest neighborhood to the SJD airport, shuttle prices are slightly cheaper than to other neighborhoods ($30 for a shared ride and $95 for a private ride). Taxis charge around $75. Note that ride-share services like Uber are not allowed to pick up customers at the airport. Once in San José, the best way to move around is by taxi or Uber. There's no need to rent a car, unless you plan to go on an excursion far from town.

PLANNING YOUR TIME

May to June is the best time to visit, right after spring break and before the rainy season starts. Summer is best for surfing, and December through April is best for whale watching (and is most expensive). Plan at least a day to explore, prioritizing the art galleries and eateries downtown. Make it a Thursday, if you can, to catch the weekly Art Walk between 5 and 9 pm.

QUICK BITES

- **Los Claros.** This is the place for a quick taco fix; $2 (fish and shrimp) or $5 (lobster) gets you some serious tacos, while $6 will buy you a killer breakfast. Two-for-one margaritas are served all day, and five beers (Corona or Pacifico) can be had for $10. ⊠ *Blvd. Antonio Mijares 1092* ☎ *624/131–5090*

- **Tacos Rossy.** At this no-frills joint, locals sink their teeth into fish tacos ($1–$3) piled high with avocados, chilies, cabbage, onions, and an assortment of spicy salsas. ⊠ *Hwy. 1, Km 33* ☎ *624/143–6755*

- **Taquería El Paisa.** This place is widely recognized as having "the best tacos in Cabo" ($1–$3); you'll be surprised by how many of them you can eat at one sitting. The *al pastor* grilled beef taco is a star alongside the customary *agua de Jamaica* (hibiscus iced tea) ($1). ⊠ *Lázaro Cárdenas, Centro, Ildefonso Green* ☎ *624/191–7409*

If being in Mexico (and not in the thick of a hopping resort scene) sounds like the ideal setting for your vacation, San José del Cabo is the place to be. San José is the quieter, more artistic of Los Cabos' two main towns; its sister across the corridor, Cabo San Lucas, has the more exciting nightlife and rowdy beaches. What you get here is a lovely downtown that's retained much of its traditional charm, with adobe houses fronted by jacaranda trees, and a peaceful, more down-to-earth experience.

With century-old buildings and many elevated sidewalks, the Centro Histórico (historic center) is a delight to explore on foot. Plaza Mijares, the open and popular *zócalo*, is graced by a fountain, lighted at night, and a stage where live music takes place frequently for the crowds who gather to stroll to nearby art galleries, enjoy ice cream, and relax after the heat of the day has let up. Several streets fronting the square are pedestrian-only, giving this historic downtown a lush and leisurely feel.

Entrepreneurs have converted many of the old homes into stylish restaurants, and new and inventive cuisine abounds—fitting for a town with an art district that is burgeoning as well. A marina, two golf courses, and a residential community are south of

Centro (town center) in Puerto Los Cabos; farther south the ever-expanding Zona Hotelera (Hotel Zone) faces a long beach on the Sea of Cortez.

Just outside San José in the lush Ánimas Bajas, farm-to-table dining concepts like Acre and Flora Farms are drawing an increasing number of visitors for fresh-as-can-be organic meals and stunning views.

◎ Sights

Many of San José's sights are located in the Centro Histórico, or historic center, a charming downtown anchored by the central Plaza Mijares. Surrounding it are a historic mission, art galleries, and colorful, pedestrian-only streets that invite you to take a relaxed stroll.

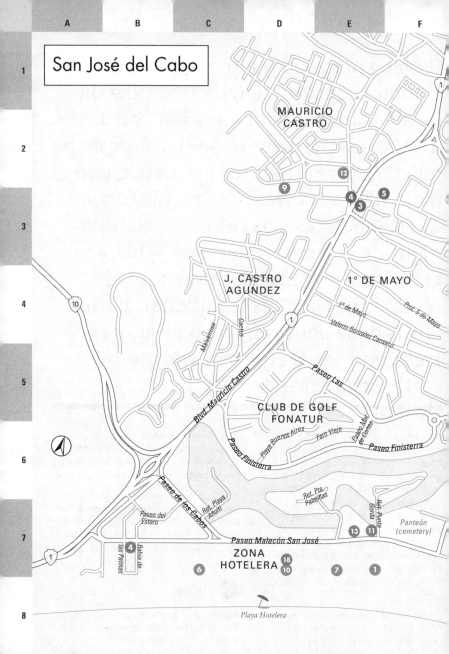

San José del Cabo

MAURICIO CASTRO

J, CASTRO AGUNDEZ

1° DE MAYO

1° de Mayo

Prol. 5 de Mayo

Valerio González Canseco

Paseo Las

CLUB DE GOLF FONATUR

Playa Buenos Aires

Faro Viejo

Paseo Mauricio Castro

Malvarrosa

Cactus

Paseo Finisterra

Paseo Mauricio Castro

Paseo Finisterra

Paseo Finisterra

Ret. Playa Añuiti

Ret. Pta. Palmillas

Ret. Punta Gorda

Ret. Punta

Panteón (cemetery)

Paseo de los Cabos

Paseo del Estero

Bahía de Las Palmas

Bahía de

Paseo Malecón San José

ZONA HOTELERA

Playa Hotelera

Bahía San José del Cabo

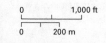

0   1,000 ft

0   200 m

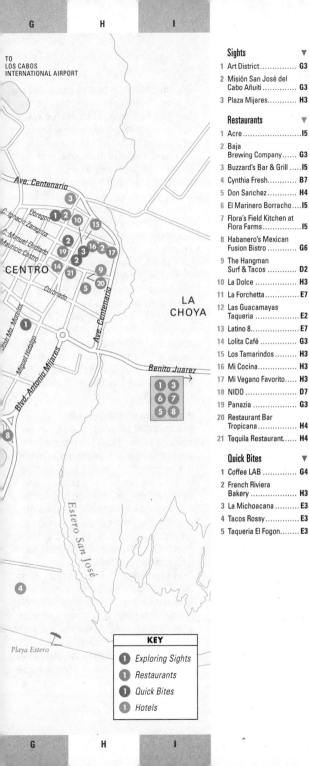

TO
LOS CABOS
INTERNATIONAL AIRPORT

Ave. Centenario

C. Ignacio Zaragoza
Obregon
C. Manuel Doblado
Mauricio Castro

CENTRO

Coronado

José Ma. Morelos

Miguel Hidalgo

Blvd. Antonio Mijares

Ave. Centenario

LA
CHOYA

Benito Juarez

Estero San José

Playa Estero

KEY

- Exploring Sights
- Restaurants
- Quick Bites
- Hotels

★ Art District

HISTORIC SITE | Within San José's historic center are four blocks packed with 16 high-quality art galleries, collectively known as the Art District. You can walk around any time, but it's worth planning your visit on Thursday afternoon to enjoy San José's popular weekly Art Walk from 5 pm through 9 pm. During this time, gallery owners open their doors and invite you to socialize with local artists and art enthusiasts from around the globe, discovering thought-provoking artwork along the way. ⊠ *Álvaro Obregón and Morelos, Distrito del Arte* ☏ *624/168–7063* ⊕ *www.artcabo.com.*

Misión San José del Cabo Añuiti

RELIGIOUS SITE | One of the most magical experiences in San José is strolling past this historic mission as its bells chime. Originally founded in 1730 near the local estuary, it was the southernmost Jesuit mission established in the Vieja California territory during Mexico's colonial days. The mission walked a tightrope between baptizing the area's indigenous Pericú and being locked in battle with them. In the 19th century, the mission was destroyed by an attack, and it wasn't until 1940 that the mission was rebuilt on its current site. The mission is currently the head of a parish comprising six churches and more than 45,000 parishioners. It holds English mass every Sunday at noon. ⊠ *Parroquia de San José del Cabo, Calle Zaragoza and Miguel Hidalgo, Centro* ☏ *624/142–0064* ⊕ *facebook.com/misionsanjosedelcabo.*

Plaza Mijares

PLAZA | FAMILY | This *zócalo* (main square) and community gathering space is the heart and soul of San José del Cabo. Surrounded by city hall and the Misión de San José, it's where all manner of events and happenings take place. The nearby streets are filled with all kinds of shops, restaurants, and art galleries, but it's here that locals gather to spend their weekend afternoons eating *antojitos* (appetizers) and enjoying performances of local street artists. ⊠ *Plaza Mijares, Centro.*

🏖 Beaches

Oh, the madness of it all. Here you are in a beach destination with gorgeous weather and miles of clear blue water, yet you dare not dive into the sea. Most of San José's hotels line Playa Hotelera on Paseo Malecón San José, and brochures and websites gleefully mention beach access. But here's the rub—though the long, level stretch of coarse brown sand is beautiful, the currents can be dangerously rough, the drop-offs are steep and close to shore, and the waves can be fierce. Although surfers love this type of water and flock here in droves, it's extremely dangerous for the casual swimmer. Warning signs are posted up and down the beach, just in case you happen to forget. Feel free to walk along the beach to the Estero San José, play some beach volleyball, or enjoy a horseback ride along the shore. For swimming, head to protected Playa Palmilla just a few miles southwest, in the Corridor.

Playa Estero (*Estuary Beach*)

BEACH—SIGHT | A sandy beach can be enjoyed at the mouth of the Estero San José, the lush estuary that starts at the north end of Hotel Zone near the Holiday Inn hotel. This oasis is home to more than 350 species of wildlife and vegetation (200-plus species of birds alone), and can be explored on foot, or via kayaks rentable at El Ganzo Beach Club. Horses are available for hire across from Holiday Inn at Bonanza Horseback Riding. Bring bug spray, as the wetlands attract lots of mosquitoes. Not recommended for swimming, it is nevertheless a worthwhile trip in an area that is otherwise not known for its lushness. Public parking is available just beyond the Holiday Inn. **Amenities:** free parking. **Best for:** walking; sunrise. ⊠ *San José del Cabo.*

Playa Hotelera
BEACH—SIGHT | FAMILY | The long, wide stretch of beach running in front of the hotels on the coast of San José del Cabo might be stunning, but the riptides and undertows make it deceivingly dangerous for swimmers. There are no public services on the beach, but you can always duck into one of the hotels for a snack, or head across the street to Plaza Del Pescador for a meal at one of the restaurants. This beach often has locals with horses to rent for a beachside ride. Due to the line of resorts, there are only a few access points to reach the sand. **Amenities:** free parking. **Best for:** walking; surfing; sunrise. ✉ *San José del Cabo.*

🍴 Restaurants

Boulevard Mijares is San José's Restaurant Row, so simply meander down the main boulevard to find one that will thrill your taste buds and delight your senses. New, organic-focused restaurants are pushing the culinary scene to the outskirts of San José del Cabo in Ánimas Bajas. These farm-to-table finds are tucked into green valleys, creating an oasis just beyond the cactus-lined dusty roads of Puerto Los Cabos.

★ Acre
$$$ | MODERN MEXICAN | Twenty-five acres are what you'll find at this farmland dining experience where design, sustainability, and modern cuisine intersect. Beyond the palm-tree forest is the main restaurant where a reed pergola casts linear shadows onto concrete floors. **Known for:** quality local ingredients; global cuisine with Mexican fusion; live DJ performances daily. [$] *Average main: $22* ✉ *Rincon De Las Animas, Calle Camino Real s/n, Las Animas Bajas* ☎ *624/171–8226* 🌐 *www.acrebaja.com.*

Baja Brewing Company
$$ | AMERICAN | Baja's popular brewery is right in the middle of San José del Cabo's Art District. Fun and upbeat, this brewpub has great music and serves filling pub meals. **Known for:** wood-fired pizza; customers watching behind-the-scenes brewing while enjoying beers at the bar; Baja beer on tap. [$] *Average main: $15* ✉ *Morelos 1277, Centro* ✣ *Between Comonfort and Obregón* ☎ *624/142–5294* 🌐 *www.bajabrewingcompany.com.*

Buzzard's Bar & Grill
$ | AMERICAN | Fronted by miles of secluded East Cape beach, this casual seaside cantina (with cheap cervezas) gets rave reviews from locals who make the 10-minute drive out of San José del Cabo. The palapa restaurant serves reasonably priced seafood entrées, such as coconut shrimp; breakfast burritos; hefty build-your-own burgers; and house flan. **Known for:** giant burritos; coconut shrimp with piña colada dipping sauce; laid-back bar with sandy floor. [$] *Average main: $9* ✉ *Old East Cape Rd., Laguna Hills* ✣ *Follow signs from San José del Cabo to Puerto Los Cabos and La Laguna* ☎ *624/113–6368* 🌐 *www.buzzardsbar.com* 💳 *No credit cards* 🕒 *Closed Aug. and Sept. No dinner Sun* ☞ *Cash only.*

Cynthia Fresh
$ | DELI | FAMILY | A hidden gem in the wide array of dining options in San José, this small restaurant and organic market serves fresh vegan and nonvegan dishes. Buy at the market and take out, or dine-in and enjoy live music and fresh margaritas. **Known for:** fresh, organic vegan food; live music and margaritas; delicious salads. [$] *Average main: $10* ✉ *Paseo Malecón San José, Plaza Caracol, Fonatur* ☎ *624/155–5874* 🕒 *Closed Sun* 💳 *No credit cards.*

Did You Know?

San José's Art District has more than a dozen galleries in just a few blocks. Local artists invite visitors to peruse during Thursday evening Art Walks.

★ Don Sanchez

$$ | MODERN MEXICAN | Award-winning chefs Edgar Roman and Tadd Chapman bring contemporary Mexican cuisine from farm to table at Don Sanchez. Brick pillars, white linens, and a wine wall comprised of nearly 100 blends make up the more formal dining area, but dinner on the patio is a must. **Known for:** butter-poached lobster with chayote pearls; fine wine and hospitality; modern Mexican menu. [$] *Average main: $20* ✉ *Blvd. Mijares s/n , Edificio Eclipse Int 3, Centro* ☎ *624/142–2444* 🌐 *www.donsanchezrestaurant.com.*

El Marinero Borracho

$ | MEXICAN FUSION | This two-story palapa restaurant, named "The Drunken Sailor," is always packed with locals and tourists alike. It's no wonder: the location across from the marina is the perfect spot to watch the sunset while enjoying a ginger mint mojito or tamarind margarita. **Known for:** unique ceviches menu; best Los Cabos dessert: avocado-lime chocolate cream pie; sunset view. [$] *Average main: $9* ✉ *Near Hotel El Ganzo, Puerto Los Cabos, Marina* ✣ *Next to Jansens Bait and Tackle* ☎ *624/105–6464* 🌐 *instagram.com/el_marinero_borracho* 🕓 *Closed Mon.*

★ Flora's Field Kitchen at Flora Farms

$$$$ | AMERICAN | FAMILY | This alfresco dining experience is built right in the center of the self-sustaining Flora Farms. It's a charming oasis featuring a farm-to-table restaurant, spa, gift shop, cooking school, organic market, and culinary cottages (private homes), all under the Flora Farms brand. **Known for:** wood-fired pizzas; farm setting with live music; produce raised on-site. [$] *Average main: $40* ✉ *Flora Farms, Las Animas Bajas* ☎ *624/142–1000, 949/200–7342 U.S. phone* 🌐 *www.flora-farms.com* 🕓 *Closed Mon. and daily 2:30–5 pm.*

The Hangman Surf & Tacos

$ | MEXICAN | By day it looks like a hole-in-the-wall, but when the sun goes down, the rummage-sale-meets-taco-stand atmosphere of this open-air local favorite truly comes to life. Get beyond the ghoulish silhouette logo—*ahorcado* means "hangman" in Spanish—and you'll find that the food is pretty good. **Known for:** outstanding tacos; reasonable prices; authentic Mexican experience. [$] *Average main: $5* ✉ *Calle Panga 30, San José del Cabo* ☎ *624/152–3989* 🌐 *facebook.com/thehangmansurfandtacos* 💳 *No credit cards* 🕓 *Closed Mon. No lunch* ☞ *Cash only.*

Habanero's Mexican Fusion Bistro

$$ | MEXICAN FUSION | Celebrity chef Tadd Chapman and partner Miguel Guerrero joined forces to re-launch this traditional Mexican restaurant in its new location and with fresh new culinary techniques. Opt for lunch specialties of octopus tacos and black scallop ceviche, and for dinner, try the seafood risotto, or the grilled NY strip with habanero chimichurri. **Known for:** home-baked banana zucchini bread; guacamole with chapulines (grasshoppers); octopus tacos. [$] *Average main: $16* ✉ *El Encanto Suites Hotel, Jose Maria Morelos 134, Centro* ☎ *624/142–2626* 🌐 *habanerosbistro.com.*

La Dolce

$$ | ITALIAN | This popular Italian restaurant right in the center of San José on the town's *zócalo* (square) is known for authentic and affordable Italian fare. Locals and visitors alike flock to this reasonably priced perennial favorite for antipasti and wood-fired-oven pizzas, a never-ending selection of pastas, and steaks and seafood dishes. **Known for:** authentic Northern Italian cuisine; handmade pizza baked with mesquite wood; great Caesar salad. [$] *Average main: $12* ✉ *Av. Zaragoza at Av. Hidalgo, Plaza Jardin Mijares, Centro* ☎ *624/142–6621* 🌐 *restauranteladolce.com* 🕓 *Closed Mon.*

Farm-fresh ingredients are served in a beautiful garden at Flora's Field Kitchen at Flora Farms.

La Forchetta

$$ | ITALIAN | FAMILY | A favorite of locals, this Italian-Mexican restaurant is the place to get Roman-style, hand-stretched pizzas. Even those who aren't fans of pizza will find something on the diverse menu, with a balanced offering of pasta, antipasti, and main courses. **Known for:** 12" hand-stretched pizzas; signature sfera di cioccolato dessert; sophisticated but family-friendly atmosphere. $ *Average main: $17* ⊠ *Paseo Malecón San José, Plaza del Pescador, Lot 24, San José del Cabo* ☎ *624/130–7723* ⊕ *www. laforchetta.mx.*

Las Guacamayas Taqueria

$ | MEXICAN | Massive globes of 15 types of margaritas and a Mexican guitarist singing American covers makes this a magnet for tourists, but it also draws locals. If you're looking for cheap and delicious Mexican food, you've come to the right place. **Known for:** outstanding marinated pork tacos; great prices; live music and outdoor seating. $ *Average main: $9* ⊠ *Calle Paseo de los Marinos,*

Centro ✛ *Near corner of Pescadores* ☎ *624/189–5284* ⊕ *facebook.com/ tacosguacamayas.*

Latino 8

$$ | LATIN AMERICAN | FAMILY | For a taste of Latin America's deliciously spicy cuisine and exuberant attitude toward life, visit this laid-back place where everything is colorful and everyone is happy. Order dishes of Mexican, Argentinian, Cuban, and Peruvian origins, among others, and try their exquisite cocktails while listening to live Latin music. **Known for:** Pan-Latin American menu; live salsa and bachata music; original cocktails. $ *Average main: $15* ⊠ *Paseo Malecón San José, Plaza del Pescador, Lot 8, Fonatur* ☎ *624/130–7267* ⊕ *www.latino8.com.*

★ Lolita Café

$ | CAFÉ | In a relaxing garden filled with retro decor, waiters in mesh trucker hats and black T-shirts deliver remarkable urban Mexican cuisine with a dash of Grandma's secret recipes. Under the shade of a mango tree, start with the trio of salsas infused with orange and chipotle, served with a basket of freshly fried tortilla chips. **Known for:** delightful breakfast under the shade of a mango tree; yummy churros and gourmet coffees; fresh squeezed juices and healthy smoothies. [$] *Average main: $8* ✉ *Manuel Doblado 24, Centro* ✣ *Between Hidalgo and Morelos* ☎ *624/130–7786* 🌐 *www.cafedelolita.com* ⏲ *Closed Mon. No dinner.*

Los Tamarindos

$$ | MEXICAN FUSION | FAMILY | A former sugarcane mill dating back to 1888, this quaint restaurant is surrounded by farmland that provides organic fruits and vegetables to many of Cabo's top eateries. Wildflowers in Mason jars and hand-painted clay dishes set the scene at this rustic spot where the menu is based on the season's harvest. **Known for:** four-hour cooking classes ($95); true farm-to-table dining experience; homemade herbal oil on breads and meats. [$] *Average main: $20* ✉ *Calle Animas Baja, Las Animas Bajas* ☎ *624/105–6031* 🌐 *www.lostamarindos.mx.*

Mi Cocina

$$$ | ECLECTIC | At this outdoor restaurant at Casa Natalia boutique hotel, fire bowls glow on the dining terrace, which is surrounded by palm trees and gentle waterfalls, blending the four elements: earth, wind, fire, and water. Tables are spaced far enough apart so that you don't have to share your whispered sweet nothings with neighbors. **Known for:** Mexican dishes with a European twist; adjoining oyster and martini bar; exceptional chicken with chocolate salsa. [$] *Average main: $25* ✉ *Casa Natalia, Blvd. Mijares 4, Centro* ☎ *624/146–7100, 888/277–3814 from U.S.* 🌐 *www.casanatalia.com* ⏲ *Closed Tues.*

Mi Vegano Favorito

$$ | VEGETARIAN | FAMILY | Serving 100% vegan food made with mostly organic ingredients, My Favorite Vegan is that cute, cool place all vegans (and even non-vegans) wish existed in every town. The vibe is relaxed and enjoyable, with a committed management that invites artists to display their work in the restaurant, DJs to play live, and sometimes even tattoo artists to set up shop for the day. **Known for:** vegan food everyone can enjoy; organic products; relaxed, artsy atmosphere. [$] *Average main: $12* ✉ *Blvd. Centenario, Centro* ☎ *624/121–1897* 🌐 *facebook.com/miveganofavorito.*

NIDO

$$ | JAPANESE FUSION | Covered by a nest-like dome and surrounded by *espejos de agua* (water mirrors), the Viceroy's sophisticated, design-forward restaurant impresses with its truly unique setting. The menu is equally original, with an eclectic mix of Japanese delicacies, Mexican fusion creations, and a gourmet raw bar. **Known for:** mesmerizing architectural style; raw bar and robatayaki (tableside Japanese grill); providing "love nest" for private dinners. [$] *Average main: $20* ✉ *Viceroy Los Cabos, Paseo Malecón San José, Lote 8, San José del Cabo* ☎ *624/104–9999, 844/222–6987 U.S. toll-free* 🌐 *www.viceroyhotelsandresorts.com/los-cabos.*

Panazia

$$ | MEXICAN FUSION | Located in San José's oldest mission, this Mexican-Asian fusion restaurant is modern and sophisticated with a series of tropical patios romantically lighted by dim fixtures and a view of the stars above. The menu highlights gourmet fusion creations by chef Paul Zamudio, such as pad Thai or dumplings, but always accompanied by Mexican flavors. **Known for:** Mexiatica (Mexican-Asian) dishes; fresh and natural raw ingredients; $15 all-you-can-eat menu. [$] *Average main: $15* ✉ *Av. Zaragoza 20, Centro* ☎ *624/142–4041* 🌐 *facebook.com/panaz1a/* ⏲ *Closed Mon.*

Restaurant Bar Tropicana

$$ | INTERNATIONAL | Reminiscent of an old colonial hacienda, this two-story restaurant draws a crowd with its live music, Sunday brunch, and large menu ranging from fresh seafood to imported steaks. The front sidewalk seating is a great place to survey the world going by. **Known for:** live music Thursday–Sunday; hacienda-style dining room; flavorful chicken enchiladas. $ *Average main: $18* ⊠ *Tropicana Inn, Blvd. Mijares 30, Centro* ☎ *624/142–1580* ⊕ *tropicanainnloscabos.com.*

Tequila Restaurant

$$ | **ECLECTIC** | A beautifully redone adobe home sets the stage for this classy dining experience on an open courtyard under the stars. A lengthy tequila list tempts diners to savor the finer brands of Mexico's national drink, and an extensive wine cellar will give you plenty of choices for what to sip as you sup. **Known for:** succulent rack of lamb; Mexican cuisine with Asian influences; beautiful garden setting. $ *Average main: $17* ⊠ *Manuel Doblado 1011, Centro* ☎ *624/142–1155* ⊕ *facebook.com/tequilarestaurante.*

☕ Coffee and Quick Bites

Coffee LAB

$ | **INTERNATIONAL** | Loved by locals and visitors alike, this beautiful place is a good spot to grab home-roasted specialty coffee (starting at $1.50), wine (starting at $6), and tapas ($2). Check their calendar online for concerts and other events. **Known for:** specialty coffee roasted in-house; engaging cultural events; co-working area. $ *Average main: $5* ⊠ *Juarez 1717, San José del Cabo* ☎ *624/105–2835* ⊕ *lab-baja.mx* ☾ *Closed Sun.*

French Riviera Bakery

$ | **CAFÉ** | The scent of fresh-baked French baguettes and a picture-perfect display of croissants, éclairs, colorful candies, and ice creams greet you at this café-bistro just off San José del Cabo's main square. In the creperie area, the cook tucks delicate crepes around eggs and cheese, ground beef and onions, or shrimp and

More on Tequila 🍴

The real stuff comes from the Tequila region in mainland Mexico, but Los Cabos folks are producing their own spirits; look for the labels from private local distilleries. Tequila brands offered with Los Cabos labels are Cabo Wabo, Hotel California tequila, Mexita, and Las Varitas brand.

pesto. **Known for:** organic local coffee; chocolate truffles; scrumptious breakfast crepes. $ *Average main: $10* ⊠ *Manuel Doblado at Av. Hidalgo, Centro* ☎ *624/105–2624.*

La Michoacana

$ | **MEXICAN** | **FAMILY** | It may be small, but La Michoacana has a grand history of providing frozen fruit-based refreshments all over Mexico. The huge selection of *paletas* (popsicles), frozen fruit bars, and ice cream is so tantalizing, it's difficult to choose just one from the colorful display. **Known for:** best popsicles in San José; authentic Mexican ice cream; dairy-free frozen fruit bars. $ *Average main: $1* ⊠ *Ignacio Zaragoza 24, Centro* ☎ *624/177-3079* ⊕ *michoacana.com.*

Tacos Rossy

$ | **MEXICAN** | Don't be fooled by the bare-bones atmosphere: Tacos Rossy serves some of the best tacos in San José. Fish tacos are the thing at this no-frills joint brimming with local families who munch on everything from peel-and-eat shrimp to ceviche and chocolate clams. **Known for:** $2 tacos and $3 margaritas; large condiment bar for dress-your-own taco; best taqueria in town. $ *Average main: $5* ⊠ *Carretera Transpeninsular, Km 33, Centro* ☎ *624/142–6755.*

Cabo Azul Resort boasts huge villas and a tranquil pool.

Taqueria El Fogon

$ | **MEXICAN** | If your to-do list includes trying authentic Mexican tacos at a local hole-in-the-wall, this is the place for you. Get your Spanish ready to order arguably the best tacos in town, plus *frijoles charros* (spicy beans) with chorizo, melted cheese, and grilled onions. **Known for:** delicious tacos al pastor; pozole on Thursday and Saturday; generously served stuffed potatoes. [$] *Average main: $3* ✉ *Manuel Doblado, Centro* ☎ *624/105–2835.*

Hotels

If you're looking for an authentic, local place to stay in Los Cabos, San José del Cabo may be it. The historic center is home to centuries-old buildings and pedestrian-only streets, a quaint town square in Plaza Mijares, and a historic church. Just beyond the center of town, and a bit farther south, is the ever-expanding Zona Hotelera, where a dozen or so hotels, timeshares, and condo projects face the long stretch of beach on the Sea of Cortez. Closer to the marina at Puerto los Cabos, the boutique El Ganzo Hotel and chain resorts like Secrets have staked their claim, with plans for further development past La Playita.

Cabo Azul Resort

$$ | **RESORT** | **FAMILY** | On the beach in San José del Cabo, this chic, whitewashed property is peaceful from the moment you walk through the 20-foot antique door to a waterfall wall and marble floors that lead to a breathtaking lobby centered by a circular rope structure that drops 1,200 feet from the ceiling. **Pros:** huge villas; sophisticated and elegant property; Kids' Club and designated pool for children. **Cons:** spotty Internet; beach not safe for swimming; not all rooms have ocean views. [$] *Rooms from: $220* ✉ *Paseo Malecón, Zona Hotelera* ☎ *624/163–5100* 🌐 *www.caboazulresort.com* 🛏 *326 rooms* 🍴 *No meals.*

★ Casa Natalia

$$ | **HOTEL** | An intimate, graceful boutique hotel, Casa Natalia is in the heart of San José's downtown and opens onto the zócalo. **Pros:** oasis in the heart of downtown; fantastic complimentary breakfast for superior rooms; lovely pool area. **Cons:** no bathtubs in the standard rooms; occasional noise from music and fiestas on Plaza Mijares; no children under 13. [$] *Rooms from: $217* ✉ *Blvd. Mijares 4, Centro* ☎ *624/146–7100, 888/277–3814 from U.S.* 🌐 *www.casanatalia.com* 🛏 *18 rooms* 🍴 *Free breakfast.*

Encanto Inn & Suites

$ | **HOTEL** | In the heart of San José's historic Art District, this gorgeous and comfortable inn has two separate buildings—one looks onto the verdant gardens and pool; the other one, across the street, is in a charming, historic building with a narrow courtyard. **Pros:** Mexican-hacienda feeling; excellent location; pet-friendly. **Cons:** staffing is minimal; spotty Wi-Fi; some rooms get street noise. [$] *Rooms from: $183* ✉ *Calle Morelos 133, Centro* ☎ *624/142–0388, 210/858–5912 from U.S.* 🌐 *www.elencantoinn.com* 🛏 *27 rooms* 🍴 *No meals.*

Holiday Inn Resort Los Cabos

$$ | **RESORT** | **FAMILY** | As the last property in San José del Cabo's Hotel Zone, the familiar Holiday Inn brand here gets high marks for its attentive, friendly, old-world Mexican attitude among the staff members. **Pros:** Chiqui Kids' Club (ages 5–12); adults-only pool; free Wi-Fi. **Cons:** rooms tend to be basic; food is run-of-the-mill buffet-style; dated style. [$] *Rooms from: $235* ✉ *Blvd. Mijares at Paseo San José, Zona Hotelera* ✣ *Cul-de-sac at end of Hotel Zone* ☎ *624/142–9229* 🌐 *www.holidayinnresorts.com/loscabos* 🛏 *397 rooms* 🍴 *All-inclusive.*

Hotel El Ganzo

$$ | **HOTEL** | At this boutique hotel with an uberchic vibe, guests can interact with artists-in-residence, musicians, and filmmakers in a creative and luxurious setting. **Pros:** an outlet for artists; free beach cruisers to explore the cactus gardens; horseback riding and estuary kayak tours. **Cons:** must spend a minimum of $30 to use the beach club; service does not match the price; no children under 18. [$] *Rooms from: $250* ✉ *Tiburón s/n, La Playita, Marina* ☎ *624/104–9000, 855/835–4269 toll-free U.S.* 🌐 *www.elganzo.com* 🛏 *70 rooms* 🍴 *No meals.*

★ Hyatt Ziva Los Cabos

$$$ | **RESORT** | **FAMILY** | This resort is great for both families and couples looking for a complete getaway, featuring 591 suites, eight restaurants ranging from French to Italian and Spanish to Japanese, seven bars, four pools (including an adults-only option), and a Kids' Club. **Pros:** great à la carte restaurant selection; spacious suites; Kids' Club and adjacent water park offer diversion for little ones. **Cons:** resort's size is a bit overwhelming; slow elevator; 30% of rooms lack ocean views. [$] *Rooms from: $300* ✉ *Paseo Malecón, Lote 5, Zona Hotelera* ☎ *624/163–7730* 🌐 *hyatt.com* 🛏 *591 rooms* 🍴 *All-inclusive.*

Royal Solaris Los Cabos

$ | **RENTAL** | **FAMILY** | Royal Solaris was the first all-inclusive in Los Cabos, and it runs smoothly like the established property it is, with plenty of entertainment options and sports activities offered. **Pros:** Kids' Club 9–5; climbing wall and mini water park; best value of the all-inclusives. **Cons:** the accommodations and food only adequate; not romantic; timeshare salespeople are pushy. [$] *Rooms from: $190* ✉ *Paseo Malecón, Lote 10, Colonia Campo de Golf, Zona Hotelera* ☎ *624/145–6800, 877/270–0440 in U.S.* 🌐 *www.hotelessolaris.com* 🛏 *390 rooms* 🍴 *All-inclusive.*

Secrets Puerto Los Cabos

$$$ | **RESORT** | The first of the all-inclusive chains to reach La Playita, this adults-only resort has swim-up rooms, ocean views, seven restaurants, and a 13,000-square-foot spa by Pevonia. **Pros:**

nightly entertainment shows; plenty of activities; caters to adults. **Cons:** beach not swimmable; annoying timeshare pitches; no kids under 18. [$] *Rooms from: $350* ✉ *Av. Paseo de los Pescadores s/n, La Playita* ☎ *624/144–2600, 866/467–3273* 🌐 *www.secretsresorts.com* 🛏 *500 rooms* 🍴 *All-inclusive.*

Tropicana Inn

$ | **HOTEL** | It's not on the beach, but this hotel in a quiet enclave along one of San José's main boulevards is a delightful, reasonable find. **Pros:** lively on-site restaurant and bar; rooms are immaculate; small on-site spa. **Cons:** positioned as adult escape but kids are allowed; poor views and lighting in some rooms; not on the beach. [$] *Rooms from: $113* ✉ *Blvd. Mijares 30, Centro* ☎ *624/142–1580* 🌐 *tropicanainnloscabos.com* 🛏 *40 rooms* 🍴 *No meals.*

★ **Viceroy Los Cabos**

$$$$ | **RESORT** | Stunning architecture, top-notch facilities, and outstanding service make this luxury resort in the heart of the Zona Hotelera arguably the best resort in San José. **Pros:** stylish rooftop restaurant with outstanding ocean views; suites include large dining areas; cool in-house cinema. **Cons:** not all rooms enjoy ocean views; not the best beach for swimming or privacy; kid-friendly policy contrasts with style of resort. [$] *Rooms from: $403* ✉ *Paseo Malecón San José, Zona Hotelera* ☎ *624/104–9999, 844/222–6987 U.S. toll-free* 🌐 *www.viceroyhotelsandresorts.com/los-cabos* 🛏 *198 rooms* 🍴 *No meals.*

Nightlife

After-dark action in San José del Cabo caters mostly to locals and tourists seeking tranquility and seclusion. There are no big dance clubs or discos in San José. What little nightlife there is revolves around restaurants, casual bars, and large hotels. A pre- or post-dinner stroll makes a wonderful addition to any San José evening. When night falls, people begin to fill the streets, many of them hurrying off to evening Mass when they hear the church bells peal from the central plaza.

A number of galleries hold court in central San José del Cabo, creating the **San José del Cabo Art District**. It's just north and east of the town's cathedral, primarily along Obregón, Morelos, and Guerrero streets. On Thursday nights (5–9 pm) from November to June, visit the **Art Walk,** where you can meander around about 15 galleries, sampling wine and cheese as you go.

BARS

Baja Brewing Co.

BARS/PUBS | The Baja Brewing Co. serves cold, on-site–microbrewed cerveza and international pub fare. You'll find entrées ranging from ahi tuna quesadillas to basil-and-blue-cheese burgers. Our favorite of the eight beers is the Baja Blond Ale; the BBC also brews Oatmeal Stout, Raspberry Lager, homemade root beer, and a dark, smooth Black Scorpion. If you can't make up your mind, order the sampler. ✉ *Morelos 1277 at Obregón, San José del Cabo* ☎ *624/142–1292* 🌐 *www.bajabrewingcompany.com.*

Cantina29 at Casa Don Rodrigo

BARS/PUBS | Come here for the ambience and cocktails (the food has mixed reviews) like the blackberry mojito or house margarita. Once the home of the owner's grandparents, the building dates back to 1927 and its original brick walls are still intact, adorned with historic family photographs. The courtyard, strung with lanterns and fairy lights, is a pleasant place to enjoy the live mariachi. ✉ *Blvd. Antonio Mijares 29, Centro* ☎ *624/166–9439, 624/142–0418* 🌐 *casadonrodrigo.com.*

★ Cielomar Rooftop

PIANO BARS/LOUNGES | This sophisticated rooftop restaurant and bar serves exquisite seafood and stylish cocktails with a side of fantastic ocean views. It's a great place to have dinner at sunset and enjoy music from international DJs at night. ⊠ *Viceroy Los Cabos, Paseo Malecón San José, Zona Hotelera* ☎ *624/104–9999* ⊕ *www.viceroyhotelsandresorts.com/los-cabos.*

La Osteria

BARS/PUBS | Live music on Thursdays and Fridays coupled with the refreshing cocktails make this one of the best spots to grab a drink in San José del Cabo. Acoustic guitars add to the quaint atmosphere you'll find in the lantern-lit, stone courtyard. Tapas make a tasty accompaniment to the house sangrias. ⊠ *Paseo del Estero, Zona Hotelera* ☎ *624/146–9696* ⊕ *facebook.com/laosteriacabo/* ☉ *Closed Sun.*

Shooters Sports Bar

BARS/PUBS | FAMILY | For a family-friendly atmosphere where you can order your choice of food and beverage and watch sports on big-screen TVs, head to Shooters, a rooftop bar overlooking the main square. It's open daily from 10 am–10 pm, for breakfast, lunch, and dinner. ⊠ *Manuel Doblado at Blvd. Mijares, San José del Cabo* ☎ *624/146–9900* ⊕ *www.shootersbar.com.mx.*

Tropicana Inn

BARS/PUBS | The Tropicana Inn's bar is a great place to mingle and enjoy live music. Conversation is usually possible on the terrace overlooking the bar and stage, though when a good band gets going, you'll be too busy dancing to talk. Flamenco and mariachi bands play Thursday through Sunday 7:30–10:30 pm. ⊠ *Blvd. Mijares 30, San José del Cabo* ☎ *624/142–1580* ⊕ *tropicanainnloscabos.com.*

🛍 Shopping

Cabo San Lucas's sister city has a refined air, with many shops in old colonial buildings just a short walk from the town's *zócalo* (central plaza). Jewelry and art are great buys—this is where you'll find the best shopping for high-quality Mexican folk art. Many of the most worthwhile shops are clustered within a few of blocks around Plaza Mijares, where Boulevard Mijares and Avenida Zaragoza both end at the zócalo at the center of San José. Thursday nights from November to June are designated Art Nights, when galleries stay open until 9 serving drinks and snacks, with various performances, demonstrations, and dancing.

ART GALLERIES

Casa Dahlia Fine Art Gallery

ART GALLERIES | Casa Dahlia Fine Art Gallery features contemporary artists from Mexico and abroad, and invites visitors to linger in its beautifully renovated historic building. ⊠ *Morelos 23, Centro* ☎ *624/166–0262 cell, 720/346–3286 in U.S.* ⊕ *www.leahporter.com* ☉ *Closed weekends.*

Frank Arnold Gallery

ART GALLERIES | Frank Arnold Gallery has two big draws: it's arguably the best gallery space in town, in a modern building by local architect Alfredo Gomez; and it holds Frank Arnold's dramatic, widely acclaimed contemporary paintings that have been compared to de Kooning, Gorky, and Hans Hofmann. The gallery also features bronze sculptures and fine-art prints. ⊠ *1137 Calle Comonfort, San José del Cabo* ☎ *624/142–4422, 559/301–1148 in U.S.* ⊕ *www.frankarnoldart.com.*

Galería Corsica

ART GALLERIES | Galería Corsica is in a spectacularly dramatic space. The gallery, which has two sister galleries in Puerto Vallarta and one in Mexico City, shows museum-quality fine art with an emphasis on paintings and large, impressive sculpture pieces. ⊠ *Álvaro Obregón*

Colorful colonial buildings line the historic downtown of San José.

10, San José del Cabo ☎ 624/146–9177 ⊕ www.galeriacorsica.com.

Galería de Ida Victoria
ART GALLERIES | Galería de Ida Victoria has been designed with skylights and domes to show off the international art contained within its three floors, which includes paintings, sculpture, photography, and prints. ✉ Guerrero 1128, San José del Cabo ✛ Between Zaragoza and Obregón ☎ 624/142–5772 ⊕ www.idavictoriagallery.com ⊗ Closed Sun.

★ Patricia Mendoza Gallery
ART GALLERIES | Explore works of art by Mexico's top contemporary artists such as Eduardo Mejorada, Javier Guadarrama, Jorge Marín, Luis Filcer, and Trubaik, among others. All of the artists represented here are known nationally and internationally in important collections and museums. ✉ Álvaro Obregón and Plaza Mijares s/n, Col. Centro, San José del Cabo ☎ 624/158–6497, 624/105–2270 ⊕ www.patriciamendozagallery.com ⊗ Closed Sun.

Silvermoon Gallery
ART GALLERIES | Silvermoon Gallery is remarkable in the Los Cabos region both for the assortment and the quality of art contained within its walls. Mexican folk art makes up most of the inventory here. Treasures include Carlos Albert's whimsical papier-mâché sculptures, Mata Ortiz pottery from the Quezada family, Huichol yarn "paintings," Alebrijes (colorful wooden animal sculptures) from Oaxaca, and fine jewelry. Owner Armando Sanchez Icaza is gracious and knowledgeable; he knows volumes about the artists whose work he carries. His silversmiths can also make custom jewelry for you within a day or two. ✉ Plaza Mijares 10, San José del Cabo ☎ 624/144–1269 ⊕ facebook.com/SilvermoonGalleryFolkArt/ ⊗ Closed Sun.

FOLK ART AND CERAMICS
Curios Carmela
ART GALLERIES | Curios Carmela displays an almost overwhelming array of Mexican textiles, pottery, glassware, hammocks, clothing, and souvenirs, but with a bit of searching you'll find some great bargains.

✉ *Blvd. Mijares 43, San José del Cabo* ☎ *624/142–1617* ⊕ *instagram.com/curi-os_carmela* ☞ *No sign on the building.*

El Armario Art & Coffee

ART GALLERIES | Calling itself "the cutest shop in town," El Amario offers a selection of Mexican folk art, ceramic pottery, candles, clay figurines, and papi-er-mâché—plus fresh coffee out on the patio. ✉ *Obregón at Morelos, San José del Cabo* ☎ *624/105–2989* ⊕ *facebook. com/armarioartandcoffee* ☽ *Closed Sun.*

La Sacristia Art & History

ART GALLERIES | La Sacristia has a fine selection of Talavera pottery, traditional and contemporary Mexican jewelry, blown glass, and contemporary paintings. The glassware is incredible. ✉ *Hidalgo 9, at Álvaro Obregón, San José del Cabo* ☎ *624/142–4007.*

HOME FURNISHINGS

Casa Paulina

HOUSEHOLD ITEMS/FURNITURE | More than just an art gallery, Casa Paulina inspires decorating ideas with items for the home. Candles, lamps, chairs, throws, and enormous clay pots are a few of the treasures you might find. ✉ *Plaza Paulina, Morelos at Comonfort, San José del Cabo* ☎ *624/142–5555* ⊕ *www.casapaulina. com.*

JEWELRY

Artwalk Shop

JEWELRY/ACCESSORIES | This small boutique at Casa Natalia has jewelry, handbags, and art made from recycled metals. Art-walk also has a good selection of brass jewelry from Mexico City. ✉ *Blvd. Mijares 4, at Casa Natalia, San José del Cabo* ☎ *624/146–7100* ⊕ *www.casanatalia. com/artwalkshop* ☽ *Closed Tues.*

MALLS

Plaza Artesanos

SHOPPING CENTERS/MALLS | With a block of 75 stalls, Plaza Artesanos has a wide selection of handmade crafts and souve-nirs, including pottery, jewelry, blankets,

clothing, hammocks, leather bags, and even pure Mexican vanilla extract. Don't be afraid to barter by starting at half the asking price and then meeting some-where in the middle. ✉ *Paseo de Las Misiones 1942, Fonatur* ☎ *624/122–1009.*

Plaza del Pescador

SHOPPING CENTERS/MALLS | **FAMILY** | An out-door mall conveniently located across the street from San José del Cabo's string of resorts, Plaza del Pescador offers guests an alternative to hotel dining. You'll find everything from sushi and gelato to tapas and a wine bar. Among the 25 shops and restaurants are a bookstore, jewelry store, fitness gym, and coffee shop. ✉ *Paseo Malecón, Local 21A, San José del Cabo* ✛ *Across from Cabo Azul Resort* ☎ *624/142–3436* ⊕ *www.plaza-delpescador.com.*

MARKETS

★ **Farmer's Market** (*San José del Cabo Mercado Orgánico*)
OUTDOOR/FLEA/GREEN MARKETS | **FAMILY** | Get your organic fix at the *Mercado Orgánico* every Saturday 9–3 between November and May. Jewelry, artwork, flowers, soaps, fruit, and vegetables are a few of the goodies you'll find here. Food stalls serve everything from tacos to pizza, and entertainment is offered for kids. You will surely leave with a bag full of fresh veggies and local art. ✉ *Comon-fort 6, Centro* ☎ *624/142–0948* ⊕ *face-book.com/Sanjomo* ☽ *Closed June–Oct.*

The Market

OUTDOOR/FLEA/GREEN MARKETS | From the creator of Flora Farms, this store sells all things organic including fresh fruit, pickled vegetables, soaps, jams, honey, coffee, and body oils. It's a great place to grab a healthy snack or stock up on produce delivered daily from Flora's local farm. ✉ *Animas Bajas, Las Animas Bajas* ☎ *624/142–1000* ⊕ *www.flora-farms. com/market* ☽ *Closed Sun.*

Continued on page 151

DID YOU KNOW?

Huichol is pronounced wee-CHOL; the people's name for themselves, however, is Wirarika (we-RAH-ri-ka), which means "healer."

THE ART OF THE HUICHOL

Updated by
Georgia de Katona

The intricately woven and beaded designs of the Huichols' art are as vibrant and fascinating as the traditions of its people, best known as the "Peyote People" for their traditional and ceremonial use of the hallucinogenic drug. Peyote-inspired visions are thought to be messages from God and are reflected in the art.

Like the Lacandon Maya, the Huichol resisted assimilation by Spanish invaders, fleeing to inhospitable mountains and remote valleys. There they retained their pantheistic religion in which shamans lead the community in spiritual matters and the use of peyote facilitates communication directly with God.

Roads didn't reach larger Huichol communities until the mid-20th century, bringing electricity and other modern distractions. The collision with the outside world has had pros and cons, but art lovers have only benefited from their increased access to intricately patterned woven and beaded goods. Today the traditional souls that remain on the land—a significant population of perhaps 6,000 to 8,000—still create votive bowls, prayer arrows, jewelry, and bags, and sell them to finance elaborate religious ceremonies. The pieces go for as little as $5 or as much as $5,000, depending on the skill and fame of the artist and quality of materials.

(left) Huichol yarn painting, National Museum of Anthropology, (top) Huichol art, Puerto Vallarta

UNDERSTANDING THE HUICHOL

When Spanish conquistadors arrived in the early 16th century, the Huichol, unwilling to work as slaves on the haciendas of the Spanish or to adopt their religion, fled to the Sierra Madre. They lived there, disconnected from society, for nearly 500 years. Beginning in the 1970s, roads and electricity made their way to tiny Huichol towns. Today, about half of the population of perhaps 7,000 continues to live in ancestral villages and *rancheritas* (tiny individual farms).

THE POWER OF PRAYER

They believe that without their prayers and offerings the sun wouldn't rise, the earth would cease spinning. It is hard, then, for them to reconcile their poverty with the relative easy living of "free-riders" (Huichol term for nonspiritual freeloaders) who enjoy fine cars and expensive houses thanks to the Huichols efforts to sustain the planet. But rather than hold our reckless materialism against us, the Huichol add us to their prayers.

THE PEYOTE PEOPLE

Visions inspired by the hallucinogenic peyote cactus are considered by the Huichol to be messages from God and to help in solving personal and communal problems. Indirectly, they provide inspiration for their almost psychedelic art. Just a generation or two ago, annual peyote-gathering pilgrimages were done

Huichol bird, Jalisco

on foot. Today the journey is still a man's chief obligation, but they now drive to the holy site at Wiricuta, in San Luis Potosi State.

SHAMANISM

A Huichol man has a lifelong calling as a shaman. There are two shamanic paths: the path of the wolf, which is more aggressive, demanding, and powerful (wolf shamans profess the ability to morph into wolves); and the path of the deer, which is playful. A shaman chooses his own path.

BEADED ITEMS

The smaller the beads, the more delicate and expensive the piece. Items made with iridescent beads from Japan are the priciest. Look for good-quality glass beads, definition, symmetry, and artful use of color. Beads should fit together tightly in straight lines, with no gaps.

YARN PAINTINGS

Symmetry is not necessary, although there should be an overall sense of unity. Thinner thread results in finer, more costly work. Look for tightness, with no visible gaps or broken threads. Paintings should have a stamp of authenticity on the back, including artist's name and tribal affiliation.

PRAYER ARROWS

Collectors and purists should look for the traditionally made arrows of brazilwood inserted into a bamboo shaft. The most interesting ones contain embroidery work, or tiny carved icons, or are painted with copal symbols indicative of their original intended purpose, for example protecting a child or ensuring a successful corn crop.

HOW TO READ THE SYMBOLS

Spiders that come out at dawn are thought to welcome the rising sun.

The deer is the animal manifestation of the god Kahumari, who intercedes in heaven on earthlings' behalf.

Anything with horns or antlers symbolizes communion and oneness with God.

Yarn painting

■The trilogy of corn, peyote, and deer represents three aspects of God. According to Huichol mythology, peyote sprang up in the footprints of the deer. Depicted like stylized flowers, peyote represents communication with God. Corn, the Huichol's

Corn symbol

staple food, symbolizes health and prosperity. An image drawn inside the root ball depicts the essence of God within it.

■The double-headed eagle is the emblem of the omnipresent sky god.

Peyote

■A nierika is a portal between the spirit world and our own. Often in the form of a yarn painting, a nierika can be round or square.

■Salamanders and turtles are associated with rain; the former provoke the clouds. Turtles maintain underground springs and purify water.

■A scorpion is the soldier of the sun.

Scorpion

■The Huichol depict raindrops as tiny snakes; in yarn paintings they descend to enrich the fields.

Snakes

Jose Beníctez Sánchez, (1938—2009) may be the elder statesman of yarn painters and has shown in Japan, Spain, the U.S., and at the Museum of Modern Art in Mexico City.

TRADITION TRANSFORMED

The art of the Huichol was, for centuries, made from undyed wool, shells, stones, and other natural materials. It was not until the 1970s that the Huichol began incorporating bright, zingy colors, without sacrificing the intricate patterns and symbols used for centuries. The result is strenuously colorful, yet dignified.

YARN PAINTINGS
Dramatic and vivid yarn paintings are highly symbolic, stylized visions of life.

MASKS AND ANIMAL STATUETTES
Bead-covered wooden or ceramic masks and animal statuettes are other adaptations made for outsiders.

PRAYER ARROWS
Made for every ceremony, prayer arrows send petitions winging to God.

VOTIVE BOWLS
Ceremonial votive bowls, made from gourds, are decorated with bright, stylized beadwork.

WOVEN SHOULDER BAGS
Carried by men, the bags are decorated with traditional Huichol icons.

For years, Huichol men as well as women wore **BEADED BRACELETS**; today earrings and necklaces are also made.

Diamond-shape **GOD'S EYES** of sticks and yarn protect children from harm.

Desert, sea, and putting greens converge at San José's popular golf clubs.

SUNDRIES AND LIQUOR

Los Barriles de Don Malaquias

CONVENIENCE/GENERAL STORES | Go beyond Cuervo and Patrón at Los Barriles de Don Malaquias, which specializes in rare tequilas. The tequila selection is complemented by a good collection of Cuban cigars. Owner Rigoberto Cuervo Rosales is often on-site to offer tequila tastings. ⊠ *Blvd. Mijares at Juárez, San José del Cabo* ☎ *624/130–7800.*

🏃 Activities

GOLF

Greens fees quoted include off- and high-season rates and are subject to frequent change.

Los Cabos has become one of the world's top golf destinations thanks to two factors: the 9-hole course opened by Mexico's tourism development agency Fonatur in San José in 1988, and the area's year-round mild to warm weather—Los Cabos never experiences even the occasional frigid winter possible in the southern United States. Green fairways dot the arid landscape like multiple oases in the desert. You'll encounter many sublime views of the Sea of Cortez, and on a few courses, play alongside it. Otherwise the motif is desert golf. Architects and designers like Jack Nicklaus, Robert Trent Jones II, Tom Weiskopf, Roy Dye, and Greg Norman have all applied their talents to courses in the area.

Club Campestre San Jose

GOLF | Here you are greeted by panoramic views stretching to the Sea of Cortez, canyons, and mountains on a Jack Nicklaus design. This public course also features dramatic elevation changes and undulating tricky multilevel putting surfaces. Attractive bunkering requires well-placed tee shots and very accurate iron play. They have used paspalum grass throughout the course that sets Club Campestre among the best manicured in the region. The only downfall is that there are no holes on the water. ⊠ *Libramiento Aeropuerto, Km 119, San José del Cabo* ☎ *877/795–8727 in U.S., 624/173–9400*

⊕ www.questrogolf.com ▣ $99–$195, depending on season ⚐. 18 holes, 6966 yards, par 71.

Puerto Los Cabos Golf Course

GOLF | This course, one of the area's most popular for visitors, features an unusual combination: two Nines were designed by Jack Nicklaus and the other by Greg Norman. The Nicklaus I Course features more expansive driving areas, whereas the Norman Nine puts more of a premium on driving accuracy. Both feature attractive bunkering and paspalum putting surfaces. The Nicklaus II Course is the most recent addition to Puerto Los Cabos and has quickly become a favorite of visitors as it affords views of the Sea of Cortez surrounded by sand dunes. ⊠ Paseo de los Pescadores, San José del Cabo ☎ 624/173–9400, 877/795–8727 ⊕ www.questrogolf.com ▣ $110–$285, depending on season ⚐. 27 holes, 3 18-hole combinations: Norman Course 3,590 yards, 18 holes, par 36; Nicklaus I Course 3,758 yards, 18 holes, par 36; Nicklaus II Course 3,436 yards, 18 holes, par 36.

GUIDED ADVENTURE TOURS

★ **Baja Outback**

TOUR—SPORTS | FAMILY | Baja Outback offers a variety of guided tours that range from four hours to several days long. The routes run through Baja backcountry, where you have the opportunity to explore the Cape's rarely seen back roads while learning desert lore from a knowledgeable guide-cum-biologist. Day trips may include anything from hiking and snorkeling to city tours and turtle release programs (August to November). Baja Outback also offers multiday tour packages designed specially for kids, with bodyboarding and sand castle building. For adventure-driven vacationers, tours include kayaking and stand-up paddleboarding near El Arco. ⊠ Campo de Golf Fonatur, Paseo de las Misiones Mzna. 1, Lote 3, San José del Cabo

☎ 624/142–9215, 855/408–3772 ⊕ www. bajaoutback.com ▣ From $75.

Baja Wild

TOUR—SPORTS | Baja Wild has a number of adventure packages that include hiking, biking, kayaking, snorkeling, surfing, and whale-watching adventures. You'll see the natural side of Cabo, with hikes to canyons, hot springs, fossil beds, and caves with rock paintings. They offer backcountry jeep tours, full-day kayak tours at Cabo Pulmo, and ATV tours in the desert. Private tours are available. ⊠ Carretera Transpeninsular, Km. 28, Plaza Costa Azul, San José del Cabo ☎ 624/122–0107, 310/860–6979 from U.S. ⊕ www.bajawild.com ▣ Tours from $100.

HIKING

Baja Wild

HIKING/WALKING | Trips with Baja Wild include hikes to canyons, small waterfalls, hot springs, a fossil-rich area, and caves with rock paintings. An all-day group hiking trip includes lunch, a guide, equipment, and transfer. ⊠ Carretera Transpeninsular, Km 28, Plaza Costa Azul, San José del Cabo ☎ 624/122–0107, 310/860–6979 from U.S. ⊕ www.bajawild.com ▣ From $150.

HORSEBACK RIDING

Cantering down an isolated beach or up a desert trail is one of the great pleasures of Los Cabos (as long as the sun isn't beating down too heavily). The following places have well-fed and well-trained horses.

Bonanza Horseback Riding

HORSEBACK RIDING | FAMILY | One of the best ways to explore the San José estuary, marina, and beach is by horseback. One- or two-hour tours are led by two professional guides who take you to the most beautiful spots around. ⊠ Blvd. Antonio Mijares, Zona Hotelera ⊹ Across from Holiday Inn Resort ☎ 624/142–2922 ⊕ facebook.com/bonanzahorse ▣ From $50 to $120.

KAYAKING

One of the most popular, practical, and eco-friendly ways to explore the pristine coves that dot Los Cabos' western shoreline is by kayak. Daylong package tours that combine kayaking with snorkeling cost anywhere from $70 to $150. Single or double kayaks can be rented by the hour for $20 to $25.

Baja Wild

KAYAKING | For a combined kayak and snorkeling trip, try Baja Wild. Daylong outdoor trips include surfing; hiking; ATV; and whale-watching trips (November through April), as well as baby sea turtle release excursions (September through November). All trips include transportation, equipment, and lunch; you can substitute scuba diving for snorkeling. ⊠ *Carretera Transpeninsular, Km 28, Plaza Costa Azul, San José del Cabo* ☎ *624/122–0107, 310/860-6979* ⊕ *www.bajawild.com* ✆ *From $150.*

SCUBA DIVING

Expert divers head to the **Gordo Banks** (100–130 feet, also known as the Wahoo Banks), which are 13 km (8 miles) off the coast of San José. The currents here are too strong for less experienced divers. This is the spot for hammerhead sharks—which are not generally aggressive with divers—plus many species of tropical fish and rays, and, if you're lucky, dolphins. Fall is the best time to go.

SPAS

Farm Spa

SPA/BEAUTY | As with every offering from the Flora Farms brand (including its popular Flora's Field Kitchen restaurant), the farm's natural surroundings play a big role in the unique indoor-outdoor space. Relaxing energy flows from the farm's own herbs, flowers, and trees. On offer are various skin therapies, a wide range of massages, and beauty treatments for men and women. Fitness classes including yoga and meditation are available by reservation only. ⊠ *Flora Farms, Las Animas Bajas* ☎ *624/178–3010,* *949/200–7342 U.S. phone* ⊕ *flora-farms.com/farm-spa* ☾ *Closed Mon.*

Paz Spa

SPA/BEAUTY | Surrounded by natural stone walls, all the treatment rooms at Cabo Azul's Paz Spa are named after semiprecious stones such as onyx, pearl, opal, lapis, jade, and amber. Specialties include 50-minute massages to 210-minute complete experiences, as well as exfoliations, wraps, facials, manicure, and pedicure. A terrace suite can accommodate up to four treatments at one time for those looking for group relaxation. Seven other rooms round out the spa itself, and two double cabanas on the beach are available for those seeking the sound of the waves as backdrop to their treatment. Popular therapies include a Papaya Sugar Polish and Shea Butter Massage, as well as an Aloe Cooling Massage. An on-site salon is open Monday to Saturday 9–5. ⊠ *Cabo Azul Resort, Paseo Malecón s/n , Lote 11 Fonatur, San José del Cabo* ☎ *624/163–5100* ⊕ *www.caboazulresort.com.*

The Spa at Viceroy Los Cabos

SPA/BEAUTY | This serene, well-equipped spa extends more than 11,000 square feet and offers everything from customary massages and beauty treatments to signature vitality pools, thermal chambers, ice fountains, and even canine massage therapy. You read that right: they will massage your dog's stress away, too. If you have to choose just one treatment, go for a Viceroy ritual or an interactive couples massage. ⊠ *Viceroy Los Cabos, Paseo Malecón San José, Zona Hotelera* ☎ *624/104–9999 ext. 76700* ⊕ *www.viceroyhotelsandresorts.com/los-cabos.*

Zen Spa at Hyatt Ziva

SPA/BEAUTY | The concept at Hyatt Ziva's spa is to explore water, earth, and air. Lounge by the communal pool or duck into one of 19 treatment rooms for revitalizing massages, romantic packages, anti-aging facials, detoxifying body wraps, and deep-cleansing scrubs using local, natural ingredients. For those interested in a quick fix, manicures and pedicures are popular, and the on-site salon can help turn a bad-hair day into something grand. ✉ *Hyatt Ziva Los Cabos, Paseo Malecón s/n , Lote 5, San José del Cabo* ☎ *624/163–7730* ⊕ *hyatt. com* ✉ *Day Pass: $145. Body treatments: $110–$285. Facials: $75–$240.*

SURFING

You can rent a board right at the beach at Costa Azul in San José del Cabo, or at the Cabo Surf Hotel, and paddle right into the gentle, feathering waves at the Old Man's surf spot. If you're at the intermediate level or above, walk a short distance eastward to La Roca (The Rock) break. Big waves are best left to the experts up north, in Todos Santos.

Baja Wild

SURFING | Baja Wild offers daylong trips to surfing hot spots throughout the Cape region for beginners and experts. A fee of $150 per person includes transportation, equipment, and instruction for a half day at Costa Azul. Full-day surf tours on the Pacific cost $150 per person. ✉ *Carretera Transpeninsular, Km. 28, Plaza Costa Azul* ☎ *624/122–0107, 310/860–6979 from U.S.* ⊕ *www.bajawild.com* ☞ *From $150.*

★ Costa Azul Surf Shop

SURFING | For epic surfing tips, rentals, and lessons, head to Costa Azul Surf Shop. They have the best quiver in Los Cabos with more than 150 hand-shaped boards from their popular Olea line. They also offer paddleboards, bodyboards, and snorkel gear. Private, two-hour lessons include transportation, the surfboard rental, a rash guard, and bottled water. All instructors are CPR certified and have 25 years of surfing experience. ✉ *Hwy. 1, Km 28, San José del Cabo* ☎ *624/142–2771* ⊕ *www.costa-azul.com.mx* ✉ *Rentals, $25 per day, $20 per day for four days or more; private lessons $150.*

WALKING TOURS

Land's End Tours

TOUR—SPORTS | One of the best ways to experience Los Cabos in a single day is through Land's End photo city tour. The outing covers the top attractions of Cabos San Lucas, the Corridor, and San José del Cabo; photographs of your adventure are captured throughout the tour and sent to you within one week by email. Tour highlights include San José's historical center, a boat trip to the arch, a visit to a glass-blowing factory, tequila tasting, shopping, and snorkeling. The six-hour tour begins at 8:15, and the price includes entrance fees, a tour guide, lunch, transportation, and photographs. Tours are offered from Monday through Saturday. ✉ *Carretera Transpeninsular, Km 5, 5 de Febrero, San José del Cabo* ☎ *624/123–4962* ⊕ *www.landsendtours. com* ✉ *$59.*

Chapter 6

LOS CABOS SIDE TRIPS

TODOS SANTOS, LA PAZ, AND EAST CAPE

Updated by
Chris Sands

6

⊙ Sights	🍴 Restaurants	🛏 Hotels	🛍 Shopping	🍸 Nightlife
★★★★★	★★★☆☆	★★★☆☆	★★★☆☆	★★★☆☆

WELCOME TO LOS CABOS SIDE TRIPS

TOP REASONS TO GO

★ **Shopping Todos Santos:** An influx of artisans and craftspeople has turned Todos Santos into the region's trendiest, highest-quality shopping destination.

★ **Lodging Value:** Todos Santos offers a selection of charming boutique inns at just a fraction of the cost—but all at full quality—of Los Cabos hostelries down the coast.

★ **The Aquarium of the World:** Jacques Cousteau gave the Sea of Cortez its nickname, and nowhere is it more fitting than the East Cape's Parque Nacional Cabo Pulmo, a protected marine sanctuary teeming with life and one of the oldest coral reefs in North America.

★ **The Best of Urban Baja:** La Paz is your best bet for the urban pleasures of a charming, low-key Mexican city, one with a grand seaside promenade to boot.

★ **A Whale of a Time:** The annual December-through-April migration of gray humpback and other whales is a guaranteed stunner.

Coming into Todos Santos from the south, Highway 19 parallels area beaches without necessarily hugging the coastline. Roads leading to the shore are in decent shape, but twist and turn at points.

To the north is La Paz, the focal point of which is the dense grid of streets in the city center, with most sights, lodgings, and restaurants either on the *malecón* (aka Paseo Álvaro Obregón) or a few blocks inland at most.

Finally, the East Cape curves over 70 miles northeast from the outskirts of San José del Cabo to the tranquil (if seasonally breezy) shores of Bahía las Palmas. Every mile you travel on the old East Cape Road is like traveling a little farther back in time toward the "Old Cabo": when the population was smaller, the beaches less crowded, and the amenities far simpler.

1 Todos Santos. Todos outgrew its surfing roots without abandoning them entirely, but you'll more likely come here for its growing number of galleries and craft shops. The arts scene has fueled a rise in gracious small inns and boutique hotels, making this popular Los Cabos–area day trip an overnight destination in its own right.

2 La Paz. Don't let La Paz's workaday hustle and bustle fool you. This seaside state capital is one of Mexico's loveliest small cities—you'll be sold after an evening stroll on the oceanfront *malecón*, ice-cream cone in hand—and the launching point for Baja's best diving, fishing, and whale-watching excursions.

3 East Cape. This lesser-visited area is paradise for outdoor activity enthusiasts, from the interior mountains of the Sierra de la Laguna in the west to the azure waters of the Sea of Cortez in the east. The big-game fishing, scuba diving, and surfing may not be as famous here as in Cabo San Lucas, but they're every bit as good.

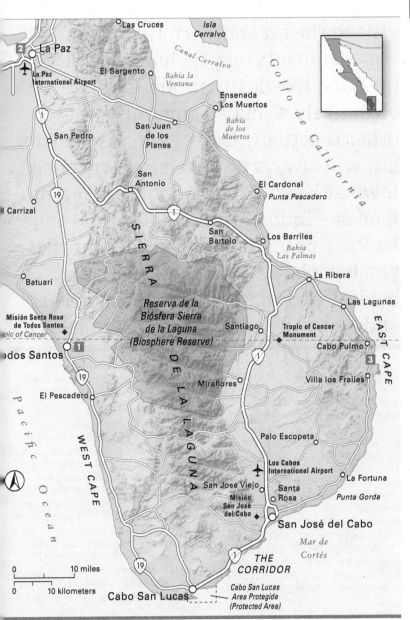

Las Cruces

Isla
Cerralvo

2 La Paz

Canal Cerralvo

La Paz
International Airport

El Sargento

Bahía la
Ventana

Golfo de California

Ensenada
Los Muertos

San Pedro

San Juan
de los
Planes

Bahía
de los
Muertos

San
Antonio

El Cardonal
Punta Pescadero

Carrizal

San
Bartolo

Los Barriles

Bahía
Las Palmas

Batuari

SIERRA

La Ribera

Las Lagunas

Reserva de la
Biósfera Sierra
de la Laguna
(Biosphere Reserve)

Santiago

Tropic of Cancer
Monument

EAST CAPE

Misión Santa Rosa
de Todos Santos

Tropic of Cancer

1

Cabo Pulmo

3

Todos Santos

DE

Miraflores

Villa los Frailes

El Pescadero

LA

Palo Escopeta

Pacific Ocean

WEST CAPE

LAGUNA

Los Cabos
International Airport

La Fortuna

San Jose Viejo

Santa
Rosa

Punta Gorda

Misión
San José
del Cabo

San José del Cabo

Mar de
Cortés

19

1

THE
CORRIDOR

0   10 miles

0   10 kilometers

Cabo San Lucas

Cabo San Lucas
Area Protegida
(Protected Area)

At the risk of sounding glib, we might suggest that you skip Los Cabos altogether. The highlights of your visit to the far southern tip of the Baja peninsula may include two very un-Cabo-like destinations. One is objectively a small community; the other is actually the region's largest city, but will always be an overgrown small town at heart. Their tranquil, reverent names—Todos Santos ("all saints") and La Paz ("peace")—are the first hint that you have left the glitz of Los Cabos behind, and that it's time to shift gears and enjoy the enchantment of Mexico.

The appeal of Todos Santos is becoming more well known, as a growing number of expats—American and European alike—move to the area. There's a lot to love here: the surf on the Pacific, just a couple of miles west of town, is good; weather is always a bit cooler than in Los Cabos; and the lush, leisurely feel of this artsy colonial town—think a smaller version of central Mexico's San Miguel de Allende—is relatively undisturbed by the many tourists who venture up from Los Cabos for the day. Todos Santos has always been the quintessential Los Cabos day trip, but it is now a destination in its own right. Break the typical pattern of day-tripping to Todos Santos and spend at least one night here amid the palms, at one of the small pleasant inns.

La Paz plants itself firmly on the Sea of Cortez side of the Baja peninsula. A couple of hours north of Los Cabos, it remains slightly outside the Cabo orbit, and it has always attracted visitors (and an expanding expat population) who make La Paz their exclusive Baja destination. Of course, 240,000-plus Paceños view their city as being the center of the universe, thank you very much. (La Paz is the capital of the state of Baja California Sur and Los Cabos is in *their* orbit.) In addition to many urban trappings, La Paz offers a growing number of outdoor-travel options. This city on the water has become all about what's in the water.

Sportfishing and scuba diving are big here, and La Paz is now a major launching point for whale-watching excursions.

The East Cape has always been "the other side" of Los Cabos, the side most tourists never see. Although lacking the resorts and luxury amenities of municipality mates Cabo San Lucas and San José del Cabo, the East Cape is every bit their equal when it comes to world-class conditions for outdoor activities like fishing, diving, and surfing. Plus, its small towns and old-school resorts have a nostalgic appeal for those who fell in love with Southern Baja when it was a sleepier and decidedly more rustic place. Much of the East Cape still remains off the grid and reachable only by dirt roads, but the recent opening of the **Four Seasons Resort Los Cabos at Costa Palmas,** and the expected arrival of a six-star **Amanvari** and **Soho House** at Costa Palmas in coming years, suggest the East Cape may soon start catching up to "the Cabos" in terms of development and popularity.

Planning

Getting Here and Around

AIR
The vast majority of tourists arrive in Baja California Sur at either Los Cabos International Airport (SJD) in San José del Cabo or Manuel Márquez de León International Airport (LAP) in La Paz. Those with private jets, meanwhile, often land at Cabo San Lucas International Airport (CSL).

BOAT
Cruise ships are a common sight in Cabo San Lucas Bay, and a few smaller (often eco-themed) cruise ships visit La Paz. Sailors seeking the trip of a lifetime can bring their boats down from San Diego, easily finding a berth in local marinas. The Baja Ha-Ha Cruisers Rally each November sees sailboats undertake this journey en masse.

Ferry service from La Paz to Topolobampo or Mazatlán is an excellent option for those who drove down the Baja California peninsula and want to continue their journey by car across mainland Mexico.

BUS
Autobuses Aguilas is the primary bus tour operator for Los Cabos and La Paz. Service is available to and from Cabo San Lucas, San José del Cabo, Pescadero, Todos Santos, La Paz, Miraflores, Santiago, Las Cuevas, and Los Barriles (all prices $15 or under one-way). Buses are air-conditioned with drop-down screens for Spanish language movies or Spanish-dubbed international releases.

Ecobaja Tours offers shuttle service to and from the Los Cabos International Airport in San José del Cabo to Todos Santos ($19), Los Barriles ($14), and La Paz ($29). All prices are one-way.

CAR
Rental cars are the recommended option for those taking side trips to destinations like Todos Santos, La Paz, and the East Cape of Los Cabos. **Avis, Hertz, Budget, Alamo, Fox, National,** and others have offices here, and rentals can be arranged from all these companies directly upon arrival at Los Cabos International Airport.

A U.S. driver's license and credit card are all that are required for rentals, and visitors should not be scared off by Spanish language street signs. Traffic lights are identical; stop signs say *alto*, but have the same color and shape; and most signs simply refer to directions for neighborhoods or destinations or are in easily recognizable pictograph form.

TAXI
Taxis may be found in the downtown areas of La Paz and Todos Santos, but are not an option in the more sparsely populated East Cape region. Always inquire about the price before getting into a taxi here, as the rates are often exorbitant. **Uber** is a more affordable option in most cases.

Hotels

While Cabo San Lucas, San José del Cabo, and their connecting corridor are awash in beachfront luxury resorts, many from high-profile hospitality brands, the options outside these areas are much more idiosyncratic. Todos Santos, for example, is famed for its boutique B&Bs, while La Paz is known for budget-friendly hotels with views along its three-mile malecón. The East Cape has one true luxury lodging—the **Four Seasons Resort Los Cabos at Costa Palmas**—but otherwise is primarily known for old-school fishing resorts.

Restaurants

A rich variety of restaurants, including fine-dining establishments and internationally themed eateries, may be found in Cabo San Lucas, San José del Cabo, Todos Santos, and La Paz. The East Cape does not offer the same variety or overall quality, although downtown Los Barriles and the **Four Seasons Resort Los Cabos at Costa Palmas** both provide excellent options.

HOTEL AND RESTAURANT PRICES

Hotel prices in the reviews are the lowest cost of a standard double room in high season. Restaurant prices in the reviews are the average cost of a main course at dinner, or if dinner is not served, at lunch.

What It Costs in U.S. Dollars			
$	$$	$$$	$$$$
RESTAURANTS			
under $12	$12–$20	$21–$30	over $30
HOTELS			
under $150	$150–$250	$251–$350	over $350

Restaurant and hotel reviews have been shortened. For full information, visit Fodors.com.

Safety

Many visitors have preconceived notions about safety in Mexico. The Los Cabos and La Paz municipalities are both very safe, but travelers should exercise the same caution and alertness they would at home, particularly if venturing into neighborhoods off the beaten path. But, since none of the primary regional tourist attractions are located in such neighborhoods, this is rarely an issue. More important is the caution against driving at night outside well-populated areas. This has nothing to do with *bandidos* (bandits), but rather the dangers of free-ranging livestock, and, in some areas, poorly tended roads.

Tours

A few Los Cabos tour operators offer round-trip transportation to La Paz and the East Cape for destination activities; swimming with whale sharks is the most common in La Paz, and diving is the most common in Cabo Pulmo on the East Cape. That means if your side trip is premised around a single activity, it may not be necessary to rent a car.

Visitor Information

Baja California Sur State Tourist Office
The Baja California Sur State Tourist Office is in La Paz, about a 5-minute drive northeast of the *malecón* (seaside promenade), on the highway to Pichilingue near Playa El Coromuel. The office is open weekdays 8–3, and both office and website are excellent resources for information about La Paz and surrounding areas. ✉ *Carretera Pichilingue–La Paz, Km 3.5, Balneario El Coromuel, La Paz* ☎ *612/124–1988* ⊕ *visitbajasur.travel.*

Todos Santos

73 km (44 miles) north of Cabo San Lucas, 81 km (49 miles) south of La Paz.

From the hodgepodge of signs and local businesses you see on the drive into Todos Santos, south on Highway 19, it appears that you're heading to the outskirts of a typical Baja town. But climb the hill to its old colonial center with its mission church and blocks of restored buildings, and the Todos Santos that is gaining rave reviews in tourism circles is revealed.

Todos Santos was designated one of the country's *Pueblos Mágicos* (Magical Towns) in 2006, joining 120 other towns around Mexico chosen for their religious or cultural significance. Pueblos Mágicos receive important financial support from the federal government for development of tourism and historical preservation. Architects and entrepreneurs have restored early-19th-century adobe-and-brick buildings around the main plaza of this former sugar town and have turned them into charming inns, whose hallmark is attentive service at prices far more reasonable than a night in Los Cabos. A good number of restaurateurs provide sophisticated, globally inspired food at hip eateries.

Todos Santos has always meant shopping, at least since about three decades ago when the first U.S. and Mexican artists began to relocate their galleries here. Day-trippers head up here from Los Cabos, enjoying lunch and a morning of shopping. The growing number of visitors who buck that trend and spend a night or two here leave feeling very satisfied indeed.

Los Cabos visitors typically take day trips here, though several small inns provide a peaceful antidote to Cabo's noise and crowds. El Pescadero, the largest settlement before Todos Santos, is home to ranchers and farmers who grow herbs and vegetables. Business hours are erratic, especially in September.

GETTING HERE AND AROUND

Highway 19, now upgraded to four lanes, connects Todos Santos south with Cabo San Lucas and north with La Paz, making the drive easier than ever. Nonetheless, we recommend making the trip before dark; the occasional cow or rock blocks the road. Autotransportes Aguila provides comfortable coach service over a dozen times a day in both directions between Los Cabos (San José and San Lucas) and La Paz, with an intermediate stop in Todos Santos. Plan on an hour from La Paz or Cabo San Lucas and 90 minutes from San José del Cabo. Ecobaja Tours offers scheduled shuttle service (about $20 one-way) four times daily between Todos Santos and Los Cabos Airport, 90 minutes away.

◉ Sights

Climb the hill north of the bus terminal to reach the original colonial town center with its stupendous views, landmark mission church, and several small inns and galleries.

Nuestra Señora del Pilar

RELIGIOUS SITE | Todos Santos was the second-farthest south of Baja California's 30 mission churches, a system the Spanish instituted to convert (and subdue) the peninsula's indigenous peoples. Jesuit priests established an outpost here in 1723 as a *visita* (circuit branch) of the mission in La Paz, a day's journey away on horseback. The original church north of town was sacked and pillaged twice during its existence, before being relocated in 1825 to this site in the center of town. Additions in the past two centuries have resulted in a hodgepodge of architectural styles, but the overall effect is still pleasing, and the structure serves to this day as the community's bustling parish church. ✉ *Calle Márquez de León* ✛ *Between Centenario and Legaspi* ☎ *612/145–0043.*

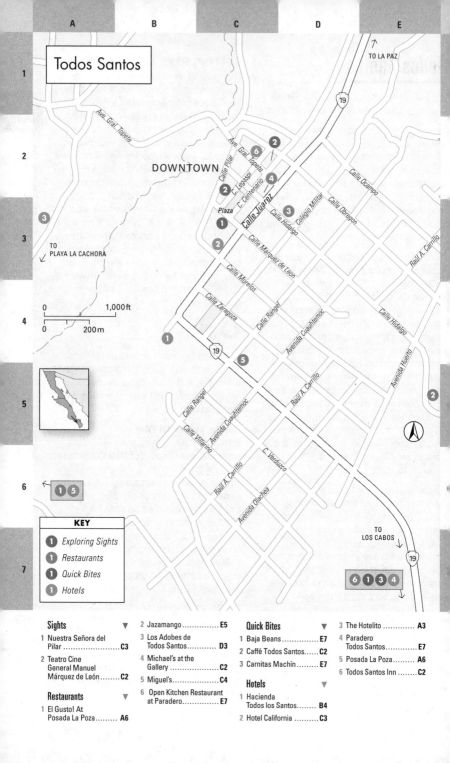

Todos Santos

DOWNTOWN

Plaza

TO LA PAZ

TO PLAYA LA CACHORA

TO LOS CABOS

Ave. Gral. Topete · Calle Pilar · Ave. Gral. Topete · C. Legaspi · C. Centenario · Calle Juarez · Colegio Militar · Calle Ocampo · Calle Hidalgo · Calle Obregon · Raúl A. Carrillo · Calle Márquez de Leon · Calle Morelos · Calle Zaragoza · Calle Rangel · Avenida Cuauhtemoc · Calle Hidalgo · Avenida Huerto · Calle Rangel · Calle Villarino · Avenida Cuauhtemoc · Raúl A. Carrillo · C. Verduzco · Raúl A. Carrillo · Avenida Olachea

0   1,000 ft
0   200 m

KEY
1 Exploring Sights
1 Restaurants
1 Quick Bites
1 Hotels

En Route to Todos Santos

Playa Los Cerritos This long, expansive beach on the Pacific Ocean, about 64 km (40 miles) north of Cabo San Lucas and on the way to the town of Todos Santos, is famous among surfers for its wonderful breaking waves in winter. Great for beginners, the waves here are consistent, accessible, and not overly powerful. Boards and lessons are available at the Costa Azul Surf Shop right on shore. This beach works best on northwest swells. Even if you don't ride the waves, you can watch them crash along the shore. The sandy beach is wide, flat, and ideal for wading and swimming close to shore. Swimming farther out is not recommended because of the strong currents. Most of the surfing crowd camps or stays in RVs near the beach, although there are no organized campsites or RV parks in the area. The developing area covers the basics with a few conveniences—including bustling Los Cerritos Club restaurant and two surf shops. Access to the beach is marked on Highway 19 (which connects Cabo San Lucas and Todos Santos) by a sign for Playa Los Cerritos at Km 64 (13 km [8 miles] south of Todos Santos). The graded dirt road to the beach is 2½ km (1½ miles) from Highway 19. **Amenities:** toilets; showers (for restaurant patrons); food concession; parking lot; camping; surfboards. **Best for:** surfing; swimming; snorkeling; walking. ✉ *64 km (40 mi) north of Cabo San Lucas, 13 km (8 mi) south of Todos Santos.*

Teatro Cine General Manuel Márquez de León

HISTORIC SITE | The mouthful of a name denotes Todos Santos's 1944 movie theater, which was quite a grand movie palace back in the day for remote, small-town Mexico. A few cultural events take place here, including the annual Todos Santos Film Festival each March. ✉ *Calle Legaspi s/n* ☎ *612/145–0225.*

🍴 Restaurants

Todos Santos's dining selection echoes the town—stylish expat with traditional Mexican—and makes a nice outing during any Los Cabos–area stay. Restaurants here do a brisk business at lunch, less so at dinner. It's well worth the trip to drive up from Los Cabos or down from La Paz for a special meal. At an hour each way, that's easier to do before dark.

El Gusto! At Posada La Poza

$$ | **ECLECTIC** | For those fortunate enough to stay at the sumptuous Posada La Poza just outside town, lunch at its equally lovely restaurant will be one of the highlights of your Los Cabos vacation. Owners Juerg and Libusche Wiesendanger call their offerings "Swiss-Mex"—Mexican food with European touches and careful attention to detail. **Known for:** Swiss-Mex cuisine; for hotel guests only, except to parties of six or more with 48 hours notice; dinner on request five nights per week. [$] *Average main: $20* ✉ *Posada La Poza, Camino a La Poza 282, La Poza* ✣ *Follow signs on Hwy. 19 and Benito Juárez to beach* ☎ *612/145–0400* 🌐 *www.lapoza.com.*

★ **Jazamango**

$$$ | **MEXICAN FUSION** | Set next to a beautiful garden that provides many of the fruits, veggies, and herbs used in the kitchen, Jazamango is a feast for the eyes as well as the taste buds, and a must-try

for first-time visitors to Todos Santos. It's helmed by well-known Mexican chef Javier Plascencia, known for his organic, sustainable approach to creating Baja-Mediterranean fusion dishes. **Known for:** atmospheric garden setting; straight-from-the-earth ingredients; Baja craft-brewed beers. Ⓢ *Average main: $27* ✉ *Calle Naranjos* ⟐ *At Esquina Jardín, Plaza Principal, Fraccionamiento Las Huertas* ☎ *612/157–0908* ⊕ *jazamango.mx* ☾ *Closed Tues.*

Los Adobes de Todos Santos

$$ | **MEXICAN** | Locals swear by the mole poblano and chiles en nogada at this pleasant outdoor restaurant. The menu is ambitious and includes several organic, vegetarian options—rare in these parts. **Known for:** mole poblano and chiles en nogada; vegetarian options available; adjacent desert garden. Ⓢ *Average main: $18* ✉ *Calle Hidalgo* ⟐ *Between Juárez and Colégio Militar* ☎ *612/145–0203* ⊕ *www.losadobesdetodossantos.com.*

Michael's at the Gallery

$$ | **ASIAN** | Everybody who dines here seems to know one another, but visitors are always welcome. The attraction at Michael's—not to be confused with Miguel's, the equally recommended Mexican place as you come into town—is an Asian menu combining Chinese, Japanese, Thai, and Vietnamese cuisines. **Known for:** patio dining behind the Galería de Todos Santos; open just three days a week; Asian dishes like Mu Shu chicken. Ⓢ *Average main: $20* ✉ *Calle Topete, Centro* ⟐ *Between Juárez and Centenario* ☎ *612/145–0500* ☾ *Closed Mon.–Thurs. No lunch.*

Miguel's

$ | **MEXICAN** | Deliciously prepared chiles rellenos are the attraction at Miguel's. The sign out front says so, and so does a faded *New York Times* article, which proclaims them the best in all of Baja. **Known for:** friendly owner; hearty chiles rellenos with shrimp and scallops; semi-outdoor dining. Ⓢ *Average main: $8* ✉ *Degollado at Calle Rangel, Centro* ☎ *612/157-4014* ▭ *No credit cards* ☾ *Closed Sun., Sept.*

★ Open Kitchen Restaurant at Paradero

$$$ | **CONTEMPORARY** | One of the region's best young chefs and a breezy open-air setting are reasons enough for guests and non-guests alike to visit the Open Kitchen Restaurant at Paradero. In addition to gorgeous desert and mountain views, the open kitchen concept offers an opportunity to watch Chef Eduardo Rios cook…and he's worth watching. **Known for:** fresh local food from a talented chef; wine from Baja's Valle de Guadalupe; ever-changing menu. Ⓢ *Average main: $30* ✉ *Paradero Todos Santos, La Mesa Km 59, Carretera Todos Santos – Cabo San Lucas* ☎ *800/614-7562* ⊕ *www.paraderohotels.com.*

🅒 Coffee and Quick Bites

Baja Beans

$ | **CAFÉ** | Although Los Cabos and Baja are not coffee-growing regions, the folks in the town of El Pescadero roast the finest beans from the Sierra Norte mountains in the Mexican state of Puebla. They turn them into the area's best gourmet coffee drinks, which may be enjoyed at tables in the adjoining garden. **Known for:** area's best gourmet coffee drinks; live music on Sundays; farmers' market on Sundays. Ⓢ *Average main: $5* ✉ *El Pescadero, Hwy. 19, Km 64* ☎ *612/130–3391* ⊕ *bajabeans.com* ☾ *No dinner.*

Caffé Todos Santos

$$ | **ECLECTIC** | Omelets, bagels, granola, and whole-grain breads delight the breakfast crowd at this casual small eatery; deli sandwiches, fresh salads, and an array of burritos, tamales, and *flautas* (fried tortillas rolled around savory fillings) are lunch and dinner highlights. Check for fresh seafood on the daily specials board. **Known for:** delicious deli sandwiches; gourmet pizzas and pastas; daily seafood specials. Ⓢ *Average main: $15* ✉ *Calle Centenario 33* ☎ *612/145–0300* ▭ *No credit cards* ☾ *No dinner Mon. Closed last two weeks of Sept.*

Carnitas Machín

$ | **MEXICAN** | It's not fancy, but this small restaurant just off the highway in El Pescadero is a good place to get acquainted with carnitas, a delicious taco style that originated in Michoacán and features pork simmered in lard until mouthwateringly tender. They serve the best version around, along with the perfect pairing: a bottle of cold Coca-Cola. **Known for:** best carnitas tacos around; Michoacán style cuisine; location just off the highway. [$] *Average main: $5* ✉ *Hwy 19, Km 61, El Pescadero* ☎ *612/203–6120.*

Hotels

The quality of lodgings in Todos Santos is high. It's a much better value to stay here than along the Corridor or in Los Cabos, and there isn't a megaresort to be found. In fact, some of the best lodging in the region is found right here, among the lush palm trees of this former sugarcane town.

Hacienda Todos los Santos

$$ | **HOTEL** | The three *casitas* (guesthouses) and four newer suites here are beautifully furnished with canopied beds and antique art; each has access to lush grounds and the oldest swimming pool in Todos Santos. **Pros:** three casitas have private terraces and kitchens; great views from upstairs rooms; good swimming pool. **Cons:** little to do here for kids; despite the central location, a car is highly recommended for local shopping and dining; no on-site restaurant. [$] *Rooms from: $190* ✉ *End of Benito Juárez* ☎ *612/145–0547* 🌐 *www.tshacienda.com* 🛏 *7 suites* 🍴 *No meals.*

Hotel California

$$ | **HOTEL** | This handsome structure with two stories of arched terraces and rich, vibrant colors on the walls is a testament to the artistic bent of owner Debbie Stewart (and no, there's no connection to the Eagles' song). **Pros:** inn feels exotic and lush; convenient location; good value. **Cons:** some street noise; service not as smooth as other hotels in town; spotty Wi-Fi. [$] *Rooms from: $150* ✉ *Benito Juárez at Morelos* ☎ *612/145–0525* 🌐 *www.hotelcaliforniabaja.com* 🛏 *11 rooms* 🍴 *No meals.*

★ **The Hotelito**

$ | **HOTEL** | Each room at this modern lodging has a private patio with lounge chairs and hammocks, plus original art and sculptural furniture that's as comfortable as it is captivating. **Pros:** saltwater swimming pool; mangoes fresh from the tree served at breakfast; five-minute walk to beach. **Cons:** 10-minute walk to downtown; aside from the petting zoo, not much for kids to do; much more convenient with a car. [$] *Rooms from: $135* ✉ *Rancho de la Cachora* ☎ *612/145–0099* 🌐 *www.thehotelito.com* 🕓 *Closed Sept.* 🛏 *4 rooms* 🍴 *Free breakfast.*

★ **Paradero Todos Santos**

$$$$ | **HOTEL** | No lodging in Todos Santos has a more spectacular location than Paradero, which is set within an organic farming community and offers panoramic vistas of desert, mountains, and the Pacific Ocean. **Pros:** suites have panoramic views and soaking tubs; great spa and one of the region's best chefs; excursions included in room rates. **Cons:** 10-minute drive from downtown Todos Santos; not for families with small children; 50 minutes from the nearest golf course. [$] *Rooms from: $550* ✉ *La Mesa , Km 59, Carretera Todos Santos – Cabo San Lucas* ☎ *800/614-7562* 🌐 *www.paraderohotels.com* 🛏 *35 suites* 🍴 *No meals.*

Posada La Poza

$$ | **HOTEL** | West of town, overlooking a bird-filled lagoon that gives way to the Pacific, this is one of the few Todos Santos properties right on the water. **Pros:** gracious owners; very generous, delicious breakfasts; gorgeous saltwater pool and hot tubs. **Cons:** no children under 12; no TV or phones; need car to stay here. [$] *Rooms from: $150* ✉ *Camino a La Poza 282, La Poza* ✣ *Follow signs on Hwy. 19 and on Benito Juárez to*

beach ☎ *612/145–0400* 🌐 *www.lapoza.com* 🛏 *8 suites* 🍴 *All-inclusive.*

★ Todos Santos Inn

$$ | B&B/INN | This converted 19th-century house, with only eight guest rooms, is unparalleled in design and comfort, owing to the loving care and attention of the owners. **Pros:** traditional Mexican elegance and hospitality; gorgeous interior courtyard; historic murals. **Cons:** street parking only; no kids under 12; street noise. [$] *Rooms from: $210* ✉ *Calle Legaspy 33* ☎ *612/145–0040* 🌐 *www.todossantosinn.com* 🛏 *8 rooms* 🍴 *Free breakfast.*

Nightlife

As tourism grows in Todos Santos, so do its nightlife options. You'll never mistake this place for Los Cabos, however, and the town is quite fine with that state of affairs. Lingering over dinner remains a time-honored way to spend a Todos Santos evening.

BARS AND WINE BARS

La Santeña

BARS/PUBS | You'll find this upscale rendition of a Mexican cantina (with a restaurant, too) in the Hotel Casa Tota. It's a great place to stop for a quiet drink. ✉ *Hotel Casa Tota, Calle Alvaro Obregón* ☎ *612/145–0590* 🌐 *www.hotelcasatota.com.*

Shut Up Frank's

BARS/PUBS | Take your pick from the sporting events shown on seven big-screen TVs at the consummate sports bar in Todos Santos. Enjoy the scrumptious burgers here, too. ✉ *Degollado at Rangel* ✣ *Across from Pemex station* ☎ *612/145–0707.*

Performing Arts

FESTIVALS

Todos Santos holds three annual arts-related festivals during the high season in January and February. It's a good idea to make reservations weeks in advance if you plan to be here at those times.

Festival de Cine de Todos Santos (*Todos Santos Film Festival*)

FESTIVALS | Todos Santos screens several new Latin American films during a festival in March. The 1940s-era Teatro Cine General Manuel Márquez de León serves as the main venue, with some films shown at other sites in Todos Santos, Pescadero, and La Paz. ✉ *Todos Santos* 🌐 *www.todossantoscinefest.org.*

Festival del Arte Todos Santos (*Todos Santos Art Festival*)

FESTIVALS | The city goes all out to celebrate Mexican dance, music, folklore, and culture for a week in early February each year. Local artists and several of the downtown galleries hold special events in conjunction with the festival. ✉ *Centro.*

Festival del Mango Todos Santos

FESTIVALS | Summer harvest festivals are among the most traditional yearly events in Baja California Sur and offer a taste of regional culture and regional produce. In Todos Santos, mangoes are celebrated each year with a festival in late July or early August (whenever the fruit ripens), highlighted by mango-flavored desserts, as well as live music, dancing, and the coronation of a festival queen. ✉ *Centro.*

Tropic of Cancer Concert Series

FESTIVALS | Former R.E.M. guitarist Peter Buck was the major force behind the Todos Santos Music Festival, held annually in January. The festival typically features seven nights of live music spread across two weekends, with an international lineup of performers appearing at Hotel California and the Todos Santos town square. Buck ruffled some local feathers with political comments at the 2016 festival, and the festival was renamed Tropic of Cancer Concert Series as a consequence. Proceeds benefit local children's charities. ✉ *Centro* 🌐 *tropicofcancerconcertseries.com.*

The markets and galleries of Todos Santos make it a top shopping destination.

🛍 Shopping

Although Todos Santos is gaining renown in all aspects of its tourism offerings, the name still means shopping to most Los Cabos–area visitors. Artists from the U.S. Southwest (and a few from Mexico) found a haven here some two decades ago. Their galleries and shops showcase traditional and contemporary work. There is a strong Baja emphasis in the art, and you'll find beautiful jewelry and fine crafts from all over Mexico.

ART GALLERIES

Benito Ortega Vargas, Sculptor

ART GALLERIES | Sculptor Benito Ortega's studio and gallery showcases evocative, often sea-inspired works in wood, bronze, stone, and other materials. ⊠ *24 Centenario, at Obregón, Centro* ☎ *612/136–2760* ⊕ *www.benitoortega. mx* ⊘ *Closed Sun.*

Ezra Katz Gallery

ART GALLERIES | Ezra Katz is considered by many to be one of the most important and original artists ever to emerge from Baja California Sur. La Paz native Katz's evocative and inspired paintings depicting the local landscape have been on display in his latest Todos Santos gallery since 2015. ⊠ *Calle Juárez at Topete, Centro* ☎ *612/158–8294* ⊕ *ezrakatz.com* ⊘ *Closed Sun. and July–Oct.*

Galería AR

ART GALLERIES | The vibrant contemporary paintings of Arturo Mendoza Elfeo are the main attraction at Galería AR. ⊠ *Centenario at Hidalgo* ☎ *612/145–0502* ⊘ *Closed Sun.*

Galería de Todos Santos

ART GALLERIES | Since opening in 1994, Michael and Pat Cope's *galería* has represented a diverse group of Mexican and American painters and sculptors working in a variety of artistic mediums. The gallery's terrace opens as an Asian restaurant, Michael's at the Gallery, on Friday and Saturday evenings. ⊠ *Calle Topete, Centro* ✛ *Between Juárez and Centenario* ☎ *612/145–0500* ⊕ *galeriato-dossantos-com.webs.com.*

Galería Logan

ART GALLERIES | The namesake gallery features the work of Jill Logan, a Southern Californian who has been in Todos Santos since 1998. Jill does bold oil-on-canvas paintings and complexly layered multimedia pieces. ⊠ *Calle Juárez at Morelos* ☎ *612/145–0151* ⊕ *www.jilllogan.com.*

BOOKS

El Tecolote Bookstore ·

BOOKS/STATIONERY | El Tecolote Bookstore is the best bookstore in the Los Cabos region. Stop here for Latin American literature, poetry, children's books, current fiction and nonfiction, and books on Baja. ⊠ *Colegio Militar ✛ Between Hidalgo and Obregón* ☎ *612/145–0295.*

CLOTHING AND FOLK ART

Manos Mexicanas

CRAFTS | Manos Mexicanas is a treasure trove of fine Mexican crafts, jewelry, decorative objects, and work by local potter Rubén Gutiérrez. Owner Alejandra Brilanti has amassed an incredible collection of affordable pieces. You are not likely to leave empty-handed. ⊠ *Manuel Márquez de León ✛ Between Juárez and Centenario* ☎ *612/145–0538* ⊘ *Closed Sun., Sept.*

Nomad Chic

CLOTHING | Eastern simplicity and the romance of travel influence Nomad Chic's eclectic collection of beach-ready apparel, jewelry, and accessories. ⊠ *Juárez at Hidalgo, Centro* ☎ *612/149–8962, 720/427–4627 in the U.S.* ⊕ *www.nomadchic.mx* ⊘ *Closed Sun.*

JEWELRY

★ Brilanti Fine Art

JEWELRY/ACCESSORIES | Brilanti Fine Art is a showcase for the stunning jewelry and design works of famed Taxco silversmith Ana Brilanti, in addition to a number of other contemporary jewelry artists—including Ana's son and the store's proprietor, José—whose work shares the same dramatic aesthetic. Be sure to look at the silver tea services and other functional pieces. You'll also find selected stone carvings and bronzes from local artists. ⊠ *Centenario ✛ Near Calle Topete* ☎ *612/145–0799* ⊘ *Closed Sept.*

MARKETS

The Pescadero-based café Baja Beans hosts a Sunday farmers' market, with arts and crafts offerings, stands featuring locally grown produce, live music, and healthy brunch options like vegetarian frittatas.

SOUVENIRS

Emporio Gallery and Store

GIFTS/SOUVENIRS | The Hotel California gift shop is a great place to stock up on souvenirs, from clothing and trinkets to jewelry and arts and crafts. ⊠ *Hotel California, Benito Juárez ✛ Between Morelos and Márquez de León* ☎ *612/145–0525* ⊕ *www.hotelcaliforniabaja.com.*

🏃 Activities

ECOTOURISM

★ Todos Santos Eco Adventures

CAMPING—SPORTS-OUTDOORS | Todos Santos Eco Adventures owns and operates two luxury tent camps in remote, protected areas of Baja California Sur. These include Camp Cecil de la Isla on Isla Espíritu Santo, part of a UNESCO World Heritage site in the Sea of Cortez, where guests are treated to real beds, luxury linens, chef-prepared meals, and wonderful adventures including kayaking, snorkeling, stand-up paddleboarding, swimming with sea lions, hiking, birding, and stargazing. The other camp is Camp Cecil de la Sierra in the Sierra La Laguna Biosphere Reserve. The Sierra camp is located in the *huerta* (farm) of a local ranching family, and also features walk-in tents with real beds, chef-prepared meals, and mountain adventures such as hiking and birding, as well as workshops with the ranching family on making traditional sweets, tortillas, and cheeses, and also leatherworking. The company also owns and operates Los Colibris Casitas

Art Walks in Todos Santos

The shops and galleries in the downtown area can be explored in an hour or two, or you can easily make a day of it. Start at **Nuestra Señora de Pilar** church in the morning, when it's cooler.

The first stop is across the street from the church at **Manos Mexicanas,** where visitors can admire the pottery of Rubén Gutiérrez. Next, turn right onto Legaspi and walk a block and a half to **Brilanti Fine Art**, a showcase for custom family-made jewelry and designs. From there, turn right on Topete to visit **Galería de Todos Santos**, which for over a quarter of a century has featured some of the best contemporary painting and sculpture in the area. Between the galleries mentioned you'll find dozens of additional shops to wander through, too.

in Todos Santos from which guests can enjoy several adventures including surfing, horseback riding, hiking, Mexican cooking classes, whale-watching, and swimming with whale sharks. ⊠ *Guaycura 88, La Poza* ⊹ *West on Calle Olachea, follow signs toward La Poza (call for detailed directions)* ☎ *612/145–0189, 619/446–6827 in U.S.* ⊕ *www.tosea.net.*

SPAS

Ojo de Agua Spa at Paradero

SPA/BEAUTY | Temazcal therapy, an experience akin to a Native American sweat lodge, headlines the healing wellness options at the recently opened hotel Paradero in Todos Santos. There's no questioning the authenticity. Paradero built an old-fashioned adobe style Temazcal lodge (shaped similarly to an Inuit igloo) and brought in a traditional shaman to lead their purifying steam rituals, which continue a tradition that dates back to the ancient Pre-Hispanic cultures of México. An array of pampering massages and body treatments are also available at the outdoor spa, as are hot and cold plunge pools. ⊠ *Paradero Todos Santos, La Mesa Km 59, Carretera Todos Santos – Cabo San Lucas* ☎ *800/614-7562* ⊕ *www.paraderohotels.com.*

SURFING

Todos Santos offers great surfing areas for beginners to experts. The advantage here is that the crowds, including the swarming masses from the cruise ships, don't head up to these waters, which makes for a much more relaxed scene in the water and on the beach.

Los Cerritos, south of Todos Santos on Highway 19, offers gentle waves to beginners during the summer and more challenging breaks for advanced surfers during the northwest swell from December to March. San Pedrito, also south of town, offers great surfing for experienced surfers during the winter swells, with a number of popular, low-key, surf-oriented motels along the beach. In summer, the surf is generally pretty mellow along this stretch, so locals and surfers who demand greater challenge head to the Corridor or areas along the east side of the Cape for more satisfying breaks.

Costa Azul Surf Shop

SURFING | Costa Azul Surf Shop is a small shop on the north end of the beach by the cliffs at Los Cerritos. The staff is friendly, and, for such a small space, there's a good selection of board rentals, as well as T-shirts, shorts, and accessories to buy. You'll see its stickers on cars all over the Cape. ⊠ *Playa Los Cerritos, Los Cerritos* ☎ *624/142–2771 San José del Cabo office.*

Did You Know?

At the Hotel California in Todos Santos (no relation to the Eagles song), you'll find the Emporio Gallery and Store, filled with curios and trinkets from around the world.

Spanish Language Schools

Side-trip destinations in the La Paz municipality, such as Todos Santos and La Paz itself, are great places to work on your Spanish skills, especially if you take advantage of the classes and programs offered by local language schools. Being such a large tourist area, English is widely spoken; resist the temptation to hang out with other English speakers and instead plunge in and practice your Spanish.

Hablando Mexicano. This language school offers personalized classes and immersion programs at all levels, including classes for kids. ⊠ *Rangel esq. Zaragoza, Todos Santos* ☎ *612/145–1167* ⊕ *www.elnopalspanish.com*

Todos Santos Surf Shop

SURFING | Swing by Todos Santos Surf Shop for board rentals, to arrange a lesson, buy gear, or get that ding in your board repaired. Other activities are also available, including day trips to Magdalena Bay during whale-watching season, and to La Paz to swim with sea lions and whale sharks. ⊠ *Calle Hidalgo* ✛ *Between Colégio Militar and Rangel* ☎ *612/145–1114* ⊗ *Closed Sun.*

La Paz

81 km (49 miles) north of Todos Santos, 178 km (107 miles) north of San José del Cabo (via Hwy. 1), 154 km (92 miles) north of Cabo San Lucas (via Hwy. 19).

Tidy, prosperous La Paz may be the capital of the state of Baja California Sur and home to about 244,000 residents, but it still feels like a small town in a time warp. This east coast development could easily be the most traditional Mexican city in Baja Sur, the antithesis of the "gringolandia" developments to the south. Granted, there are plenty of foreigners in La Paz, particularly during snowbird season. But in the slowest part of the off-season, during the oppressive late-summer heat, you can easily see how La Paz aptly translates to "peace," and how its residents can be called *Paceños* (peaceful ones).

Travelers use La Paz as both a destination in itself and a stopping-off point en route to Los Cabos. There's always excellent scuba diving and sportfishing in the Sea of Cortez. La Paz is the base for divers and fishermen headed for Cerralvo, La Partida, and the Espíritu Santo islands, where parrotfish, manta rays, neons, and angels blur the clear waters by the shore, and marlin, dorado, and yellowtail leap from the sea. Cruise ships are more and more often spotted sailing toward the bay, as La Paz emerges as an attractive port. (Only small ships can berth at La Paz itself; most cruise liners dock at its port of Pichilingue, about 16 km [10 miles] north of town.)

La Paz officially became the state capital in 1974 and is its largest settlement (though the combined Los Cabos agglomeration is quickly catching up). All bureaucracy holds court here, and it's the site of the ferry port to Mazatlán and Topolobampo, the port of Los Mochis, on the mainland. There are few chain hotels or restaurants, but that's sure to change as resort developments come to fruition around the area.

La Paz region, including parts of the coastline south of the city, is slated as the future building site of several large-scale, high-end resort developments with golf courses, marinas, and vacation homes. Economic doldrums of recent years put brakes on those projects, but as Mexico's tourism finally and cautiously begins to rebound, plans have moved to the forefront again.

GETTING HERE AND AROUND

Aeropuerto General Manuel Márquez de León (LAP) is 11 km (7 miles) northwest of La Paz. Alaska Air partner Horizon Air flies daily from Los Angeles. Aereo Calafia connects La Paz with Los Cabos. Several airlines connect La Paz with Mexico City and various domestic airports in Mexico. Flying into the Aeropuerto Internacional de Los Cabos, two hours away near San José del Cabo, offers a far better selection of fares and itineraries. Ecobaja Tours operates shuttles six times daily between Los Cabos Airport and La Paz for just under $30 one-way. In La Paz taxis are readily available. Taxis between La Paz airport and downtown are relatively inexpensive (less than $20) and convenient. A ride within town costs under $10; a trip to Pichilingue costs around $20. In La Paz the main Terminal de Autobus is on the malecón at Independencia. Bus companies offer service to Todos Santos (one hour), Los Cabos (two hours).

Baja Ferries connects La Paz with Topolobampo, the port at Los Mochis, on the mainland, with daily high-speed ferries. The trip takes six hours and costs $64 per person. Baja Ferries also connects La Paz and Mazatlán; it's a 12-hour trip and costs $73 per person. You can buy tickets for ferries at La Paz Pichilingue terminal. The ferries carry passengers with and without vehicles. If you're taking a car to the mainland, you must obtain a vehicle permit before boarding. Ferry officials will ask to see your Mexican auto-insurance papers and tourist card, which are obtained when crossing the U.S. border into Baja.

ESSENTIALS

AIRLINES Aereo Calafia. ☎ 612/123–2643 ⊕ www.calafiaairlines.com. **Aeropuerto Manuel Márquez de León.** ☎ 612/124–6307 ⊕ www.aeropuertosgap.com.mx. **Horizon Air.** ☎ 800/252–7522 ⊕ www.alaskaair.com.

BUS CONTACTS Autobuses Aguila. ⊠ Terminal Turística, Av. Álvaro Obregón 125, Malecón ✥ Between Independencia and 5 de Mayo ☎ 800/026–8931 ⊕ www.autobusesaguila.com. **Ecobaja Tours.** ⊠ Terminal Turística, Av. Álvaro Obregón 125, Malecón ✥ Between Independencia and 5 de Mayo ☎ 612/123–0000 ⊕ www.ecobajatours.com.

CURRENCY EXCHANGE Banamex. ⊠ Carlos Esquerro 110, Zona Comercial ☎ 800/021–2345 ⊕ www.banamex.com.

EMERGENCIES Highway Patrol. ☎ 612/122–0477. **Police.** ☎ 911.

FERRY LINES Baja Ferries. ⊠ La Paz Pichilingue Terminal ☎ 612/123–6600, 800/337–7437 ⊕ www.bajaferries.com.mx.

HOSPITALS Centro de Especialidades Médicas. ⊠ Calle Delfines 110 ☎ 612/124–0402 ⊕ www.cemlapaz.com.

⊙ Sights

Catedral de Nuestra Señora de la Paz
RELIGIOUS SITE | The downtown church, Catedral de Nuestra Señora de la Paz, is a simple, unassuming stone building with a modest gilded altar but beautiful stained-glass windows. The church was built in 1861 near the site of La Paz's first mission, which no longer exists. The two towers of the present cathedral were added a half century later. ⊠ Revolución de 1910, Centro ✥ Between 5 de Mayo and Independencia ☎ 612/122–2596.

Malecón
PROMENADE | Officially the Malecón Álvaro Obregón, this seaside promenade is La Paz's seawall, tourist zone, and social center all rolled into one. It runs for 5 km (3 miles) along Paseo Álvaro Obregón and has a broad palm-lined walkway, statues of whale sharks, dolphins, sharks, and other local denizens of the deep, as well as several park areas in the directly adjacent sand. Paceños are fond of strolling the malecón at sunset when the

The Steinbeck Connection

For an account of the Baja of years past, few works beat John Steinbeck's *The Log from the Sea of Cortez*, published in 1951. It recounts a six-week voyage he took in 1940 with marine biologist Ed Ricketts for the purpose of cataloging new aquatic species on the gulf side of Baja California. (*Phialoba steinbecki*, a previously unknown species of sea anemone discovered during the excursion, was later named for the author.)

Steinbeck lamented what he was sure would one day be the inevitable tourism growth to arrive on the peninsula. The author was mistaken on one key point however: he was certain the megaboom would come to La Paz and not to then-sleepy Cabo San Lucas.

heat of the day finally begins to subside. (You will see people swimming here, and the water is cleaner than it used to be, but the beaches outside town are a far surer bet in that regard.) ⊠ *Paseo Álvaro Obregón.*

Malecón Plaza

PLAZA | A two-story white gazebo is the focus of Malecón Plaza, a small concrete square where musicians sometimes appear on weekend nights. An adjacent street, Calle 16 de Septiembre, leads inland to the city. ⊠ *Paseo Álvaro Obregón at Calle 16 de Septiembre.*

Museo Regional de Antropología y Historia de Baja California Sur

MUSEUM | **FAMILY** | La Paz's culture and heritage are well represented at the Museo de Antropología, which has re-creations of indigenous Comondu and Las Palmas villages, photos of cave paintings found in Baja, and copies of Cortés's writings on first sighting La Paz. All exhibit descriptions are labeled in both English and Spanish. If you're a true Baja aficionado and want to delve into the region's history, this museum is a must; otherwise, a quick visit is all you need. ⊠ *Calle Altamirano at Calle 5 de Mayo, Centro* ☎ *612/122–0162* 🖼 *$3.*

Plaza Constitución

PLAZA | Plaza Constitución, the true center of La Paz, is a traditional *zócalo* (main square) that also goes by the name Jardín Velazco. Concerts are held in the park's gazebo and locals gather here for art shows and fairs. Day-to-day life here entails shoeshines and local bingo games. ⊠ *Bordered by Av. Independencia, Calles 5 de Mayo, Revolución de 1910, and Madero, Centro.*

Serpentario de La Paz

ZOO | Better that you encounter all the creatures that slip and slither here in the safety of Mexico's largest serpentarium than out in the wilds of Baja. More than 100 species are on display in indoor and outdoor exhibits, including turtles, pythons, rattlesnakes, and a rather large iguana. For less than $3, visitors may take photos with their choice of two pythons or a baby crocodile. Labeling is entirely in Spanish, but the staff offers guided tours in English with advance notice. A gift shop sells reptile-themed souvenirs. ⊠ *Calle Brecha California, Centro* ✛ *Between Nueva Reforma and Guaycura* ☎ *612/122–5611* ⊕ *www.elserpentario.org* 🖼 *$8.*

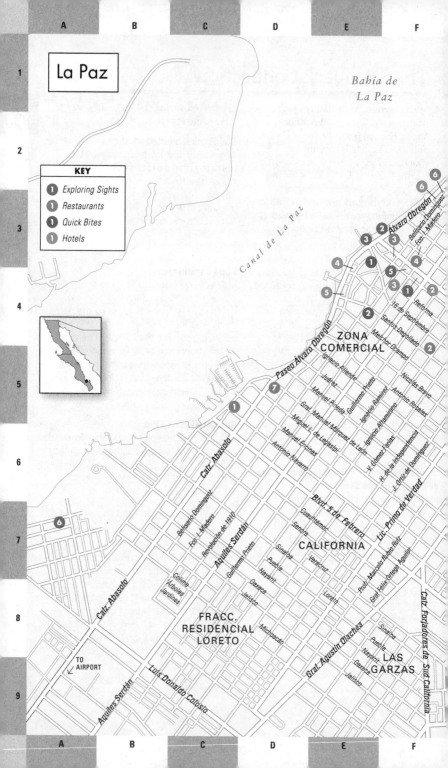

Sights ▼

1 Catedral de Nuestra
  Señora de la Paz................... **F4**
2 Malecón **F3**
3 Malecón Plaza **E3**
4 Museo Regional de
  Antropología y Historia de
  Baja California Sur **G4**
5 Plaza Constitución................. **F3**
6 Serpentario de La Paz............. **A7**

Restaurants ▼

1 Bandido's Grill..................... **C5**
2 El Bismark **F5**
3 J & R Ribs Costillería **F3**
4 Las Tres Vírgenes.................. **F3**
5 Mar y Peña **H5**
6 Mariscos Los Laureles............. **F2**
7 Rancho Viejo **D5**

Quick Bites ▼

1 Caffé Gourmet..................... **E3**
2 Tacos Hermanos González **E4**

Hotels ▼

1 Club El Moro....................... **H1**
2 el ángel azul **F4**
3 Hotel Arte Museo Yeneka **F4**
4 Hotel Perla......................... **E3**
5 Hotel Seven Crown Malecón...... **E4**
6 Hotel y Restaurant
  Nuevo Pekin....................... **F3**
7 La Concha Beach Club
  Resort and Condominiums........ **H1**
8 Marine Waterfront Hotel.......... **H1**

🏖 Beaches

Around the malecón, stick to ambling along the sand while watching local families enjoy the sunset. Just north of town the beach experience is much better; it gets even better north of Pichilingue. Save your swimming and snorkeling energies for this area. All facilities listed here exist on the weekends. Their existence on weekdays may be spottier.

Playa Balandra

BEACH—SIGHT | A rocky point shelters a clear, warm bay at Playa Balandra, 21 km (13 miles) north of La Paz. Several small coves and pristine beaches appear and disappear with the tides, but there's always a calm area where you can wade and swim. Snorkeling is fair around Balandra's south end where there's a coral reef. You may spot clams, starfish, and anemones. Kayaking and snorkeling tours usually set out from around here. If not on a tour, bring your own gear, as rentals aren't normally available. Camping is permitted but there are no hookups. The smallish beach gets crowded on weekends, but on a weekday morning you might have the place to yourself. Sand flies can be a nuisance here between July and October. **Amenities:** camping; food concession; parking lot; toilets. **Best for:** snorkeling; swimming; walking. ⊠ La Paz.

Playa Caimancito

BEACH—SIGHT | Situated just beyond La Concha Beach Club Resort, 5 km (3 miles) north of La Paz, Caimancito is home to a scenic stretch of sand and some sun-shading palapas. Locals swim laps here, as the water is almost always calm and salty enough for easy buoyancy. There aren't any public facilities here, but if you wander over to the hotel for lunch or a drink, you can use its restrooms and rent water toys. **Amenities:** parking lot. **Best for:** sunsets; swimming; walking. ⊠ La Paz.

Sunrise, Sunset 👁

La Paz sits on the east coast of the Baja peninsula, but a convoluted curvature of the shoreline here positions the city to look out west over the Sea of Cortez. That means that you can enjoy beautiful sun *sets* over the water here at the end of the day.

Playa El Tecolote

BEACH—SIGHT | Spend a Sunday at Playa El Tecolote, 25 km (15 miles) north of La Paz, and you'll feel like you've experienced the Mexico of old. Families set up house on the soft sand, kids race after seagulls and each other, and all ages wade together in the water. Vendors rent out beach chairs, umbrellas, kayaks, and small, motorized boats; a couple of restaurants serve simple fare such as ceviche and *almejas* (chocolate clams). These eateries are usually open throughout the week, though they sometimes close on chilly days. Facilities include restrooms and trash cans. Camping is permitted, but there are no hookups. **Amenities:** camping; food concession; parking lot; playground; toilets. **Best for:** sunsets; swimming; walking. ⊠ Carretera La Paz–El Tecolote.

Playa Pichilingue

BEACH—SIGHT | **FAMILY** | Starting in the time of Spanish invaders, Pichilingue, 16 km (10 miles) north of La Paz, was known for its preponderance of oysters bearing black pearls. In 1940 a disease killed them off, leaving the beach deserted. Today it's a pleasant place to sunbathe and watch sportfishing boats haul in their daily catches. Locals set up picnics here on weekend afternoons and linger until the blazing sun settles into the bay. Restaurants consisting of little more than a palapa over plastic tables and chairs serve oysters *diablo,* fresh clams, and plenty of cold beer. Pichilingue curves northeast along the bay to the terminals where the ferries from Mazatlán and Topolobampo arrive and many of the sportfishing boats depart. If La Paz is on your cruise itinerary, you'll likely dock at Pichilingue, too. One downside to this beach: traffic buzzes by on the nearby freeway. The water here, though not particularly clear, is calm enough for swimming. **Amenities:** food concession; parking lot; toilets. **Best for:** sunset; walking. ⊠ *La Paz.*

🍽 Restaurants

Bandido's Grill

$ | **BURGER** | **FAMILY** | Bandido's has come a long way since opening nearly a decade ago with three plastic tables and a grill fixed under the hood of an old pickup truck. The unique truck-grill is still around, but the restaurant's latest alfresco setting suggests it may be transitioning from working-class pit stop into romantic burger joint. **Known for:** popular with locals; hearty burgers and ribs; old-time rock and roll. Ⓢ *Average main: $12* ⊠ *Calle Navarro at Topete, Centro* ☎ *612/128–8338.*

El Bismark

$$ | **MEXICAN** | The original Bismark is a bit out of the way, but it attracts families who settle down for hours at long wooden tables, while telenovelas (Latin American soap operas) play on the TV above the bar. Tuck into seafood cocktails, enormous grilled lobsters, or carne asada served with beans, guacamole, and homemade tortillas. **Known for:** seafood cocktails; long dining experience; good for families. Ⓢ *Average main: $16* ⊠ *Av. Degollado at Calle Altamirano, Centro* ☎ *612/122–4854.*

J & R Ribs Costillería

$$ | **BARBECUE** | For those who reach a saturation point with Mexican cuisine, there's always American-style barbecue at J & R Ribs Costillería. Half and full racks of *costillas* (ribs) are specialties

here, as are brisket and sides of cornbread and macaroni and cheese. **Known for:** racks of ribs; picnic-table dining; brownies and ice cream in bourbon sauce. Ⓢ *Average main: $20* ⊠ *Calle 5 de Mayo at Belisario Dominguez* ☎ *612/137–2312, 612/122–7977* ⊕ *www.ribsjr.com* Ⓜ *23000.*

★ Las Tres Vírgenes

$$ | **INTERNATIONAL** | Poll locals on their favorite restaurant in La Paz, and Las Tres Vírgenes is likely to be the runaway winner. Chef and Tijuana native Jesús Chávez has endeared himself to Paceños over the past dozen years with consistently excellent mesquite-grilled fare, from seafood and enormous burgers (try the Baja 1000 with "double beef, double cheese, double everything") to slow-braised Angus short ribs, Tomahawk bone-in rib eye, and Brazilian-style picaña. **Known for:** #1 favorite among locals; romantic courtyard dining; great cocktails. Ⓢ *Average main: $18* ⊠ *Calle Francisco I. Madero 1130, Centro* ✛ *Between Constitución and Miguel Hidalgo y Costilla* ☎ *612/123–2226.*

Mariscos Los Laureles

$$ | **SEAFOOD** | A small stand that looks as if it might have been rolled along the street by a vendor is just the entryway decoration for this well-established restaurant. Whether you eat at a bench at the stand outside or dine within in the air-conditioning, if you like seafood, you will enjoy Los Laureles. **Known for:** excellent seafood; many types of fruits de mer; fresh seafood cocktails. Ⓢ *Average main: $14* ⊠ *Paseo Álvaro Obregón at Salvatierra, Centro* ☎ *612/128–8532.*

Mar y Peña

$$ | **SEAFOOD** | The freshest, tastiest seafood cocktails, ceviches, and clam tacos imaginable are served in this nautical restaurant crowded with locals. If you come with friends, go for the *mariscada*, a huge platter of shellfish and fish for four. **Known for:** huge portions; often busy; extremely fresh and tasty seafood

dishes. $ Average main: $16 ⊠ Calle 16 de Septiembre, Centro ✛ Between Isabel la Católica and Albáñez ☎ 612/122–9949 ⊗ Closed Christmas and New Year's Day.

Rancho Viejo

$$ | **MEXICAN** | Everything is delicious, and prices are reasonable at this cheerful little restaurant painted in bright yellow and orange. Meats are the specialty here, but just about everything on the menu is good and choices are abundant. **Known for:** tasty tacos de arrachera; open 24 hours; abundant choices. $ Average main: $12 ⊠ Márquez de León at Dominguez, Centro ☎ 612/128–4647, 612/125–6633.

☕ Coffee and Quick Bites

Caffé Gourmet

$ | **CAFÉ** | Not far from hotels, restaurants, and important downtown sights, this small café is a great place to recharge with a morning espresso, chai, or smoothie, along with great pastries. Wi-Fi is available here, so you can catch up on your email. **Known for:** great pastries; Wi-Fi available; centrally located. $ Average main: $3 ⊠ Esquerro at Calle 16 de Septiembre ☎ 612/122–7710 ⊗ Closed Mon.

Tacos Hermanos González

$ | **MEXICAN** | La Paz has plenty of great taco shacks, but none are better than the small stand owned by the González brothers, who serve hunks of fresh fish wrapped in corn tortillas and offer bowls of condiments with which to decorate your taco. The top quality draws sizable crowds. **Known for:** area's best taco stand; lots of condiments to add; draws big crowds. $ Average main: $3 ⊠ Madero at Degollado, Centro ☎ 612/237–2019 ▭ No credit cards.

Hotels

The alternative to staying in the city is the 18-km (11-mile) highway leading north from La Paz to its port of Pichilingue, lined with a few small seaside hotels.

Club El Moro

$ | **RESORT** | Possibly the best bargain on the malecón, although a bit away from the city center itself, this vacation-ownership resort has very reasonable suite rentals on a nightly and weekly basis. **Pros:** handsome architecture; pool; private balconies. **Cons:** some dated decor; rooms facing pool area can be noisy; lengthy walk to downtown shopping and dining. $ Rooms from: $73 ⊠ Hwy. 11 to Pichilingue, Km 2 ☎ 612/122–4084, 866/375–2840 ⊕ www.clubelmoro.com.mx ⤵ 26 rooms ⦿| No meals.

★ el ángel azul

$ | **HOTEL** | Owner Esther Ammann converted La Paz's historic courthouse into a comfortable retreat in the center of the city. **Pros:** lovely owner; attentive service; historic building. **Cons:** street parking only; kids under 12 not permitted; a bit of a walk to the malecón. $ Rooms from: $80 ⊠ Av. Independencia 518, at Guillermo Prieto, Centro ☎ 612/125–5130 ⊕ www.elangelazul.com ⤵ 10 rooms ⦿| No meals.

Hotel Arte Museo Yeneka

$ | **HOTEL** | Twenty budget-friendly rooms fringe a courtyard strewn with art and artifacts, each individually decorated and adorned with hand-painted accents to reflect this hotel's bohemian sensibility. **Pros:** affordable room rates; complimentary tequila shots each evening; centrally located. **Cons:** patchy Wi-Fi; noisy ceiling fans and air-conditioning units; no views. $ Rooms from: $50 ⊠ Calle Madero 1520, Centro ☎ 612/125–4688 ⊕ www.hotelyeneka.com ⤵ 20 rooms ⦿| Free breakfast.

Hotel Perla

$ | **HOTEL** | The legendary low-rise of the oldest hotel in Baja California Sur faces the malecón, and although it sometimes shows its age (it has seen plenty of action since 1940), the location is unbeatable. **Pros:** central location; friendly staff; great sunset views from street-facing rooms. **Cons:** room facing street can be noisy; kitschy furnishings; property is historic, but shows age. [$] *Rooms from: $80* ✉ *Paseo Álvaro Obregón 1570, Malecón* ☎ *612/122–0777* 🌐 *www.hotelperlabaja.com* 🛏 *110 rooms* 🍴 *No meals.*

Hotel Seven Crown Malecón

$ | **HOTEL** | This very reasonable, modern, minimalist hotel is perfectly situated to one side of the malecón's action. **Pros:** central location; affordable; rooftop restaurant with bay views. **Cons:** very simple rooms; some rooms facing street can be noisy; weak and patchy Wi-Fi. [$] *Rooms from: $60* ✉ *Paseo Álvaro Obregón 1710, Centro* ☎ *612/128–7787* 🌐 *www.sevencrownhotels.com* 🛏 *72 rooms* 🍴 *No meals.*

Hotel y Restaurant Nuevo Pekin

$ | **HOTEL** | The most budget-friendly accommodations on the malecón are also the most unusual, given they were built on top of a Chinese restaurant. **Pros:** super cheap; air-conditioning, TV, and Wi-Fi included; great location with bay views. **Cons:** dated decor; short walk to downtown, though the attached restaurant has the best Chinese in town; no frills furnishings. [$] *Rooms from: $30* ✉ *Paseo Álvaro Obregón 875* ☎ *612/125–5335* 🌐 *www.nuevopekin.com* 🛏 *32 rooms* 🍴 *No meals.*

La Concha Beach Club Resort and Condominiums

$ | **RESORT** | **FAMILY** | On a long beach with calm water, this older resort (built in 1984) has a water-sports center and a notable restaurant. **Pros:** renovated rooms in good shape; lower-priced rooms are good value; private beach. **Cons:** you'll need a car to stay here; some decor is a bit dated; no meals included. [$] *Rooms from: $58* ✉ *Hwy. 11 to Pichilingue, Km 5* ☎ *612/121–6161* 🌐 *www.laconcha.com* 🛏 *99 rooms* 🍴 *No meals.*

Marine Waterfront Hotel

$ | **RESORT** | Here's a hotel with remodeled rooms and a full-service marina, meaning easy concierge access to activities like fishing, scuba diving, and kayaking. **Pros:** great value; nice on-site drinking and dining options; good location between downtown and nearby beaches. **Cons:** you'll need a car; spotty Wi-Fi; not all rooms have water views. [$] *Rooms from: $64* ✉ *Hwy. 11 to Pichilingue, Km 2.5, Col. Lomas de Palmira* ☎ *612/121–6254* 🌐 *www.waterfronthotel.com.mx* 🛏 *89 rooms* 🍴 *Free breakfast.*

🍸 Nightlife

BARS AND DANCE CLUBS

El Parnazo

BARS/PUBS | Liter-sized bottles of beer called *caguamas* (slang for "giant sea turtles"), or sometimes *ballena* (whale), line the shelf behind this popular sports bar and zigzag through the spacious interior. But oversized beers served with chilled steins aren't the only notable things about the bar, located a few steps from the malecón on Calle 16 de Septiembre. The nachos, burgers, and chicken wings are all excellent, as are the mojitos and margaritas. Big games are shown on big wall-mounted TVs, and the staff will honor requests for U.S. sports (if they have access to the channel). ✉ *Calle 16 de Septiembre 15* ☎ *612/129–7272.*

★ La Miserable

CAFES—NIGHTLIFE | Don't let the name fool you: good times are typically had by all at this downtown mezcalería, thanks to its congenial late-night atmosphere and many rare and unusual examples of México's "other" national spirit. The bar's collection of smoky, agave-derived mezcals are primarily sourced from small mainland distillers, including the potent

Did You Know?

Just north of La Paz, Playa Balandra has small coves and pristine beaches that appear and disappear with the tides. The shallow, clear water is ideal for snorkeling.

and flavorful house brand. Local artwork and vintage photos adorn the colorfully painted walls, and bar staff play a lively mix of popular hits and hard-driving rock and roll. Bottled beer is stocked for those with an aversion to strong liquors, and there are always a few traditional Mexican specialties featured on the chalkboard menu. ⊠ *Calle Belisario Dominguez 274, Centro* ⊹ *Between 5 de Mayo and Constitución* ☎ *612/129–7037* ☞ *Closed Sun.*

La Terraza

BARS/PUBS | The best spot for both sunset- and people-watching along the malecón is La Terraza at the Hotel Perla. The place makes killer margaritas, too. ⊠ *Hotel Perla, Paseo Alvaro Obregón 1570, Malecón* ☎ *612/122–0777* ⊕ *www. hotelperlabaja.com.*

Las Varitas

MUSIC CLUBS | This club heats up after midnight, with live music acts playing Banda, Norteño, and other Mexican musical styles. Ladies Night is Friday 9–11, with cheap drinks and performances by male exotic dancers. ⊠ *Av. Independencia 111, at Domínguez, Centro* ☎ *612/125–2025.*

🎭 Performing Arts

El Teatro de la Ciudad

THEATER | La Paz's cultural center seats more than 1,100 and stages shows by visiting and local performers. ⊠ *Av. Navarro 700, Centro* ⊹ *Between Ignacio Manuel Altamirano and Héroes de Independencia* ☎ *612/125–0204.*

🛍 Shopping

ART AND SOUVENIRS

Artesanías La Antigua California

CRAFTS | Antigua California has the nicest selection of Mexican folk art in La Paz, including wooden masks and lacquered boxes from the mainland state of Guerrero. Hats, T-shirts, and

other souvenir apparel are also sold. ⊠ *Carlos M. Esquerro 1680-A, Malecón* ☎ *612/125–5230.*

Got Baja?

GIFTS/SOUVENIRS | You'll find a nice selection of Baja-themed souvenirs, including quality T-shirts, at this downtown shop that shares space with Doce Cuarenta Café & Repostería. There's also a branch in Todos Santos. ⊠ *Calle Madero 1240, Centro* ⊹ *Between 5 de Mayo and Constitución* ☎ *612/178–0067* ⊕ *www. gotbaja.mx.*

Ibarra's Pottery

CERAMICS/GLASSWARE | The Ibarra family oversees the potters and painters at their namesake shop. Their geometric designs and glazing technique result in gorgeous mirrors, bowls, platters, and cups. ⊠ *Calle Guillermo Prieto 625, Centro* ⊹ *Between Torre Iglesias and República* ☎ *612/159–1526* ⊗ *Closed Sun., Aug. and Sept.*

BOOKS

Allende Books

BOOKS/STATIONERY | This bookstore stocks La Paz's best selection of English-language works, mainly about Baja and México, as well as laminated nature field guides and works of popular fiction. A new owner and location has led to an expanded inventory, a new coffee bar and courtyard seating area, and a more central downtown setting. ⊠ *Calle 21 de Agosto, Centro* ⊹ *Between 16 de Septiembre and Agustin Arriola Martinez* ☎ *612/138–1589* ⊕ *www.allendebooks.com.*

🏃 Activities

BOATING AND FISHING

The considerable fleet of private boats in La Paz now has room for docking at several marinas, including Marina Palmira north of the malecón, and Marina de La Paz and Marina Cortez to the south. Most hotels can arrange trips. Fishing tournaments are typically held in July, August, and October.

Fishermen's Fleet

BOATING | The Fishermen's Fleet has day-long fishing on *pangas* (skiffs), as well as multiday excursions to Magdalena Bay. ✉ *La Paz* ☎ *612/122–1313, 408/884–3932 in U.S.* ⊕ *www.fishermensfleet.com.*

Mosquito Fleet

BOATING | The Mosquito Fleet has 22-foot pangas starting at $400 or a 26-foot panga at $500 for two to three people, plus 28-foot cabin cruisers from $650 for four people. Lunches onboard are an additional $16 per person, fishing licenses are $18 each, and bait is $50 per boat. ✉ *Hwy. to Pichilingue, Km 5* ✛ *Between downtown and Pichilingue* ☎ *612/127–1614, 877/408–6769 in U.S.* ⊕ *www.bajamosquitofleet.com.*

KAYAKING

The calm waters off La Paz are perfect for kayaking, and you can take multiday trips along the coast to Loreto or out to the nearby islands.

Baja Expeditions

KAYAKING | Baja Expeditions, one of the oldest outfitters working in Baja (since 1974), offers several kayak tours, including multinight trips. A support boat carries all the gear, including ingredients for great meals. Seven-day trips in the Sea of Cortez with camping on remote island beaches start at $1,995 per person, based on double occupancy. ✉ *Calle Sonora 585, Manglito* ✛ *Between Topete and Abasolo* ☎ *612/125–3828, 800/843–6967 in U.S.* ⊕ *www.bajaexpeditions.com.*

Nichols Expeditions

KAYAKING | Nichols Expeditions arranges kayaking tours to Isla Espíritu Santo and between Loreto and La Paz, with camping along the way. It also offers a combination of sea kayaking in the Sea of Cortez with whale-watching in Magdalena Bay. ✉ *497 N. Main St., Moab* ☎ *800/648–8488 in U.S.* ⊕ *www.nicholexpeditions.com* ✉ *8-day sea kayaking trip $1,695; 9-day sea kayaking and whale watching trip $1,595.*

SCUBA DIVING AND SNORKELING

Popular diving and snorkeling spots include the coral banks off Isla Espíritu Santo, the sea-lion colony off Isla Partida, and the seamount 14 km (9 miles) farther north (best for serious divers).

Cortez Club

SCUBA DIVING | The Cortez Club is a full-scale water-sports center with equipment rental and scuba, snorkeling, kayaking, and sportfishing tours, as well as the complete slate of PADI instructional courses. ✉ *Hwy. to Pichilingue, Km 5* ✛ *Between downtown and Pichilingue* ☎ *612/121–6120, 877/408–6769 in U.S.* ⊕ *www.cortezclub.com* ✉ *Two-tank dives from $165.*

Fun Baja

DIVING/SNORKELING | Fun Baja offers land tours, scuba and snorkel excursions with sea lions, seasonal whale-watching trips, and camping safaris to Isla Espíritu Santo. ✉ *Hyatt Place La Paz, Hwy. to Pichilingue, Km 7.5, Lomas de Palmira* ☎ *612/106–7148* ⊕ *www.funbaja.com* ✉ *Two-tank scuba trips from $145.*

TOUR OPERATORS

Adventures in Baja

SNORKELING | Snorkel and swim with whale sharks off the coast of La Paz with a small group tour from this company. Lunch and round-trip transportation from a Los Cabos resort is included. ✉ *La Paz* ☎ *612/104–6340* ⊕ *www.adventuresinbaja.com* ☞ *From $220.*

Baja Expeditions

SCUBA DIVING | Dive at pristine sites near Isla Espíritu Santo or "glamp" overnight on the island with customizable activities. Snorkel with whale sharks in sheltered coves off the coast of La Paz or with sea lions at Los Islotes. It's all possible with Baja Expeditions' 45-foot catamaran *El Mechudo*, which can carry up to eight people for snorkel and dive charters. ✉ *Calle Sonora 585, Manglito* ✛ *Between Topete and Abasolo* ☎ *612/125–3828, 800/843–6967 in U.S.*

A diver gets up close and personal with a sea lion in the waters of the Sea of Cortez.

⊕ *www.bajaexpeditions.com* ✉ *Scuba diving from $175 per person.*

WHALE-WATCHING

La Paz is a good entry point for whale-watching expeditions to **Bahía Magdalena,** 266 km (165 miles) northwest of La Paz on the Pacific coast. Note, however, that such trips entail about six hours of travel from La Paz and back for two to three hours on the water. Only a few tour companies offer this as a day-long excursion because of the time and distance constraints.

Many devoted whale-watchers opt to stay overnight in Puerto San Carlos, the small town by the bay. Most La Paz hotels can make arrangements for excursions, or you can head out on your own by renting a car or taking a public bus from La Paz to San Carlos, and then hire a boat captain to take you into the bay. The air and water are cold during whale season from December to April, so you'll need to bring a warm windbreaker and gloves. Captains are not allowed to "chase" whales, but that doesn't keep

the whale mamas and their babies from approaching your *panga* (skiff) so closely you can reach out and touch them.

An easier expedition is a whale-watching trip in the Sea of Cortez from La Paz, which involves boarding a boat in La Paz and motoring around until whales are spotted. They most likely won't come as close to the boats and you won't see the mothers and newborn calves at play, but it's still fabulous watching the whales breeching and spouting nearby.

Baja Expeditions

WHALE-WATCHING | Seasonal four-day, three-night gray whale–watching excursions are offered for $2,995 per person, double occupancy. Tours are typically scheduled in February and March, and include flights, meals, an expert natural guide, and comfortable glamping conditions at Laguna San Ignacio. ✉ *Calle Sonora 585, Manglito* ✛ *Between Topete and Abasolo* ☎ *612/125–3828, 800/843–6967 in U.S.* ⊕ *www.bajaexpeditions.com.*

Cortez Club

WHALE-WATCHING | The water-sports center Cortez Club runs extremely popular full-day whale-watching trips in winter. Transportation, guide, breakfast, and seafood lunch are included. ⊠ *Hwy. to Pichilingue, Km 5* ✛ *Between downtown and Pichilingue* ☎ *612/121–6120, 877/408–6769 in U.S.* ⊕ *www.cortezclub. com* ✉ *$199 per person.*

East Cape

At its northernmost point, Los Barriles, it is 78 km (49 miles via Hwy. 1) from San José del Cabo and 106 km (65 miles) from La Paz.

First-time visitors may think Los Cabos is only Cabo San Lucas, San José del Cabo, and their connecting 20-mile tourist corridor, but that's not true at all. Yes, those two towns are the genesis of the name Los Cabos (The Capes), but the Los Cabos municipality as a whole comprises nearly 1,500 square miles, including more than a dozen smaller towns and at least one microregion full of natural treasures: the East Cape. Known as "the other side" of Los Cabos, the off-the-grid area is home to rustic fishing resorts, great surfing and diving in Cabo Pulmo National Park, pristine beaches with no vendors, and spectacular views that make it well worth a trip.

The East Cape proper begins at the outskirts of San José del Cabo and then traces the coast for nearly 70 miles, all the way to Los Barriles. Los Barriles is the largest East Cape coastal community (with more than 1,000 residents, many of whom are retired expats), and the only one that is not in the Los Cabos municipality but in La Paz.

The East Cape also includes small inland towns like Miraflores and Santiago, easily accessed from the Carretera Transpeninsular (Federal Highway 1). The highway provides the safest and quickest means to reach most East Cape communities; either directly in the case of Buena Vista and Los Barriles, or via the turnoff at La Ribera that loops back to San José del Cabo along the largely dirt Camino Cabo Este, or East Cape Road. The latter is the only way to reach tucked-away communities like Cabo Pulmo, whose national park includes a marine sanctuary with one of the oldest living coral reefs in North America.

With the exception of the newly opened Four Seasons Resort Los Cabos at Costa Palmas (in La Ribera), luxury is in short supply along the East Cape. Rather, this off-the-grid region provides a snapshot of what Cabo San Lucas and San José del Cabo were like 50 years ago, before they were developed into international tourist destinations. In other words, it's the last chance to see "Old Cabo."

GETTING HERE AND AROUND
BUS
Buses do travel to the East Cape, despite its off-the-radar status. Autobuses Aguila leaves every morning and afternoon from Plaza Golden Palace in Cabo San Lucas, picking up passengers in San José del Cabo before continuing on through Miraflores, Santiago, La Ribera, and Los Barriles on the way to La Paz. Tickets for all these destinations are less than $10 from Cabo San Lucas. But buses are a less-than-ideal mode of transportation for East Cape travel, since these small towns largely lack central shopping, dining, and resort areas within walking distance of bus stops. Los Barriles is the lone exception, since everything visitors could want (hotels, restaurants, beach, activities) is on or within easy walking distance of Calle 20 de Noviembre, the town's main drag. Every other destination requires a car.

CAR

Cars are the best way to travel the East Cape. Rentals are available throughout Cabo San Lucas and San José del Cabo, including at the airport and on-site at some upscale resorts. The airport toll road from Cabo San Lucas to the airport in San José del Cabo dramatically reduces the travel time to reach the East Cape by means of the Carretera Transpeninsular (Federal Highway 1), and at a reasonable cost (about $10). Miraflores can be reached in about one hour by this route; Los Barriles in just under two hours.

Coastal road Camino Cabo Este, accessible from Highway 1 at La Ribera, is also widely used. It remains almost completely dirt, with slow speed limits (20 to 25 mph) in most of the 45-mile route between Cabo Pulmo and San José del Cabo. Driving this dirt road should never be attempted without a four-wheel drive vehicle, and not at all during or in the days immediately after a rainstorm. Visitors should also avoid driving at night, on all roads, due to the possibility of hazardous encounters with the region's free-ranging *chinampo* cattle.

Eventually, the Camino Cabo Este will be completely paved. An alternative does exist, however, in that many local dive companies offer round-trip transportation for Cabo Pulmo scuba trips, and a few adventure providers, like High Tide Los Cabos, offer jeep tours of the region.

◉ Sights

Mirador Santiago de Yola

VIEWPOINT | Mirador in Spanish means lookout, and this rustic observation platform (be careful with the rickety steps!) offers magnificent views of the lagoons and palm groves of Santiago, as well as the surrounding mountains. Access to the mirador requires a short drive down a dirt road, and those willing (and with the four-wheel drive capability) to take

the dirt road farther will discover the magical **Rancho Ecológico Sol de Mayo**, a canyon area with a stunning waterfall and rock-bounded swimming hole, as well as the small rural community of **San Dionisio**, where local guides will lead you on hiking and climbing expeditions into the Sierra de la Laguna. ⊠ *Santiago* ✛ *Accessible from Calle Francisco J. Múgica. Ask for directions at the gas station near the main square.*

Misión de Santiago

RELIGIOUS SITE | For a little area history, visit Santiago's lovely Catholic church, built in the 1950s. A plaque outside the church commemorates one of the most turbulent and important events in the region: the Rebellion of the Pericúes in 1734. The Pericú were the indigenous inhabitants of present day Los Cabos. In an uprising against the Jesuits, who founded four missions in Baja California Sur during the early decades of the 18th century, the Pericú destroyed all four: La Paz, Santiago, San José del Cabo, and Todos Santos, and killed two Jesuit priests. The tribe of Pericú in Santiago were known as the Coras, and their name, their place name for Santiago (Aiñiní), and their rebellion are reminders of their connection to the land. ⊠ *Maestros Misioneros de 1930 at Guadalupe Victoria, Santiago* ✛ *Across from the public library.*

Monumento a las Madres

MEMORIAL | In a salute to mothers, this pedestal-mounted sculpture was inaugurated in 1929 at the urging of local schoolchildren and is one of the oldest tributes of its kind in Mexico. It was certainly built before there were paved roads in Miraflores, since Avenida Union—one of the main thoroughfares in the small farming community—splits to accommodate it. For now, it remains one of the few reasons for tourists to stop here, although a regularly scheduled organic farmers' market is rumored to

Continued on page 190

A WHALE'S TALE

by Kelly Lack and Larry Dunmire

Seeing the gray whales off Baja's western coast needs to be on your list of things to do before you die. "But I've gone whale watching," you say. Chances are, though, that you were in a big boat and might have spotted the flip of a tail 100 yards out. In Baja your vessel will be a tiny panga, smaller than the whales themselves; they'll swim up, mamas with their babies, coming so close that you can smell the fishiness of their spouts.

Grey Whales Guerrero Negro

WHEN TO GO

Gray whales and tourists both head south to Baja around December—the whales in pods, the snowbirds in RV caravans—staying put through to April to shake off the chill of winter. So the beaches, hotels, restaurants, and bars during whale-watching season will be bustling. Book your room two to three months ahead to ensure a place to stay. The intense experience that awaits you at Magdalena Bay, San Ignacio, or Scammion's Lagoon is worth traveling in high season.

THE GRAY WHALE:
Migrating Leviathan

Yearly, gray whales endure the longest migration of any mammal on earth—some travel 5,000 miles one way between their feeding grounds in Alaska's frigid Bering Sea and their mating/birthing lagoons in sunny Baja California. The whales are bottom-feeders, unique among cetaceans, and stir up sediment on the sea floor, then use their baleen—long, stiff plates covered with hair-like fibers inside their mouths—to filter out the sediment and trap small marine creatures such as crustaceanlike Gammarid amphipods.

DID YOU KNOW?

Gray whales' easygoing demeanor and predilection for near-shore regions makes for frequent, friendly human/whale interactions. Whalers, however, would disagree. They dubbed mother grays "devilfish" for the fierce manner in which they protect their young.

A humpback whale shows off the spectacular breaching behavior for which the species is famous.

WHALE ADVENTURES

Calafia Whales (*www.tourballenas.com*) offers the most convenient gray whale adventure option to those already enjoying their Los Cabos vacations. Round trip-transportation whisks guests from resort to airport to Magdalena Bay and back in a single-day (in time for dinner even), with at least three hours in-between devoted to up-close encounters with gray whales.

Whale Watch Cabo (*www.whalewatch-cabo.com*) gets clients to Magdalena Bay a little slower, but the six-hour van ride (both ways) is worth it for six hours of dedicated whale encounters over the course of the two-day adventure, as well as the incredible scenery en route. One-night in a hotel and all meals are included, as are the photos taken by your expert guide.

WHALE NURSERIES: THE BEST SPOTS FOR VIEWING

If you want an up-close encounter, head to one of these three protected spots where the whales gather to mate or give birth; the lagoons are like training wheels to prep the youngsters for the open ocean.

Laguna Ojo de Liebre (Scammon's Lagoon). Near Guerrero Negro, this lagoon is an L-shaped cut out of Baja's landmass, protected to the west by the jut of a peninsula.

Laguna San Ignacio. To reach the San Ignacio Lagoon, farther south than Scammon's, base yourself in the charming town of San Ignacio, 35 miles away. This lagoon is the smallest of the three, and along with Scammon's, has been designated a U.N. World Heritage site.

Bahía de Magdalena. This stretch of ocean, the farthest south, is kept calm by small, low-lying islands (really just humps of sand) that take the brunt of the ocean's waves. Very few people overnight in nearby San Carlos; most day-trip in from La Paz or Loreto.

WHAT TO EXPECT

The experience at the three lagoons is pretty standard: tours push off in the mornings, in pangas (tiny, low-lying skiffs) that seat about eight. Wear a water-resistant windbreaker— it will be a little chilly, and you're bound to be splashed once or twice.

The captain will drive around slowly, cutting the motor if he nears a whale (they'll never chase whales). Often the whales will approach you, sometimes showing off their babies. They'll gently nudge the boat, at times sinking completely under it and then raising it up a bit to get a good, long scratch.

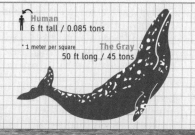

Human
6 ft tall / 0.085 tons

* 1 meter per square   The Gray
50 ft long / 45 tons

Baja whale watching, gray whale

East Cape in One Day

If you do just one thing in the East Cape, make it snorkeling or diving in **Cabo Pulmo National Park**. This protected marine sanctuary is like an undersea fantasia, with the highest concentration of sea life found anywhere in the Sea of Cortez, from unforgettable tornado-like columns of big eye jacks to dolphins, giant sea turtles, moray eels, manta and mobula rays, and several species of sharks.

Cabo San Lucas-based companies like **Cabo Adventures** can provide round-trip transportation to Cabo Pulmo. Driving is part of the fun, though, and allows more freedom to explore on your own schedule. To get there, take either the coast road (primarily dirt) 45 miles from San José del Cabo or the inland Hwy 1, about 65 miles.

Local guides from Cabo Pulmo dive centers will show you the eight fingers of offshore coral reef and prime sites to see incredible marine life. Afterwards, relive your undersea adventures with tacos and beer at **Tacos and Beer**, of course. This little comfort food restaurant offers gorgeous beachfront views and laid-back, local atmosphere, not to mention tasty offerings from the local microbrewery.

Between drive time and dive time, this will take up the majority of the day. Remember, driving at night is never recommended in rural areas due to the dangers of collisions with free-ranging livestock. If there are a few hours of free time left, however, head 30 miles up the road to Buena Vista and spring for the day pass ($30) at **Hotel Buena Vista Beach Resort**. The roomy hot tub gets its hot water from underground thermal hot springs, the pool and beach views are beautiful, generations of family recipes are featured at the beachfront **El Navegante**, and kids will love the Ping-Pong tables.

be in the works. If so, the market could prove to be an even bigger draw, given that Miraflores is famed regionally for its high-quality organic produce, and provides the fruits and vegetables for many of the best restaurants in Los Cabos. ⊠ *Av. Union 13, Miraflores.*

★ **Parque Nacional Cabo Pulmo**

NATIONAL/STATE PARK | At this 27 3/4-square-mile national park, a 20,000-year-old coral reef has been legally protected since 1995 and is home to more than 2,000 different kinds of marine invertebrates—as well as more than 800 species of marine life, from mantas and giant sea turtles to dolphins and sea lions. The park comprises both land and sea, and is renowned among diving aficionados for its eight fingers of hard coral reef,

plus its immense abundance of colorful tropical fish. The best months to visit are August, September, and October, when visibility is highest. The park isn't difficult to access. Head southwest from La Ribera and it's just 8 km (5 miles) from the end of the paved road; it's bordered by Playa Las Barracas in the north and Bahía Los Frailes to the south. It can also be reached by the dirt road running along the coast from San José del Cabo. It'll take you two hours or more this way, but the coast along this route is unmatched. (Though, if it's raining, stick to the paved route.) There are two main dive centers, **Cabo Pulmo Dive Center** and **Cabo Pulmo Sport Center**, offering full gear rentals, kayaks, snorkel gear, and sportfishing tours. ⊠ *Camino Cabo Este, Cabo Pulmo* ⊕ *www.cabopulmopark.com* ⊠ *$5.*

Did You Know?

The East Cape is best known for Parque Nacional Cabo Pulmo, a pristine park covering land, sea, and a vibrant coral reef.

Trópico de Cáncer

MEMORIAL | A globe-shaped monument marks the spot where the Tropic of Cancer line (the northernmost circle of latitude at which the sun can be seen directly overhead on the summer solstice) crosses Baja California Sur. The line separates Earth's temperate zone and the tropics. Of course, Baja is Baja, and you won't detect any difference in climate no matter which side of the line you are on. The geographical milepost is easily seen from the highway, but it's worth getting out of the car to explore the series of shops surrounding it, which offer arts and crafts from local communities. On the western, Pacific Ocean side of Baja California Sur, the Tropic of Cancer line runs between Pescadero and Todos Santos, though it's noted only by a sign. ✉ *Federal Hwy 1, Km 81, Santiago* ✣ *Between Miraflores and Santiago.*

Beaches

Nine Palms

BEACH—SIGHT | There are more than nine palms here, but who's counting? People who brave the dirt road to this off-the-beaten-track beach are here to surf the rippable right-hand point break. It's about an hour drive northeast from San José del Cabo, along with two other great surf spots, Shipwrecks and Punta Perfecta, which are clustered around La Fortuna and Boca de la Vinorama. The best time to surf is during the summer months, when southwesterly swells provide optimal conditions. But for those seeking only sun, sand, and breathtakingly beautiful views, Nine Palms is a year-round pleasure. **Amenities:** none. **Best for:** surfing, swimming, walking. ✉ *Camino Cabo Este, La Fortuna.*

★ Playa La Ribera

BEACH—SIGHT | White sand lines this quiet public beach in La Ribera, a sleepy town just north of Cabo Pulmo National Park. The beach feels almost untouched, with calm water that's great for sportfishing, kayaking, paddleboarding, swimming, and snorkeling. The Four Seasons is just down the beach. **Amenities:** toilets. **Best for:** solitude; snorkeling; swimming. ✉ *Camino Cabo Este, Km 13.5, La Ribera.*

Playa Los Barriles

BEACH—SIGHT | Playa Los Barriles runs the entire length of town, curving gently towards Bahía de las Palmas. Amazingly, it is almost completely free of people, except from November to March, when wind-sports companies offer rentals during the gusty season and it becomes a jumping-off point for activities including kiteboarding, kitesurfing, windsurfing, and foilboarding. Those seeking sun and sea views recline on chaise lounges at beachfront resorts, and those seeking a congenial atmosphere hang out at restaurants or beach bars set just off the main shoreline. **Amenities:** none. **Best for:** walking; swimming; fishing; wind sports. ✉ *Los Barriles.*

🍴 Restaurants

Bay View Bar and Grill

$$ | MEXICAN | Diners on the shaded deck of this restaurant at Hotel Palmas de Cortez enjoy magnificent views of the Bay of Palms, with its azure waters, pristine miles-long beach, and picturesque array of fishing boats. The menu has both Mexican favorites (burritos, enchiladas, and quesadillas) and American ones (cheeseburgers, club sandwiches, and rib-eye steaks), but as at all good East Cape restaurants, seafood is the most satisfying choice. **Known for:** beautiful beach and bay views; fresh local seafood; burgers and steaks. [$] *Average main: $20* ✉ *Hotel Palmas de Cortez, 20 de Noviembre 2, Los Barriles* ☎ *624/205–3607, 624/141–0044* 🌐 *vanwormerresorts.com/restaurants.*

★ Casa de Brasa

$$$$ | SEAFOOD | This brasserie at the Four Seasons is a showcase for all things Baja. A modern reimagining of a traditional Baja *palo de arco* (pergola) shades the alfresco setting; guests are fêted with fresh regional seafood, including tuna, dorado, cabrilla, and chocolate clams; and, of course, there are sweeping views of the beautiful beach. **Known for:** Sea of Cortez views; great service and fresh seafood; Baja wines, premium tequilas, and mezcals. $ *Average main: $31* ✉ *Four Seasons Resort Los Cabos at Costa Palmas, Calle Eureka, La Ribera* ☎ *624/689–0292* ⊕ *www.fourseasons. com/loscabos.*

El Navegante

$$$ | MEXICAN | The dinner menu is forever changing at this family-owned and-run restaurant at Hotel Buena Vista Beach Resort, and that's a good thing. Whether you order soup and salad, steak, or fresh catch of the day prepared any way you like it, this is a one-of-a-kind dining experience with amazing sea views. **Known for:** fresh catch of the day; ever-changing menu; gorgeous ocean-view patio dining. $ *Average main: $25* ✉ *Calle Bonito, Buena Vista* ☎ *624/142–0099* ⊕ *hotel-buenavista.com.*

Lazy Daze Beach Bar

$ | MEXICAN | Lazy days in Los Barriles are best spent at this palapa-shaded spot, which is about 10 feet from a beach volleyball court and only a few steps more from the pristine *play a* that hugs the Bay of Palms for miles in either direction. Put your bare toes in the sand while sipping on margaritas, piña coladas, or ice-cold cervezas and noshing on your standard chicken wings or fish tacos. **Known for:** beachfront setting; ice-cold cervezas; daily food specials. $ *Average main: $10* ✉ *Barricuda Blvd., Los Barriles* ☎ *624/124–8041* ⊕ *lazydazebeachbar.com.*

Palomar Restaurant-Bar

$$ | MEXICAN | Palomar has been an institution in Santiago since 1963, when it was favored by celebrities such as Bing Crosby and John Wayne, and it continues to serve fresh seafood alongside delicious handmade tortillas. Enjoy your food in a shaded garden courtyard, and stop at the bar afterwards to admire the photo collection (owner Sergio Gómez is happy to point out photos of his mother with Crosby and other celebrity snapshots). **Known for:** historical memorabilia; friendly service; fresh catches. $ *Average main: $15* ✉ *Maestros Misiones de 1930, Santiago* ☎ *624/142–0604* ⊘ *Closed Sun.*

☕ Coffee and Quick Bites

Tacos and Beer

$ | MEXICAN | In need of refreshments after a magical day snorkeling in Cabo Pulmo National Park? Stop by Tacos and Beer, and soak up the *muy tranquilo* vibes while you eat delicious seafood tacos and admire views so paradisiacal they look like the set of a Corona commercial. **Known for:** Baja-style fish tacos; locally brewed beer; gorgeous views of Playa Cabo Pulmo and Sea of Cortez. $ *Average main: $5* ✉ *Camino Cabo Este, Cabo Pulmo* ☎ *624/191–3081* ▭ *No credit cards.*

Taquería Pinches Tacos del Toro

$ | MEXICAN | This is the place to go in La Ribera for filling comfort food and local atmosphere, not that there are a lot of other options in this small East Cape community besides the Four Seasons. Although it looks like virtually any roadside Mexican taquería, from the thatched-palm roof to the red-and-white-checkered plastic tablecloths, the quality is a cut above. **Known for:** tacos al pastor; breakfast omelets; aguas frescas. $ *Average main: $5* ✉ *Camino Cabo Este, La Ribera* ☎ *624/228-6295* ▭ *No credit cards.*

🛏 Hotels

Though much of the area is rustic and no-frills, the arrival of a Four Seasons as well as the planned openings of an Amanvari and Soho House are putting the East Cape on the map for travelers who want luxurious, secluded escapes.

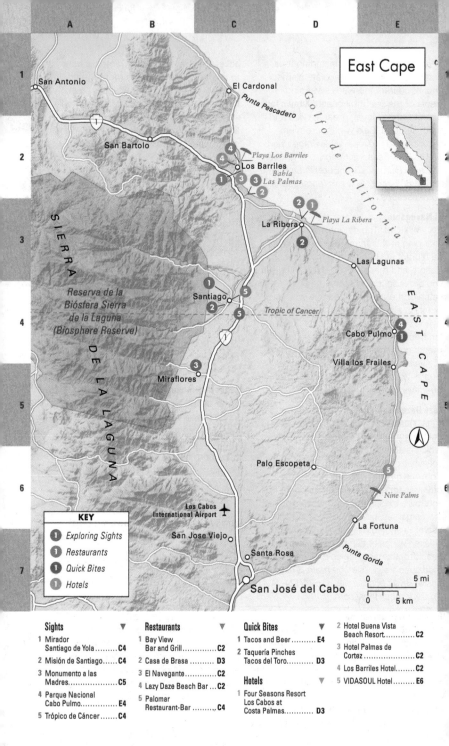

East Cape

San Antonio

San Bartolo

El Cardonal

Punta Pescadero

Golfo de California

Playa Los Barriles

Los Barriles

Bahía Las Palmas

La Ribera

Playa La Ribera

Las Lagunas

Reserva de la Biósfera Sierra de la Laguna (Biosphere Reserve)

Santiago

Tropic of Cancer

Cabo Pulmo

Villa los Frailes

Miraflores

Palo Escopeta

Nine Palms

Los Cabos International Airport

San Jose Viejo

La Fortuna

Santa Rosa

Punta Gorda

San José del Cabo

SIERRA DE LA LAGUNA

EAST CAPE

0   5 mi

0   5 km

KEY
- ① Exploring Sights
- ① Restaurants
- ① Quick Bites
- ① Hotels

Sights ▼
1 Mirador
   Santiago de Yola..........**C4**
2 Misión de Santiago......**C4**
3 Monumento a las
   Madres....................**C5**
4 Parque Nacional
   Cabo Pulmo..............**E4**
5 Trópico de Cáncer.......**C4**

Restaurants ▼
1 Bay View
   Bar and Grill..............**C2**
2 Casa de Brasa **D3**
3 El Navegante..............**C2**
4 Lazy Daze Beach Bar ...**C2**
5 Palomar
   Restaurant-Bar **C4**

Quick Bites ▼
1 Tacos and Beer **E4**
2 Taquería Pinches
   Tacos del Toro...........**D3**

Hotels ▼
1 Four Seasons Resort
   Los Cabos at
   Costa Palmas............**D3**

2 Hotel Buena Vista
   Beach Resort.............**C2**
3 Hotel Palmas de
   Cortez **C2**
4 Los Barriles Hotel........**C2**
5 VIDASOUL Hotel.........**E6**

★ Four Seasons Resort Los Cabos at Costa Palmas

$$$$ | **RESORT** | More than two miles of pristine beach and breathtaking Baja flora surround this five-star resort, where rooms all have spectacular sea views, access to ample amenities, and the personalized luxury only Four Seasons can deliver. **Pros:** chic, contemporary interiors; top-rate spa, on-site dining, and golf course; balconies or plunge pools in every room. **Cons:** expensive; remote location; far from Cabo San Lucas and San José del Cabo. [$] *Rooms from: $1,350* ✉ *Calle Eureka, La Ribera* ☎ *624/689–0292* 🌐 *www.fourseasons.com/loscabos* 🛏 *141 rooms* 🍴 *No meals.*

Hotel Buena Vista Beach Resort

$ | **RESORT** | **FAMILY** | Underground hot springs are the secret ingredient at this benchmark fishing getaway in Buena Vista; for proof, check out the amazing hot tub. **Pros:** amazing fishing; beautiful beach; enormous swimming pool. **Cons:** no refrigerators; only two rooms have TVs; dated decor in some rooms. [$] *Rooms from: $110* ✉ *Calle Bonito, Buena Vista* ☎ *624/142–0099* 🌐 *hotelbuenavista.com* 🛏 *60 rooms* 🍴 *No meals.*

Hotel Palmas de Cortez

$ | **HOTEL** | This tried-and-true fishing resort in Los Barriles continues to impress with its central beachfront location and beautifully landscaped interlocking swimming pools, its on-site dining at Bay View Bar and Grill and Umi Sushi Bar, plus a spa and tennis court. **Pros:** gorgeous swimming pools; fishing charters; on-site dining options. **Cons:** dated decor in older rooms; many rooms lack ocean views; pricey by Los Barriles standards. [$] *Rooms from: $120* ✉ *Calle 20 de Noviembre 2, Los Barriles* ☎ *624/141–0044, 877/777–8862 in the U.S.* 🌐 *vanwormerresorts.com* 🛏 *74 rooms* 🍴 *No meals.*

Los Barriles Hotel

$ | **HOTEL** | Just about every hotel in Los Barriles could aptly be described as old-school, and while this budget-friendly hotel certainly fits the bill, its 20 rooms are comfy and air-conditioned, with two queen-sized beds, mini-refrigerators, and walk-in showers with hand-painted tiles. **Pros:** budget-friendly rates; nice swimming pool; complimentary coffee in the morning. **Cons:** no televisions in the rooms; decor is dated; no beach or ocean views. [$] *Rooms from: $70* ✉ *Apartado, Postal 50, Los Barriles* ☎ *624/141–0024* 🌐 *losbarrileshotel.com* 🛏 *20 rooms* 🍴 *No meals.*

VIDASOUL Hotel

$ | **HOTEL** | Local art and modern architecture, plus beautiful Sea of Cortez and beach views make this solar-powered, eco-friendly lodging one of the top East Cape accommodations. **Pros:** trendy decor; beautiful beach; supercomfy memory foam beds. **Cons:** only accessible via the old dirt East Cape Road; more than a one-hour drive from San José del Cabo; remote from shopping and nightlife areas. [$] *Rooms from: $120* ✉ *Camino Cabo Este 1000, Boca de la Vinorama* ☎ *624/154–6966* 🌐 *www.vidasoul.com* 🛏 *16 rooms* 🍴 *No meals.*

🍸 Nightlife

Crossroads Restaurant

MUSIC CLUBS | On most days, this restaurant at the boutique solar-powered VIDASOUL Hotel is a quiet place to enjoy an organic chicken Marsala or piccata, a margarita, and gorgeous beachfront views of the Sea of Cortez. But on Friday and Saturday nights in-season (November through May), live bands play, and it becomes the best of the scant nightlife options between Los Barriles and San José del Cabo. Locals and visitors alike party down, East Cape style, and the restaurant closes when the last guest goes to bed. ✉ *Camino Cabo Este 1000, Boca de la Vinorama* ☎ *624/154–6966, 626/840–0485 in the U.S.* 🌐 *www.vidasoul.com.*

Smokey's Grill and Cantina

BARS/PUBS | If you're wondering where locals in Los Barriles go after 5 p.m., the answer is Smokey's. This sports-bar style cantina is the *de facto* after-work meeting place for cocktails and cervezas, not only for those working in Los Barriles, but also for much of the East Cape. For visitors the main attraction is the barbecue straight from curing in the on-site smokehouse. Highlights include the pulled pork and the char-grilled chicken breast slathered in Maker's Mark and barbecue sauce. ⊠ *Calle 20 de Noviembre 113, Los Barriles* ☎ *624/141–0294.*

🛍 Shopping

★ Plaza Turística y Artesanal Trópico de Cancer

CRAFTS | The globe-shaped Tropic of Cancer monument inspires many visitors to stop for photos, but the gift shops at the plaza are worth a visit, too. In fact, this may be the best collection of local arts and crafts found anywhere in Los Cabos. Government employees run the various gift shops, each of which spotlights art and local specialty items, including furniture, fruit preserves, piñatas, regional liqueurs, and more. All items are sourced from the communities of Cabo San Lucas, San José del Cabo, Santiago, and other towns and villages throughout the Los Cabos municipality. There is also a beautiful shrine to the Virgin of Guadalupe that is a stop on a local pilgrimage that takes place each year on the day of the virgin (Dec. 12 in Mexico) and ends in nearby Miraflores. ⊠ *Carretera Transpeninsular, Km 81, Santiago* ☺ *Closed Sun.*

Activities

The East Cape is a world-class playground for a wide variety of outdoor sports, from fishing, diving and surfing to camping, hiking, climbing, and more.

Fishing has long been the major tourist attraction in small towns like Los Barriles and Buena Vista, where the larger resorts either maintain their own fishing fleets or have relationships with local charter boats to refer guests looking to get their hooks into marlin, tuna, dorado, wahoo, roosterfish, and more.

Scuba diving has increasingly become more popular since the offshore coral reef at Cabo Pulmo became protected as part of a larger national park in 1995. The effect of this protected status has been remarkable, and Cabo Pulmo now boasts the highest density of marine life of any area in the Sea of Cortez, an abundance that includes sharks, dolphins, giant sea turtles, mobula rays, and hundreds of colorful tropical fish species.

Some East Cape attractions are more seasonal. For example, each winter when strong El Norte winds blow down the Sea of Cortez, small towns like Los Barriles and La Ventana become windsports meccas. Not only do windsurfers flock here, but also kiteboarders, kitesurfers, foilboarders, and others seeking to take advantage of the ideal 18- to 24-knot winds. If winter means wind, summer means surf off some of the East Cape's pristine beaches thanks to often ideal southwesterly swells.

Inland town Santiago, meanwhile, is the jumping-off point for those who love hiking, camping, and climbing. ATVs are particularly popular in Los Barriles, where expats tool around town on them, but rentals are readily available throughout the region.

GOLF

Costa Palmas Golf Club

GOLF | Tee time access at this gorgeous Robert Trent Jones Jr.-designed course is currently restricted to Four Seasons guests and Costa Palmas homeowners, but will also be an amenity for guests at Amanvari and Soho House when those properties open nearby. In the meantime, traffic is light on this 7,221-yard layout, which features spectacular scenery on all 18 holes, including breathtaking backdrops from the nearby Sierra de la Laguna mountain range, and a finish next to the yacht-filled marina. Five sets of tee boxes are on hand for players of various skill levels, as well as two on-site comfort stations/cafés that can be enjoyed by all: Bouchie's and Lucha Libre. Twilight greens fees take effect after 2 p.m. ⊠ *Four Seasons Resort Los Cabos at Costa Palmas, Calle Eureka-Buenavista, La Ribera* ☎ *624/689–0292* ⊕ *www.fourseasons.com/loscabos/golf* ⚲ *18 holes, 7221 yards, Par 72* ⚲ *$300 greens fees for Four Seasons guests; $200 twilight.*

SNORKELING AND SCUBA DIVING

Adventures in Baja

SCUBA DIVING | Transplanted Englishwoman Karen Bradfield is the owner and chief guide for Adventures in Baja, which specializes in small group eco-tours (no plastics used, period) for some of the region's most memorable activities, from whale-watching in Cabo San Lucas and swimming with whale sharks in La Paz to scuba diving in Cabo Pulmo. A national parks certification helps for the latter, as does years of experience with the myriad dive sites in this 27 1/2-square-mile marine sanctuary. Round-trip transportation from Cabo San Lucas is included. ⊠ *Cabo San Lucas* ☎ *612/104–6340* ⊕ *www.adventuresinbaja.com* ⚲ *$235 per person for Cabo Pulmo dive.*

Cabo Pulmo Dive Center

SCUBA DIVING | Cabo Pulmo Dive Center provides some of the more exceptional dives in the area and has everything you need, including certification classes (multiday). This 5-star PADI-certified outfit is a local family-run shop. It's right on the beach and offers full diving services, as well as cheap rooms at the adjoining solar-powered Cabo Pulmo Beach Resort from $100 per night. ⊠ *Camino Cabo Este, Cabo Pulmo* ☎ *624/141–0726* ⊕ *www.cabopulmo.com* ⚲ *Two-tank diving from $120 without equipment rentals; snorkeling from $60 without equipment rentals.*

Cabo Pulmo Sport Center

DIVING/SNORKELING | Cabo Pulmo Sport Center offers snorkeling tours of Cabo Pulmo National Park with a certified guide. A mask, fins, water and snacks are included. The center also has a casita and a couple of simple bungalows for rent (from $59 per night), should you decide to extend your stay. ⊠ *Camino Cabo Este, Cabo Pulmo* ⚲ *Acceso Principal a la Playa (Main Beach Access)* ☎ *624/157–9795* ⊕ *www.cabopulmosportcenter.com* ⚲ *$60.*

SPA

Oasis Spa at Four Seasons Resort Los Cabos

FITNESS/HEALTH CLUBS | FAMILY | Romantic experiences are a specialty at Oasis Spa, where two of the eight on-site treatment rooms are set aside solely for couples. But other massages are expertly applied, too, including the signature 90-minute version which incorporates hot stones and indigenous herbs. Deep tissue, Thai, reflexology, and pampering four-hands massages are also on the menu, as are beauty services courtesy of the Rossano Ferretti Salon, including haircuts and a shampoo blow-dry, beard shaping and trims, and shape-ups for kids. Those who want to maintain their workout regimen on vacation will find a state-of-the-art fitness center with Sea of Cortez views, as well as tennis and basketball courts, and an Olympics-style lap pool. ⊠ *Four Seasons Resort Los Cabos at Costa Palmas, Calle Eureka, La Ribera* ☎ *624/689–0292* ⊕ *www.fourseasons.com/loscabos/spa/.*

SPORTFISHING

Outside Parque Marino Nacional Cabo Pulmo (where you aren't allowed to fish), just north of Cabo Pulmo, there are a number of excellent spots to try your luck at hooking a marlin, tuna, giant sea bass, or snapper. Many resorts in Los Barriles or Buena Vista were built with charter fishing in mind, and it's easy to book a fishing trip through the resort. Or stop by some of the local dive shops and make arrangements for them to take you out.

Hotel Palmas de Cortez

FISHING | Hotel Palmas de Cortez is the gold standard for charter fishing in Los Barriles, offering four sizes of fishing vessels, ranging from a super panga (a 25-foot boat which can accommodate three anglers for $415 per day) to a super-deluxe cruiser (35- or 36-foot boat for six anglers starting at $900), all of which leave from the beachfront dock. Lower rates are available to those who opt for lodging and fishing packages, and a weigh-in station is on hand for the several big tournaments based at the hotel each year, including the East Cape Dorado Shootout in July and the East Cape Gold Cup Wahoo Jackpot in August. ⊠ *Calle 20 de Noviembre 2, Los Barriles* ☎ *624/141–0044, 877/777–8862 in the U.S.* ⊕ *vanwormerresorts.com* ☞ *From $415.*

WIND SPORTS

Exotikite Kiteboarding

WATER SPORTS | Meet the kiteboarding king of Los Barriles. Like most wind-sports specialists in Los Barriles, Exotikite is only open during the windy season (Nov. to Apr.), offering rentals and intensive, professionally guided lesson packages, with "La Playa" studio accommodations available next door. Surfing and foilboarding lessons are also offered, as are SUP rentals. ⊠ *Accesso a la Playa, Los Barriles* ☎ *624/165–2612, 541/380–0948 in the U.S.* ⊕ *www.exotikite.com.*

Vela Baja

WINDSURFING | Vela Baja is open every day during the East Cape wind-sports season (mid-November to mid-March), arranging guided tours for windsurfing, kiteboarding, mountain biking, free diving, and stand-up paddleboarding. Windsurfing is their specialty, with rentals available by the hour ($35), half-day ($60), or day ($80). Lessons start at $90. ⊠ *Hotel Playa del Sol, Calle 20 de Noviembre Unica, Los Barriles* ☎ *624/150–4146* ⊕ *velabaja. com.*

BAJA CALIFORNIA

7

WITH ENSENADA AND THE VALLE DE GUADALUPE WINE REGION

Updated by
Marlise Kast-Myers

⊙ Sights	🍴 Restaurants	🛏 Hotels	🛍 Shopping	🍸 Nightlife
★★★☆☆	★★★★★	★★★★☆	★★★★☆	★★★☆☆

WELCOME TO BAJA CALIFORNIA

TOP REASONS TO GO

★ **Scenic Driving:** Driving along the Pacific coast south of Tijuana on the Carretera Transpeninsular (Highway 1) is half the fun of traveling to Baja's historic missions and remote beaches.

★ **Sampling Mexico's Wine:** The Valle de Guadalupe, near Ensenada, is a gorgeous valley blanketed with sprawling vineyards and boutique hotels ranging from eco-lofts to country inns.

★ **Whale-Watching:** Gray whales swim to Baja California every winter to mate and calve in three lagoons on the peninsula's western coast.

★ **Shopping for Handicrafts:** In Ensenada stores are filled with unique souvenirs in addition to the usual sunglasses and sombreros.

★ **Beach Towns:** Soak up the sun and party on Rosarito Beach, just across the border from California, or indulge in fried lobster by the sea in Puerto Nuevo.

Flanked by the Pacific Ocean to the west and the Sea of Cortez to the east, Baja California (also called Baja California Norte, or simply Baja Norte) comprises the northern half of the Baja peninsula. The majority of the narrow state is accessible by the Carretera Transpeninsular (Highway 1), but it's easy to feel as if you've gone far off the grid when a hundred miles of barren land stands between you and the nearest town or gas station. Embrace the feeling; Baja is really Mexico's Wild West and has the stark desert landscapes, secluded coves, and striking mountains to prove it.

1 Rosarito. Just 16 km (10 miles) south of the U.S. border are Rosarito's beautiful wide beaches, fronted by a less-than-beautiful town full of touristy bars targeting college students looking for a weekend of partying.

2 Puerto Nuevo. San Diegans cross the border for the fried lobster that made this sleepy fishing village famous.

3 Valle de Guadalupe. Explore the Ruta de Vino dotted with award-winning wineries, farm-to-table restaurants, and boutique hotels with unpretentious hosts.

4 Ensenada. A seaport town sandwiched by beaches, Ensenada is home to some of the best fish tacos and margaritas Mexico has to offer.

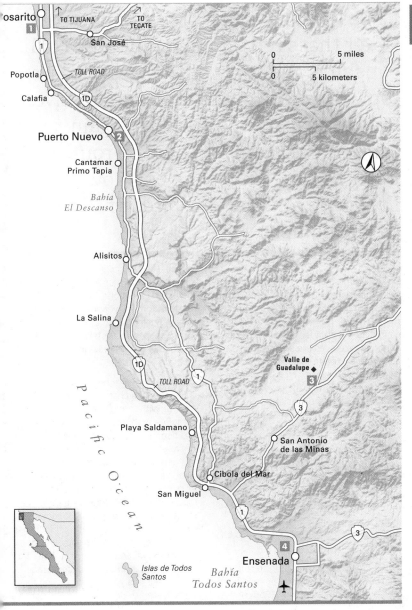

osarito

TO TIJUANA

TO TECATE

San José

1

TOLL ROAD

Popotla

Calafia

1D

Puerto Nuevo 2

Cantamar
Primo Tapia

Bahía
El Descanso

Alisitos

La Salina

1D

TOLL ROAD 1

Valle de
Guadalupe
3

3

Playa Saldamano

San Antonio
de las Minas

Cibola del Mar

San Miguel

1

Pacific Ocean

Islas de Todos
Santos

Bahía
Todos Santos

Ensenada 4

3

0   5 miles
0   5 kilometers

The northern Baja peninsula (aka Baja California) may be far from Los Cabos in the south, but it's no less dreamlike: its beaches have fine brown sand, water that's refreshing but not too cold, sunshine, and some of the West Coast's top waves. The beach towns themselves are not as inspiring, but then again, they can serve as sunny detours en route to Baja's biggest draws: the port town of Ensenada and the vineyards of the Valle de Guadalupe.

Baja California's proximity to Southern California makes it a popular weekend road trip destination. Rosarito, just thirty minutes away from the U.S. border, is a nightlife hot spot for rowdy American spring breakers, as are several towns along the Carretera Transpeninsular (Highway 1). The party crowd can interrupt the serenity that these towns offer midweek before the masses arrive, its wide and long beaches often full of ATVs and horses trotting in the sand. But the longer you stay, the more you'll find that partying is just a small part of the picture. The true riches of Rosarito are found in the authentic Mexican experience, in interactions with the genuine locals, in the courtyard shops and eateries, and in the punchy waves near the pier or further along the coast at Km 38 and Las Gaviotas.

Twenty minutes south is Puerto Nuevo, a small fishing village whose famous fried lobster put it on the map in 1956. These days it's best to stop in for lunch en route to other destinations; be prepared for the reality that many vendors and parking attendants in town may approach to ask you to shop, park, or take a look at a menu. Still, if lobster is on the mind, it's a must-visit town.

The jewel of Baja's beachside towns is Ensenada, a charming fisherman's enclave with the feel of a small village, complete with beachside trinket stores and fish taco stands (the town's beaches, conversely, are not a big draw). Along this part of the peninsula, towns are close together, and the essentials (gas, food, lodging) are never far. Ensenada's main "downtown" drag along Calle Primera is worth checking out, though not for everyone. You'll get a repeat of Rosarito's party scene alongside its souvenir shops, tattoo parlors, and motels, but there are a smattering of boutiques, food carts, and restaurants well worth pausing for.

Thirty minutes inland, Valle de Guadalupe is Baja Norte's pièce de résistance, showcasing Mexico's finest wines and trendiest places to stay. Along the Ruta del Vino are endless vineyards, olive groves, orange orchards, and architectural masterpieces at hip B&Bs. From country inns and luxurious haciendas to container hotels and glamping tents, there's no shortage of lodging—or wine tastings—in this region. Capitalizing on the fertile land are talented young chefs serving refreshing, experimental takes on regional cuisine, their farm-to-table restaurants operating right in the middle of dreamy ranches.

Planning

Getting Here and Around

The main artery of the Baja peninsula is a road of legend: Carretera Transpeninsular (Highway 1) winds down from Tijuana to Los Cabos through deserts and coastal bluffs, past fertile estuaries, and through bleak towns that eke out a few crops from the dry soil. A faster alternative to the coastal road is Highway 1D connecting Tijuana to Ensenada. Three toll booths in Tijuana, Rosarito Beach, and Ensenada charge MX$50 to pass.

If you're driving into Baja California from San Diego during peak hours, you might try heading 35 km (19 miles) east to the much less congested border crossing at Tecate. From there Highway 3 takes you south through the Valle de Guadalupe to Ensenada.

Highway 3 continues southeast from Ensenada over the San Martír Pass, where it meets Highway 5. From here you can head north to Mexicali or south to San Felipe, where the road ends. In northern Baja, Highway 2 hugs the border from Mexicali to Tijuana. Although the hairpin turns make for beautiful

overlooks during the day, the road east of Tecate is best avoided at night.

If you're driving in from the United States, purchase Mexican insurance (required) from any of the brokers near the border. It's also possible to rent a car in Tijuana or Mexicali from any of the major chains. The only San Diego–based rental agency allowing vehicles to cross into Mexico is California Baja Rent-A-Car. Rates include insurance coverage for both sides of the border. Pack plenty of water and make sure your tires are in good shape: although the major highways are well-maintained, a number of smaller roads are unpaved.

There are few international flights into Tijuana, Baja California's only major airport; most travelers access the area from the border at San Diego. Aeroméxico flies to Los Cabos, to La Paz on the Baja Peninsula, and to several cities in mainland Mexico. Alaska Airlines, Spirit, Southwest, United, Delta, and American all fly into Los Cabos. It's also possible to park in the secured lot in San Diego at the Cross Border Xpress (CBX). This pedestrian bridge allows passengers to cross the border between Mexico and the United States.

Restaurants

With a modern history not much older than the Carretera Transpeninsular, most Baja California towns have appropriated their local cuisine from the cultures of mainland Mexico. In many regions, the best lunches and dinners are had at curbside taco stands, where fried fish is served atop tortillas—with shredded cabbage and salsa to add at your discretion. There are exceptional restaurants popping up in Ensenada and Valle de Guadalupe where award-winning chefs are offering a farm-to-table experience. When restaurants are limited, opt for the local hot spot, which is always a better option than paying premium for half-baked takes on "international cuisine."

Hotels

Expect private bathrooms, daily housekeeping service, Wi-Fi, a secure parking lot, and clean quarters in all but the most basic of establishments. Many hotels offer breakfast for an extra fee, and swimming pools are prevalent. Luxury is never far in Baja Norte; almost every touristed locale has at least one "Resort & Spa" that tacks on Jacuzzis, massages, and dollar signs to the above basics (especially along the coast near Ensenada). Be aware that only camping (no hotels) is available in some of Baja Norte's smaller towns, including those on Highway 1 between Ensenada and San Quintín, and those on Highway 3 between Ensenada and San Felipe.

What It Costs in U.S. Dollars

	$	$$	$$$	$$$$
RESTAURANTS				
	under $12	$12–$20	$21–$30	over $30
HOTELS				
	under $150	$150–$250	$251–$300	over $300

Restaurant and hotel reviews have been shortened. For full information, visit Fodors.com.

When to Go

Like the American Southwest, Baja California's weather is conducive to year-round travel, though "peak season" will have a different meaning for beach goers and marine-life enthusiasts. The deserts can be sweltering between May and October, and parts of the Pacific coast are chilly between November and February. Whale-watching season on the Pacific runs roughly from December to late March, and although fishing is possible all year-round, local experts consider the summer months the best time to hook a big one.

Rosarito

29 km (18 miles) south of Tijuana.

Southern Californians use Rosarito (population 70,000) as a weekend getaway, and during school vacations, especially spring break, the crowd becomes one big party. Off-season, the area becomes a ghost town. The beach here, which stretches from the power plant at the north end of town to about 8 km (5 miles) south, is long with beautiful sand and sunsets, but it's less romantic for the party scene that booms every few minutes.

If staying the night, head out to the beach near the pier in front of Rosarito Beach Hotel, or hire a horse at the north or south end of Boulevard Benito Juárez for $45 per hour. Wine tours can be booked through Rosarito Beach Hotel.

GETTING HERE AND AROUND

Rosarito is off of Highway 1 about 30 minutes south of the border. Follow the exit road directly into town.

CAR RENTAL Alamo. ⊠ *Blvd. Cuauhtemoc 1705, Zona Río* ☎ *664/686–4040* ⊕ *www.alamo.com.mx.* **California Baja Rent-A-Car.** ⊠ *9245 Jamacha Blvd., Spring Valley* ☎ *619/470–7368* ⊕ *www.cabaja.com.*

◉ Sights

Claudius

WINERY/DISTILLERY | As Rosarito's only wine production facility, this winery brings grapes from neighboring valleys to create remarkable blends, such as their 2016 Merlot. All the wines by owner Julio Benito Martin are organic and are best appreciated with the winemaker himself, who has passion behind every pour. The tasting room is ideal for those who want to enjoy local wines near the border without driving the distance to Valle de Guadalupe. ⊠ *Blvd. Hisense 3722, col Amp Benito Juárez* ☎ *661/850–1339* 🍷 *5 wine tastings $18* ⊗ *Closed Sat. and Sun.*

Just across the border from the U.S., Rosarito's beaches are popular with the spring break crowd.

Beaches

Rosarito Beach

BEACH—SIGHT | Directly behind Rosarito Beach Hotel is your best bet for a true Baja beach experience. Fine sand, a wide strand, palapa umbrellas, and rolling waves near the pier make this a top choice south of the border. As Rosarito's most popular beach, it's also the hub for water sports and beach activities, meaning sunbathing might be interrupted by ATVs, horses, and partiers. Plenty of bars and restaurants are scattered nearby in downtown, and decent waves can be found between Rosarito and La Fonda at Km 59; the best breaks are around Km 38 approaching Puerto Nuevo. Point breaks and beach breaks abound the farther south you go, and you'll be treated to stunning coastlines where no-name breaks might beckon you toward the water. Park in a secured, paid lot (there's one at Rosarito Beach Hotel); and never leave valuables in your vehicle. Equipment rental, food, and restrooms can be found at Rosarito Beach Hotel. **Amenities:** food and drink; parking (fee); toilets; water sports. **Best for:** partiers; surfing; walking. ✉ *Blvd. Benito Juárez 31, Playas de Rosarito.*

Restaurants

Colectivo Surf Tasting Room

$ | **SEAFOOD** | If you need fuel after a day at the beach, walk across the street at Km 41 to this two-story blue collective where you'll find everything from poke bowls to coffee to craft beer and mezcal. A tribute to surfing and all-things-local, Colectivo Surf serves produce from local farmers, fish from *pangueros* (fisherman) along Baja's coast, organic wine from Valle de Guadalupe, and small batch beers from their own brewery. **Known for:** live music Thurs.–Sun.; crispy fish tacos; artisanal beers on tap. [$] *Average main: $10* ✉ *Carretera libre Tijuana Rosarito–Ensenada, Km 41, Playas de Rosarito* ✥ *Five minutes south of Rosarito* ☎ *661/125–4144* 🌐 *www.colectivosurf.com.*

El Nido Steakhouse

$$$ | STEAKHOUSE | A dark, wood-paneled restaurant with leather booths, Mexican antiques, and a large central fireplace, this is one of Rosarito's oldest eateries, and the best in town for atmosphere. Diners unimpressed with newer, fancier places come here for grilled venison, lamb, and quail from the owner's farm in the Baja wine country. **Known for:** tortillas made table-side; strong margaritas; charming patio. $ *Average main: $30* ✉ *Benito Juárez 67* ☎ *661/612–1430* ⊕ *www.elnidorosarito.net.*

★ Mi Casa Supper Club

$$ | INTERNATIONAL | What began as an underground supper club in the home of Dennis and Bo Bendana is now the leading restaurant in Rosarito. Inspired by the founders' international travels, the decor reflects their love for Morocco and Bali while the menu from chef Guillermo Trexo celebrates the Mediterranean and Mexico. **Known for:** red velvet churros with dark chocolate; Sunday brunch and live music; seven-course tasting menu. $ *Average main: $18* ✉ *Estero 54, San Antonio Del Mar* ☎ *664/609–3459* ⊕ *www.micasasupperclub.com* ⊗ *Closed Mon.–Wed. No breakfast or lunch Thurs.–Fri.*

Susanna's

$$ | ECLECTIC | In addition to the fresh Southern California cuisine, many come to this restaurant to connect with the charming owner Susanna who moved to Rosarito years ago to open a furniture shop. Her love for fine food prevailed, thus turning her store into a restaurant that makes people feel right at home. **Known for:** fresh California cuisine; homemade breads; sweet dressings and glazes. $ *Average main: $16* ✉ *Blvd. Benito Juárez 4356, Publo Plaza, Playas de Rosarito* ☎ *661/613–1187* ⊕ *www.susannasinrosarito.com* ⊗ *Closed Tues.*

🛏 Hotels

Rosarito Beach Hotel & Spa

$$ | HOTEL | Charm and location have the slight edge over comfort at this landmark hotel built in 1924. **Pros:** close to the beach; antique charm; good Sunday brunch. **Cons:** older furnishings; overpriced; slow elevator. $ *Rooms from: $190* ✉ *Blvd. Benito Juárez 31, Centro, 22710* ✛ *In front of Rosarito Beach Pier* ☎ *661/612–0144, 800/343–8582* ⊕ *www.rosaritobeachhotel.com* ⇝ *495 rooms* ⦿ *No meals.*

🅨 Nightlife

Papas & Beer

BARS/PUBS | Papas & Beer, one of the most popular bars in Baja Norte, draws a young, energetic spring-break crowd for drinking and dancing on the beach. The $3.50 beers and mechanical bull make for an entertaining combination. ✉ *Corona-do 400, 22710 Playas de Rosarito* ✛ *On beach off Blvd. Benito Juárez* ☎ *661/612–0444* ⊕ *www.papasandbeer.com.*

🏃 Activities

Rosarito Ocean Sports

KAYAKING | FAMILY | The ocean sports center in the heart of Rosarito rents kayaks, paddleboards, snorkeling gear, Jet Skis, and scuba diving equipment. ✉ *Blvd. Benito Juárez, 890-7, Playas de Rosarito* ☎ *661/100–2196* ⊕ *www.rosaritooceansports.com* ⛵ *Kayak rental $20/hr; diving trips from $100.*

Puerto Nuevo

19 km (12 miles) south of Rosarito.

Southern Californians regularly cross the border to indulge in the classic Puerto Nuevo meal: lobster fried in hot oil and served with refried beans, rice, homemade tortillas, salsa, and lime. In 1956 local Susana Diaz Plascencia first created the fried-lobster recipe that put Puerto Nuevo on the culinary map. Now at least 20 restaurants are packed into this village; nearly all offer the same menu, but the quality varies drastically; some establishments cook up live lobsters, while others swap in frozen critters. In most places prices are based on size; a medium lobster with all the fixings will cost you about $20.

Though the fried version is the Puerto Nuevo classic, some restaurants also offer steamed or grilled lobsters.

The town itself is dated, with waitstaff standing curbside to pressure tourists in passing cars to stop in for the day's catch. Watch your step along steep and uneven sidewalks where gaping holes can easily ruin a vacation. Still it's the best spot along the coast to try fresh lobster at an unbeatable price. Expect a table-side serenade of mariachi music. For lodging you're better off renting a beach house in the neighboring community of Las Gaviotas or heading to a hotel north in Rosarito or south in Ensenada. Most accommodations in the town of Puerto Nuevo are in desperate need of a face-lift.

Artisans' markets and stands throughout the village sell serapes, paintings, ponchos, sombreros, T-shirts, and sour tamarind candy; the shops closest to the cliffs have the best selection.

GETTING HERE AND AROUND
Puerto Nuevo sits just beside the Carretera Transpeninsular (Highway 1). When you pull off the highway and enter the town, find a parking spot (free unless otherwise marked) and hop out. There's no other transport to speak of (or needed) in this five-block hamlet.

🍴 Restaurants

La Casa de la Langosta
$$ | SEAFOOD | FAMILY | Seafood soup and grilled fish are options at the "House of Lobster," but clearly the lobster, fried

Puerto-Nuevo style, is the star. This is one of the best spots in town to try the deep-fried recipe created by Susana Diaz Plascencia in 1956; otherwise, try their fresh lobster steamed or stewed with seafood and salsa inside a traditional molcajete stone. **Known for:** fresh marlin soup; large portions; lobster prepared five different ways. $ *Average main: $20* ✉ *Av. Renteria 3, Km 44* ☎ *661/614–1072* ⊕ *www.casadelalangosta.com.*

🛏 Hotels

Puerto Nuevo Hotel & Villas
$ | RESORT | FAMILY | This '90s-era Puerto Nuevo property is comprised of a hotel and villas and is located just beyond the archway into Puerto Nuevo's lobster village. **Pros:** nice-size rooms; convenient location; good ocean views. **Cons:** rooms a little spartan; dark rooms; loud beach music. $ *Rooms from: $132* ✉ *Carretera Tijuana–Ensenada, Km 44.5* ✛ *Just past Puerto Nuevo in Ensenada direction* ☎ *661/614–1488, 877/315–1002* ⊕ *www.puertonuevohotelyvillas.com* ⇄ *257 rooms* ⏋ *No meals.*

Valle de Guadalupe

80 km (50 miles) southeast of Rosarito.

The Valle de Guadalupe, 15 minutes northeast of Ensenada on Carretera 3, is filled with vineyards, wineries, and rambling hacienda-style estates. Although Mexican wines are still relatively unknown in the United States, the industry is exploding in Mexico, and the Valle de Guadalupe is responsible for some 90% of the country's production. In 2004 there were five wineries in production, and today there are more than 120. Along with this splurge of growth comes award-winning chefs setting up "farm-to-fork" restaurants where nearly everything on their menu is harvested right outside their door. Designers, architects, and hoteliers are getting in on the action with dreamy properties ranging from villas and ranches to haciendas and eco-lofts. Lavender fields and bougainvillea add a splash of color to hillsides framing alfresco eateries with menus that will put most culinary destinations to shame. It's the patchwork of vineyards producing impressive blends that's keeping visitor count high.

With a region that combines the right heat, soil, and a thin morning fog, some truly world-class boutique wineries have developed in the Valle de Guadalupe, most in the past decade. Many of these are open to the public; some require appointments. Several tour companies, including Bajarama Tours (☎ *646/178-3252*), leave from Ensenada on tours that include visits to wineries, a historical overview, transportation, and lunch. Better yet, visit the wineries yourself by car, as they all cluster in a relatively small area. Also worth a look is winemaker Hugo D'Acosta's school, which brings in some 30 young winemakers to use common facilities to make their own blends. The facilities are on the site of an old olive oil press (a few antique presses remain in the outlying buildings), and the grounds are augmented with artwork made from recycled wine bottles and other materials.

It seems that it's not only Mexican wine that's being discovered, but the potential of Guadalupe as a "wine destination," along with the mixed blessings that accompany such discovery. Consequences of its growth include overdevelopment and water shortages. Many locals are fighting to keep it from becoming the next Napa Valley.

WHEN TO GO

The ideal time to visit Valle de Guadalupe's wine country is in April to May or October to November to avoid the scorching heat and busloads of tourists. The annual Grape Harvest Festival (Fiestas de la Vendimia) is in August. This 21-day celebration brings in thousands of wine lovers who commemorate the harvest with wine tastings, cultural blessings, live music, and elaborate feasts. Be sure to make hotel reservations well in advance.

GETTING HERE AND AROUND

If you're not on a tour, a private car (or hired taxi) is essential for touring the wine country. Main roads through the valley are paved. Once you branch off toward vineyards, you'll likely be on dirt roads, although progress is being made to smooth out roads to the larger wineries. The turnoffs for the major wineries are well marked; if you're looking for a smaller destination, you may end up doing a few loops or asking a friendly bystander. The general area is not too spread out, but you'll need to drive from one winery to the other. Watch out for hidden stop signs at nearly every street crossing. You can arrange a half- or full-day tour with many of the taxi drivers in Ensenada, and some drivers in Tecate may also be willing to take you. Expect to pay around $120 for a full day of transportation.

ESSENTIALS

Banks are few and far between in this area, so get cash before arriving. Nearly every business accepts credit cards and U.S. dollars. There are two gas stations in town: one at the entrance to the valley near Ensenada, and the second where Highway 3 meets Highway 1.

◉ Sights

Adobe Guadalupe

WINERY/DISTILLERY | Adobe Guadalupe makes an array of fascinating old-world-style blends named after angels. Don't miss the Kerubiel, which is a blockbuster blend; the Serafiel, Gabriel, and Miguel are also excellent. Gaining wide notice is the Jardín Romántico—80% Chardonnay—and of course the powerful mezcal, appropriately named Lucifer. Tastings are offered daily 10–6 and include four reds

Adobe Guadalupe Winery and Inn was one of the first vineyards in the region and names its wines after angels.

for $15 (free to hotel guests). Be sure to visit the wine store and tapas food truck on your way out. ✉ *Off Carretera Tecate–Ensenada, Guadalupe* ✛ *Turn at sign and drive 6 km (4 miles)* ☎ *646/155–2094* ⊕ *www.adobeguadalupe.com.*

Baron Balché

WINERY/DISTILLERY | Despite up-and-coming wineries fighting for the spotlight, this premier producer is still considered the Rolls-Royce of Valle de Guadalupe's wineries. Logos on the premium line are based on Mayan numbers, with outstanding selections like the Balché UNO, a Grenache with hints of raspberry and caramel. The Balché CERO 100% Nebbiolo is the king of their wines, having aged four years in the barrel. Even their younger wines are exceptional, but expect to pay a hefty price to try them. Tastings for top selections will cost you about $50, but considering you are sampling $250 bottles of wine, it just might be worth it. Be sure to end your wine tour here, otherwise the rest of your tastings might pale in comparison. ✉ *Ej. El Porvenir* ☎ *646/155–2141* ⊕ *www.baronbalche.com.*

Casa de Piedra

WINERY/DISTILLERY | The brainchild of Hugo D'Acosta, Casa de Piedra is part of an impressive portfolio that includes Paralelo, Aborigen, and La Borde Vieille, known for its Mexican and French blends. Try Casa de Piedra's flagship wine Contraste or their newer sparkling wines. The space is interesting and modern, designed by the winemaker's architect brother. Visits are by reservation only. ✉ *Carretera Tecate–Ensenada, Km 93.5, San Antonio de las Minas* ☎ *646/155–5267* ⊕ *www. vinoscasadepiedra.com* ⊘ *Closed Sun.*

El Cielo

WINERY/DISTILLERY | Considered a giant among the region's vineyards, this winery produces 38,000 cases of wine, has its own concert venue, private villas, and the popular restaurant Latitude 32. Most stop by to sample the fine blends named after constellations in honor of the owner's love for astronomy. Behind the barrel is winemaker Jesus Rivera, responsible for much of the success of neighboring wineries where he previously consulted.

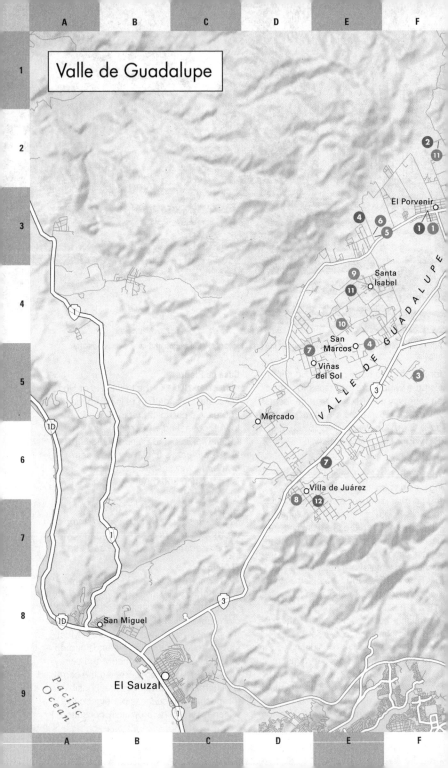

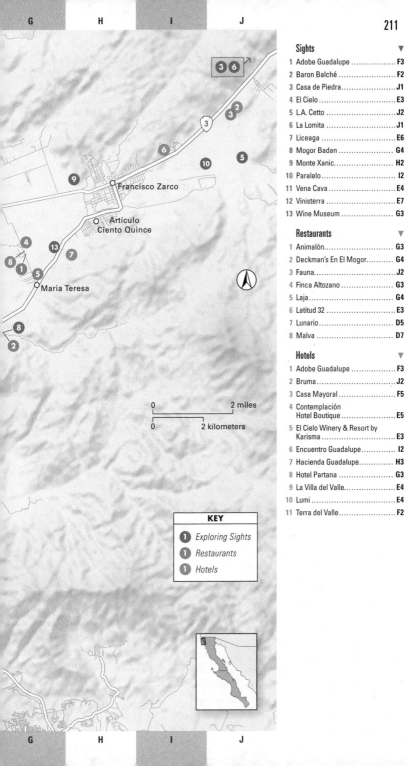

Sights ▼

1 Adobe Guadalupe **F3**
2 Baron Balché **F2**
3 Casa de Piedra..................... **J1**
4 El Cielo **E3**
5 L.A. Cetto **J2**
6 La Lomita **J1**
7 Liceaga **E6**
8 Mogor Badan **G4**
9 Monte Xanic....................... **H2**
10 Paralelo............................ **I2**
11 Vena Cava **E4**
12 Vinisterra **E7**
13 Wine Museum **G3**

Restaurants ▼

1 Animalón............................ **G3**
2 Deckman's En El Mogor.......... **G4**
3 Fauna................................ **J2**
4 Finca Altozano **G3**
5 Laja **G4**
6 Latitud 32 .... **E3**
7 Lunario.............................. **D5**
8 Malva **D7**

Hotels ▼

1 Adobe Guadalupe **F3**
2 Bruma............................... **J2**
3 Casa Mayoral **F5**
4 Contemplación
  Hotel Boutique **E5**
5 El Cielo Winery & Resort by
  Karisma **E3**
6 Encuentro Guadalupe.............. **I2**
7 Hacienda Guadalupe.............. **H3**
8 Hotel Partana **G3**
9 La Villa del Valle................... **E4**
10 Lumi **E4**
11 Terra del Valle...................... **F2**

Francisco Zarco

Artículo
Ciento Quince

Maria Teresa

KEY

1 *Exploring Sights*
1 *Restaurants*
1 *Hotels*

0   2 miles

0   2 kilometers

For an elegant Chardonnay, try Capricornius, or for an Italian grape blend of Nebbiolo and Sangiovese, the Perseus aged 24 months in French oak barrels is also wonderful. The Orion is one of their most popular reds. For the jewel of El Cielo, go big with their reserved collection, Estrellas (stars) that have been preserved up to 20 years. Tastings and tours are available daily for $17. ⊠ *Parcela . 118, Km 7.5* ☎ *646/155–2220* ⊕ *www. vinoselcielo.com.*

★ L.A. Cetto

WINERY/DISTILLERY | L.A. Cetto is a giant that produces more than 1.2 million cases of wine each year, making it the closest thing to a California wine country experience south of the border. When tasting or buying, avoid the more affordable wines, and go straight for the premiums. Having earned over 530 international awards, they are well known for their lovely Nebbiolo and Chardonnay, and their nicely balanced Don Luis Concordia. Don't miss the Peninsula Espaldera, a Sangiovese-Aglianico blend with aromas of black fruit and toffee. The largest winery in Mexico, this is also one of the busiest in the area. Tours take place daily 10–5 on the half hour. ⊠ *Carretera Tecate–Ensenada, Km 73.5* ☎ *646/155–2179, 646/197–5498* ⊕ *www. lacetto.mx.*

★ La Lomita

WINERY/DISTILLERY | Owned by Fernando Pérez Castro, this new-generation winery creates rich wines made with 100% local grapes. With six labels under their barrel, their blends are sold to top restaurants and hotels in Mexico City, Riviera Maya, and Cabo. The preferred Sacro—a mix of Cabernet Sauvignon and Merlot—has hints of pomegranate, cherry, pepper, berries, and maple syrup, while the Tinto de la Hacienda has characteristics of compote and jam. For something unique, try Pagano, their rebel baby Grenache that comes in a square bottle. The circular tasting room overlooks a pit of shiny wine tanks where vines dangle from

above. It's the place where cool people sip, especially San Diego day-trippers who Instagram their pours in front of murals by Mexican artist Jorge Tellaeche. Tastings are Thursday to Sunday 12–4. ⊠ *Plot 13, San Marcos Village, San Antonio de las Minas* ☎ *646/156–8466* ⊕ *www.lomita.mx* ⊟ *Tastings $20* ⊘ *Closed Mon. and Tues.*

Liceaga

WINERY/DISTILLERY | Neighboring Casa de Piedra, this winery produces a variety of Merlot- and Cabernet-heavy blends. Try Liceaga's "L," a complex and elegant wine with hints of cherry, blackberry, cassis, plum and pepper. The tasting room is open most days 11–5, and they have live music Saturdays from July through September. ⊠ *Carretera Tecate–Ensenada, Km 93, San Antonio de las Minas* ☎ *646/155–3281* ⊕ *www.vinosliceaga. com* ⊟ *Four tastings, $9.*

Mogor Badan

WINERY/DISTILLERY | One of the area's few vineyards to offer organic wines, this 1950s ranch has gained renown for whites such as their remarkably fragrant Chasselas del Mogor. Their newer Pirineo blends a contemporary Mexican Grenache with a French Syrah. Wine tastings are available by reservation only on weekends 11–5 in their underground cave. After wine tasting, dine at the neighboring garden restaurant, operated by the talented chef Drew Deckman. ⊠ *Rancho El Mogor, Carretera Tecate–Ensenada, Km 85.5, San Antonio de las Minas* ☎ *646/156–8156* ⊟ *3 tastings with appetizers, $25.*

Monte Xanic

WINERY/DISTILLERY | Tastings at Monte Xanic take place at the edge of a lovely pond and include three reds and two whites for $15. Most impressive is their consistency, right down to the cheapest table wines. Tastings and tours are available by appointment only. Be sure to check out the impressively styled cellar. ⊠ *Careterra Tecate–Ensenada, Km 70* ☎ *646/117–0027* ⊕ *www.montexanic.com.mx.*

Paralelo

WINERY/DISTILLERY | Paralelo was built by the Hugo d'Acosta clan as "parallel" to Casa de Piedra. The winery makes two red blends—the excellent and balanced Arenal and the heavier, minerally Colina—as well as a Sauvignon Blanc Emblema. A reservation is necessary. ✉ *Carretera Tecate–Ensenada, Km 73.5* ☎ *646/156–5268* 🎟 *Tastings $5* 🕒 *Closed Sun.*

★ Vena Cava

WINERY/DISTILLERY | Even if you're not into wine, a visit to this award-winning winery is well worth a visit. Winemaker Phil Gregory blended his passion for sustainable practices and wine making into the architecture of this funky wine cave made from old fishing boats. Bursting with character, these 1930s vessels once sailed the waters off the coast of Ensenada. Today they serve as the domes that cap the wine cellar, housing Vena Cava's labels considered among the best blends in Mexico. Vena Cava is one of the few wineries to produce natural wines, free of sulfites and with no added yeast. The Big Blend Tempranillo is elegant, gentle, and fruit-forward, and the 2016 Cabernet Sauvignon is remarkably smooth. This fine balance of science and art have become an obsession for the talented winemaker who uses French barrels and organic grapes from local valleys. Tastings are offered 11–5 on the hour for $20. Stay awhile and enjoy a meal at the food truck out front, serving an urban take on Baja cuisine. ✉ *Rancho San Marcos* ☎ *646/156–8053* 🌐 *www.venacavawine.com.*

Vinisterra

WINERY/DISTILLERY | Within Vinisterra, expect to find Tempranillo and Cabernet-Merlot blends which are big and juicy. Tastings are available from 11–5. Four tastings will run you about $9 to $40 depending on your selection. Call well in advance for reservations. ✉ *Carretera Tecate–Ensenada, Km 94.5, San Antonio de las Minas* ☎ *646/178–3350, 646/178–3310* 🌐 *www.vinisterra.com* 🕒 *Closed Tues.*

Wine Museum (*Museo de la Vid y el Vino*)

MUSEUM | For a better understanding of the wine-making process, the Museo de la Vid y el Vino in the heart of Valle de Guadalupe has exhibits on wine history, viticulture, and wine-inspired art. The museum showcases a vast collection of agricultural tools, more than 100 wines from the region, and a wine-tasting room where local blends are introduced daily. Don't miss the spectacular panoramic view of the valley and the outdoor amphitheater surrounded by vineyards. ✉ *Carretera Tecate–Ensenada, Km 81.37* ☎ *646/156–8165, 646/156–8166* 🌐 *www.museodelvinobc.com* 🎟 *$4* 🕒 *Closed Mon.*

🍴 Restaurants

★ Animalón

$$$$ | INTERNATIONAL | Pull up an equipale barrel chair and savor lunch under the canopy of a 200-year-old oak tree at this open-air restaurant, chef Javier Plascencia's tribute to local producers and the Valle lifestyle. Featured dishes change almost weekly, but you might find duck confit, kanpachi tostadas, lobster tallarines, and rib eye with sweet corn. **Known for:** tasting menu with wine pairing; superlative hospitality and setting; creative appetizers. [$] *Average main: $65* ✉ *Carretera Tecate–Ensenada, Ejido Km 83* ☎ *646/688–1973* 🌐 *www.animalon-baja.com* 🕒 *Closed Mon. and Tues. and Nov.–March.*

Deckman's En El Mogor

$$ | MEXICAN FUSION | Dining at Deckman's is like stepping into the quintessential Pinterest photo, replete with an open-air kitchen, straw floor, and wooden tables adorned with wildflowers. As if the chirping birds, adobe structure, soft jazz, and vineyard views weren't enough, you'll find a revolving menu built around seasonable products from

Continued on page 217

VIVA VINO

About an hour and a half south of San Diego, just inland from Ensenada, lies a region that's everything Ensenada is not. The 14-mile-long Valle de Guadalupe is charming, serene, and urbane, and—you might find this hard to believe if you're a wine buff—is a robust producer of quality vino.

There's no watered-down tequila here. Red grapes grown include Cabernet Sauvignon, Merlot, Tempranillo, and Syrah, while whites include Chardonnay, Sauvignon Blanc, and Viognier. Drive down and spend a day at the vineyards and wineries that line la Ruta del Vino, the road that stretches across the valley, or better yet, base yourself here. The inns and restaurants in the Valle de Guadalupe welcome guests with refined material comforts, which complement the region's natural desert-mountain beauty and lovely libations.

(top) Adobe Guadalupe, (bottom left) Grapes from the Guadalupe Valley, Ensenada, (bottom right) Adobe Guadalupe

WINERY-HOPPING

Some wineries along la Ruta del Vino are sizeable enterprises, while others are boutique affairs. Here are a few choice picks.

THE FULL-BODIED EXPERIENCE

Serious oenophiles should visit the midsize **Monte Xanic**, which is a serious contender for Mexico's finest winery. Tastings are by appointment; don't miss the Gran Ricardo, a high-end Bordeaux-style blend. **L. A. Cetto** is bigger than Monte Xanic, but it offers a well-orchestrated experience with tastings. Free tours are offered daily every half-hour from 10–5. Look for celebrity winemaker Camillo Magoni's wonderful Nebbiolo. A spectacular terrazza overlooks Cetto's own bullring and a sweeping expanse of wine country.

SIZE ISN'T EVERYTHING

Tiny, cozy **Casa de Piedra** is the legendary Hugo D'Acosta's winery. Tours and tastings of D'Acosta's high-end wines are by reservation only. Call ahead to visit the even smaller, but equally impressive, **Vinisterra**, where eccentric Swiss winemaker Christoph Gärtner turns out a small-production line of showstoppers called Macouzet, plus one of the only wines in the world made from mission grapes; these grapes come from vines descended from those planted by the Spanish in the 1500s for ceremonial services.

BACK TO THE BEGINNING

The imbibing of fermented fruit dates from the Stone Age (or Neolithic period; 8,500–4,000 BC), but the production of wine in the Americas is comparatively adolescent. Mexico actually has the New World's oldest wine industry, dating from 1574, when conquistadors and priests set off north from Zacatecas in search of gold; when none turned up, they decided to grow grapes instead. In 1597, they founded the Hacienda de San Lorenzo, the first winery in the Americas, in the modern-day state of Coahuila. By the late 1600s, Mexican wine production was so prolific, the Spaniards shut it down so it wouldn't compete with Spanish wine—sending Mexico's wine industry into a three-century hibernation. Now, most Mexican wine producers have moved to the thriving Valle de Guadalupe (a cooler, more favorable climate for vineyards).

L.A. Cetto sparkling wines, Valle de Guadalupe

HOW TO EXPERIENCE WINE COUNTRY

LIVE THE VALLEY If you fancy tranquility and a perfectly starry sky, and don't mind an early bedtime, you're best off staying at one of the intimate, romantic haciendas in the middle of the valley itself, where you'll also benefit from your hosts' knowledge of the area. One of the first small wineries in Baja, Adobe Guadalupe is also a gracious bed-and-breakfast run by Tru Miller. A delightful and committed host—Tru might take you to neighboring wineries on horseback. **La Villa del Valle**, a luxury inn, is larger but just as nice, with spectacular countryside views and amenities like a Jacuzzi and a food truck. Be sure to visit its cellar at neighboring Vena Cava Winery, made entirely of recycled boats.

DO IT BY DAY If you can't live without city buzz and nightlife, Ensenada has tons of it, and staying there is another viable option. In downtown Ensenada you can also visit **Bodegas de Santo Tomás**, one of Baja's oldest wineries. The city is less than an hour's drive to most of the wineries. It's also possible to visit the valley on a day trip from Tijuana or San Diego.

WINOS UNITE You can expect clear, sunny days in the valley for virtually the whole year, although evening temperatures dip into the 40s F (single digits Celsius) from December through March. A good time to visit is during the first two weeks of August, when the region comes alive for the **Fiestas de la Vendimia**, a harvest festival that's full of special wine tastings, dinners, and parties—both at the wineries and in Ensenada proper.

(pictured top and bottom) Adobe Guadalupe

the neighboring Mogor Ranch. **Known for:** one of best restaurants in Mexico; farm-to-table experience; artisanal-ranch menu. $ *Average main: $20* ⊠ *Carretera Ensenada–Tecate, Km 85.5, San Antonio de Las Minas* ☏ *646/188–3960* ⊕ *www.deckmans.com* ⊘ *No breakfast. Closed Tues. and Wed.*

Fauna

$$$$ | **MEXICAN FUSION** | Imagine a restaurant where communal tables sit among sunflowers, where rosemary sprigs burn like incense, and where chefs are free to create an experimental menu. That's Fauna, tucked within the Bruma property and run by prodigy-chef David Castro Hussong, who consistently pours out culinary magic. **Known for:** ever-changing menu with highlights like tender lamb; garden setting; impressive presentation. $ *Average main: $40* ⊠ *Bruma, Carretera Ensenada–Tecate, Km 73* ☏ *646/103–6403* ⊕ *www.faunarestaurante.mx.*

Finca Altozano

$$ | **MODERN MEXICAN** | From the moment you see guests clinking glasses atop wine-barrel towers, you know you're in for a memorable dining experience. On the edge of sprawling vineyards, this rustic setting under tin roofs has a seasonal menu to match. **Known for:** regional ingredients; oak-grilled quail; famous wine-barrel towers. $ *Average main: $18* ⊠ *Carretera Tecate–Ensenada, Km 83, Ejido Francisco Zarco* ☏ *646/156–8045* ⊕ *www.fincaltozano.com* ⊘ *No breakfast.*

★ Laja

$$$$ | **MEXICAN** | Set aside three hours for this extraordinary dining experience inside a cozy little house. Celebrity chef Jair Téllez's ambitious prix-fixe menus (there are four-course and eight-course versions) change frequently, but may include chione clam soup, yellowtail tartare, and braised beef with butternut squash and cauliflower purée, all served with excellent regional wines. **Known for:** eight-course wine pairing; twist on

Mexican and international flavors; farm-to-table with everything local. $ *Average main: $120* ⊠ *Highway 3, Km 83* ☏ *646/155–2556* ⊕ *www.lajamexico.com* ⊘ *Closed Sun.–Tues. and late Nov.–early Jan. No dinner Wed. Last orders taken at 8:30 pm Thurs.–Sat.*

Latitud 32

$$$ | **STEAKHOUSE** | Named for its location on the map, this upscale restaurant at El Cielo Vineyards specializes in grilled cuts and Baja-Yucatán cuisine. Suggested El Cielo wines are listed next to each menu item to assure a perfect pairing with dishes baked in annatto, sour orange, and other unique indigenous spices. **Known for:** Baja-Yucatán fusion; certified Angus cuts; panoramic views. $ *Average main: $30* ⊠ *Parcela 118, Km 7.5, at El Cielo* ☏ *646/155–2220* ⊕ *www.vinoselcielo.com.*

Lunario

$$$$ | **MODERN MEXICAN** | **FAMILY** | This jaw-dropping restaurant at Lomita winery is your chance to try a four-, six-, or eight-course tasting menu with a wine pairing. Grab a table overlooking the vineyards or head indoors, where a glass-roofed dining room allows the stars to shine over your table. **Known for:** spectacular wines from Lomita and Carrodilla wineries; observatory-esque dining room; menu featuring local ingredients. $ *Average main: $65* ⊠ *Ejido el Porvenir, at Lomita winery* ☏ *646/156–8469* ⊕ *www.restaurantelunario.com* ⊘ *Closed Mon.–Thurs.*

Malva

$$ | **ECLECTIC** | With sprawling views of vineyards, this restaurant and open-air kitchen is shaded by a thatched palapa and surrounded by acres of farmland where chef Roberto Alcocer gathers ingredients. Beer, wine, vegetables, fruit, cheese, bread, meat, eggs, honey—nearly everything served is from the on-site farm, making this a true farm-to-table experience. **Known for:** locally sourced food; tasting menu featuring Mexican flavors; Baja seafood and ranch-grown foods. $ *Average main: $20* ⊠ *Carretera Ensenada–Tecate, Km 96, at Mina Penelope Vinicola, San Antonio de las Minas* ☎ *646/155–3085* ⊕ *www.minapenelope.com* ⊗ *Closed Tues.*

🛏 Hotels

Properties in Valle de Guadalupe range from ranch-style B&Bs amid orchards, to eco-lofts on boulder-strewn hillsides. A welcome drink is fairly standard at most hotels, and some even include breakfast and wine tasting in the room rate. Don't expect to find TVs or nightlife in these parts, since wine tasting and early nights are top priorities. Some hotels request that toilet paper not be flushed due to gray water systems and clogging drains. Depending on where you're staying, remote properties are at the end of long dusty roads pitted with potholes. Ask the front desk for a Fast Track Pass to avoid the border wait at San Ysidro. Charging stations for electric cars are available at newer hotels and restaurants.

Adobe Guadalupe

$$$ | **B&B/INN** | Brick archways, fountains, and a pasture with white horses set a tone of endless tranquility at Tru Miller's magnificent country inn surrounded by vineyards. **Pros:** on-site food truck serves great tapas; electric car charging stations; rates include wine tasting and breakfast. **Cons:** weekends usually booked six months in advance; chilly pool; no children under 12. $ *Rooms from: $275* ⊠ *Off Highway 3 through Guadalupe village* ⊹ *6 km (4 miles) along same road, right turn at town of Porvenir* ☎ *646/155–2094* ⊕ *www.adobeguadalupe.com* ⤶ *6 rooms* ⦿ *Free breakfast.*

Bruma (*Casa 8*)

$$$$ | **B&B/INN** | Inside the luxury compound at Bruma, you'll find a winery, the top-notch Fauna restaurant, villas, and the architectural masterpiece, Casa 8; its eight suites are joined by a main house

complete with a common living room, kitchen, pool, and sundeck. **Pros:** contemporary design; excellent restaurant; luxurious property. **Cons:** pricey hotel; noise carries between rooms; booking process could use improvement. $ *Rooms from: $350* ⊠ *Otro Carretera Tecate–Ensenada, Km 74* ☎ *646/ 116–8031* ⊕ *www.bruma.mx* ⤶ *8 rooms* ⦿ *Free breakfast.*

Casa Mayoral

$ | **B&B/INN** | This road less traveled leads to four cozy cabins in a farmy setting with clucking chickens, vegetable gardens, and hammocks swaying under the shade of an orange grove. **Pros:** close to top restaurants; gated property; sustainable cabins with valley views. **Cons:** low water pressure; bumpy road and remote; nothing fancy. $ *Rooms from: $105* ⊠ *Carretera Tecate–Ensenada, Km 88.24* ☎ *664/257–2410* ⊕ *www.casamayoral.com* ⤶ *6 rooms, 1 house* ⦿ *Free breakfast.*

★ Contemplación Hotel Boutique

$ | **HOTEL** | At the push of a button, remote-controlled blackout curtains unveil vineyard views from this property's freestanding villas with floor-to-ceiling windows. **Pros:** gourmet cuisine at Salvia Blanca; remakable rates; kindhearted staff. **Cons:** no pool; inconsistent hot water; minibars aren't always stocked. $ *Rooms from: $105* ⊠ *Parcela 325 Calle Merlot, Ejido el Porvenir* ☎ *646/311–0995* ⊕ *www.contemplacionhotel.com* ⤶ *12 rooms* ⦿ *Free breakfast.*

★ El Cielo Winery & Resort by Karisma

$$$ | **RESORT** | As the largest hotel in the area, "Heaven" is the closest thing the Valle has to the big resort experience common in Riviera Maya, but without all the traffic or all-inclusive magnitude. **Pros:** gated property with 24-hr security; separate breakfast restaurant, Polaris; one-stop shop in luxury. **Cons:** $3 charge for extra Nespresso coffee pods; restauant is pricey; pool time must be booked in advance. $ *Rooms from:*

Did You Know?

Baja California produces about 70 percent of Mexico's wine; its main wine region, Valle de Guadalupe, is home to more than 100 wineries.

$300 ✉ *Carretera El Tigre–El Porvenir, Km 7.5 , Parcela 117 El Porvenir* 🌐 *www.elcielovalledeguadalupe.com* 🛏 *99 rooms* 🍴 *No meals.*

Encuentro Guadalupe

$$$$ | **HOTEL** | With freestanding steel box-cabins perched on a boulder-strewn hill, this property has architect Jorge Gracia to thank for its innovative design. **Pros:** pet-friendly; unique design; rate includes continental breakfast and wine tasting. **Cons:** no kids under 13; must sign liability waivers at check-in; room rates don't match quality of service. [$] *Rooms from: $550* ✉ *Carretera Tecate–Ensenada, Km 75, San Antonio de las Minas* ☎ *646/155–2775* 🌐 *www.grupoencuentro.com.mx* 🛏 *21 rooms* 🍴 *Free breakfast.*

Hacienda Guadalupe

$$$ | **HOTEL** | Privacy, comfort, and quality are the pillars of this hacienda-style property that draws a loyal clientele for the central location and reasonable rates. **Pros:** great value; gorgeous waterfall pool; hospitality at its best. **Cons:** restaurant closed Tuesday and Wednesday; no TVs; low water pressure. [$] *Rooms from: $264* ✉ *Carretera Tecate–Ensenada, Km 81.5* ☎ *646/155–2859* 🌐 *www.haciendaguadalupe.com* 🛏 *16 rooms* 🍴 *No meals.*

Hotel Partana

$$ | **HOTEL** | In the heart of Baja's wine country sits this modern 10-room boutique hotel within walking distance of Valle's top restaurants. **Pros:** rooms are built in between vines; modern amenities and artisanal toiletries; private accommodations each have a rooftop terrace. **Cons:** not a full-service hotel; loose gravel pathway to room; patchy Wi-Fi. [$] *Rooms from: $250* ✉ *Next to Finca Altozano, Carretera Tecate-Ensenada, Km 83* ☎ *646/668–1970* 🌐 *www.hotelpartana.com* 🛏 *10 rooms* 🍴 *No meals.*

La Villa del Valle

$$$$ | **B&B/INN** | Perched on a hilltop overlooking Vena Cava winery, this luxury inn is reminiscent of a Tuscan villa. **Pros:** convenient on-site food truck; wine tasting, teatime, snacks included in rate; excellent breakfasts. **Cons:** no kids under 13; guests are not given keys to lock rooms; two-night minimum stay. [$] *Rooms from: $315* ✉ *Off Carretera Tecate-Ensenada, Km 88* ✣ *Between San Antonio de las Minas and Francisco Zarco. Exit at Rancho Sicomoro and follow signs* ☎ *646/156–8007, 818/207–7130 in U.S.* 🌐 *www.lavilladelvalle.com* 🛏 *6 rooms* 🍴 *Free breakfast.*

Lumi

$$ | **HOTEL** | **FAMILY** | It's love that launched this stunning Nordic-inspired container hotel, starting with a romance between a Finnish woman and a Mexican man who turned their marriage into a passion project that beautifully blended both cultures. **Pros:** pets stay free; sauna great on cold nights; bikes for use. **Cons:** often booked; must reserve sauna; remote property. [$] *Rooms from: $169* ✉ *Camino Vecinal, Ejido El Porvenir* ☎ *686/261–8030* 🌐 *www.lumi.mx* 🛏 *6 container cabins; 4 tents* 🍴 *Free breakfast.*

Terra del Valle

$ | **B&B/INN** | Beyond the lavender fields and orange groves of this 12-acre property are ranch-style adobe suites insulated with bales of hay and equipped with surprising amenities like organic bath products, plush robes, and private terraces. **Pros:** excellent value; swimming pool; Jacuzzi and bikes for use. **Cons:** soft mattresses; usually booked; remote location on dirt road. [$] *Rooms from: $140* ✉ *Rancho La Concha, Camino San José de la Zorra s/n, Ejido El Porvenir* ☎ *646/117–3645* 🌐 *www.terradelvalle.com.mx* 🛏 *5 rooms* 🍴 *Free breakfast.*

🔘 Shopping

Baja Divina

GIFTS/SOUVENIRS | After lunch at Finca Altozano, pop into this small boutique next door where you'll find ponchos, hats, jewelry, artwork, and apothecary products from the valley. ✉ *Carretera Tecate–Ensenada, Km 83* ✚ *Ejido Francisco Zarco, next to Finca Altozano.*

La Casa de Doña Lupe

FOOD/CANDY | Near L.A. Cetto, Dona Lupe's boutique sells organic jams, chili marmalades, olive spreads, cheeses, salsas, oils, wines, and other local delicacies. Products can be shipped to the United States. ✉ *San Antonio de las Minas* ✚ *Off Carretera Tecate–Ensenada, turn left and follow road past L.A. Cetto to yellow building* ☎ *646/193–6291* ⊕ *www.lacasadonalupe.com.*

🏃 Activities

Quinta Monasterio Spa

SPA/BEAUTY | The creative makers of Quinta Monasterio wine combine tastings with spa treatments, which incorporate grapes, lavender, citrus, and olive oil directly from their property. Housed in an innovative two-story container, the small spa accommodates one to four guests and includes massages, facials, exfoliations, manicures, pedicures, and aromatherapy in the sauna created from old wine barrels. Spa packages include lunch and a glass of wine; appointments are by reservation only. ✉ *Quinta Monasterio 12, San Antonio de las Minas* ✚ *Take Highway 3 to el Ejido Porvenir, turn right and follow signs* ☎ *646/156–8023* ⊕ *www.viniphera.com.*

Ensenada

65 km (40 miles) south of Puerto Nuevo.

The Yumano people were the original inhabitants of what is now Ensenada; the Spanish arrived in 1542 to the seaport that Sebastián Vizcaíno named Ensenada-Bahía de Todos Santos (All Saints' Bay) in 1602. Since then the town has drawn a steady stream of explorers and developers. After playing home to ranchers and gold miners, the harbor gradually grew into a major port for shipping agricultural goods, and today Baja's third-largest city (population 523,000) is one of Mexico's largest sea and fishing ports in addition to a popular weekend destination for Southern Californians.

There are no beaches in Ensenada proper other than a man-made cove at Hotel Coral, but sandy stretches north and south of town are satisfactory for swimming, sunning, surfing, and camping. Estero Beach is long and clean, with mild waves; the Estero Beach Resort takes up much of the oceanfront, but the beach is public. Although not safe for swimming, the beaches at several of the restaurants along the Carretera Transpeninsular (Highway 1) are a nice place to enjoy a cocktail with a view. Surfers populate the strands off Highway 1 north and south of Ensenada, particularly San Miguel, Tres Marías, and Salsipuedes, while scuba divers prefer Punta Banda, by La Bufadora. Lifeguards are rare, so be cautious.

Both the waterfront and the main downtown street, Calle Primera, are pleasant places to stroll. If you're driving, be sure to take the Centro exit from the highway, since it bypasses the commercial port area.

GETTING HERE AND AROUND

If you're flying into Tijuana, from Aeropuerto Alberado Rodriguez (TIJ) you can find buses that also serve Rosarito and Ensenada. Or you can hop on a bus at Tijuana Camionera de la Línea station, just inside the border, with service to Rosarito and Ensenada along with city buses to downtown. To head south from Tijuana by car, follow the signs for Ensenada Cuota, the toll road Carretera 1D along the coast. Tollbooths accept U.S. and Mexican currency; there are three tolls of about $2.50 each between Tijuana and Ensenada. Restrooms are available near toll stations. Ensenada is an hour south of Tijuana on this road. The alternative free road—Carretera Transpeninsular Highway 1, or Ensenada Libre—is curvy and not as well maintained. (Entry to it is on a side street in a congested area of downtown Tijuana.)

Highway 1 continues south of Ensenada to Guerrero Negro, at the border between Baja California and Baja Sur, and on to Baja's southernmost resorts; there are no tolls past Ensenada. Highway 1 is fairly well maintained and signposted.

Although there are several rental car companies in Tijuana, Alamo is one of the few that includes insurance and tax in the quoted rate, rather than tacking on hidden fees at arrival. California Baja Rent-A-Car is the only agency to rent vehicles for Mexico on the San Diego side of the border. Rates start at $60 per day. Drivers must carry mandatory third-party liability, an expense that is not covered by U.S. insurance policies or by credit card companies.

If driving your own vehicle across the San Ysidro border, ask your hotel if they offer a Fast Track Pass, which helps eliminate the long border wait on the return. Otherwise expect to wait around three hours on an average weekend. Border wait times are available at ⊕ bwt.cbp.gov.

Taxis are a reliable means of getting around Ensenada, and you can flag them down on the street.

VISITOR INFORMATION Ensenada Tourist Information Office. ⊠ *Blvd. Costero 546, Zona Playitas* ✛ *Just south of cruise ship terminal* ⊕ *www.bajanorte.com.*

◉ Sights

Avenida López Mateos (*Calle Primera*)
NEIGHBORHOOD | Avenida López Mateos, commonly known as Calle Primera, is the center of Ensenada's traditional tourist zone and shopping district. Hotels, shops, restaurants, and bars line the avenue for eight blocks, from its beginning at the foot of the Chapultepec Hills to the dry channel of the Arroyo de Ensenada. The avenue also has sidewalk cafés, art galleries, and most of the town's souvenir stores, where you can find pottery, glassware, silver, and other Mexican crafts. ⊠ *Av. López Mateos.*

La Bufadora
BODY OF WATER | Legend has it that La Bufadora, an impressive tidal blowhole (la bufadora means the buffalo snort) in the coastal cliffs at Punta Banda, was created by a whale or sea serpent trapped in an undersea cave. The road to La Bufadora along Punta Banda—an isolated, mountainous point that juts into the sea—is lined with olive, craft, and tamale stands; the drive gives you a sampling of Baja's wilderness. If you're in need of some cooling off, turn off the highway at the sign for La Jolla Beach Camp. The camp charges a small admission fee for day use of the beachside facilities, but it's a great place to do a few "laps" of lazy freestyle or breaststroke at La Jolla Beach. At La Bufadora, expect a small fee to park, and then a half-mile walk past T-shirt hawkers and souvenir stands to the water hole itself. A public bus runs from the downtown Ensenada station to Maneadero, from which you can catch a minibus labeled Punta Banda that goes to

La Bufadora. Guided tours from Ensenada to La Bufadora will run you about $15. ☒ *Carretera 23, Punta Banda* ✛ *31 km (19 miles) south of Ensenada.*

La Cava de Marcelo

FARM/RANCH | FAMILY | For many, a visit to Baja Norte must include an afternoon drive to the cheese caves of Marcelo in Ojos Negros, just 45 minutes outside Ensenada. With Swiss-Italian roots, owner Marcelo Castro Chacon is now the fourth generation to carry on the *queso* tradition since it first began in 1911. A visit to the farm includes a tour of the milking facilities and a tasting of seven cheeses and their signature Ramonetti red wine. Milder selections seasoned with basil, black pepper, and rosemary are more popular with locals than their sharper cheeses, aged up to two-and-a-half years, loved by out-of-towners. As Mexico's only cheese cave (and the first in Latin America), this beloved factory produces 450 pounds of cheese per day. Milking takes place at 5 pm daily and the small on-site shop sells the remarkable marmalade and wine that accompany your cheese tasting. Those with time and an appetite can dine under the shade of a peppertree for a lunch menu integrating Marcelo's cheeses and organic fruits and vegetables from his farm (expect flies in summer). The cactus salad and portobello mushrooms with melted cheese make the ideal starters to the regional trout served with roasted garlic. The fig mousse alone is worth a visit. Be aware that cell service is limited and the road here is winding. ☒ *Rancho La Campana, Carretera Ensenada–San Felipe, Km 43, 48 km (30 miles) east of Ensenada, Ojos Negros* ✛ *Off Highway 3, follow signs to La Cava de Queso* ☎ *646/117–0293* 🍽 *$10 tour and tasting* ⓧ *Closed Mon.–Wed.*

Las Bodegas de Santo Tomás (*Cava Miramar*)

WINERY/DISTILLERY | One of Baja's oldest wine producers gives tours and tastings at its downtown Ensenada winery and bottling plant. Santo Tomás's best wines are the Alisio Chardonnay, the Cabernet, and the Tempranillo; avoid the overpriced Único. The winery also operates the enormous wineshop, a brick building across the avenue. The Santo Tomás Vineyards can be found on the eastern side of Highway 1 about 50 km (31 miles) south of Ensenada in Santo Tomás Valley, fairly near the ruins of the Misión Santo Tomás de Aquino, which was founded by Dominican priests in 1791. They have a third facility, Cava San Antonio de las Minas, at the entrance to Valle de Guadalupe at Km 94.7. ☒ *Av. Miramar 666, Centro* ☎ *646/178–3333* ⊕ *www.santo-tomas.com* 🍽 *4 tastings $6.*

Mercado de Mariscos (*Mercado Negro*)

MARKET | At the northernmost point of Boulevard Costero, the main street along the waterfront, is an indoor-outdoor fish market where row after row of counters display piles of shrimp, tuna, dorado, and other fish caught off Baja's coasts. Outside, stands sell grilled or smoked fish, seafood cocktails, and fish tacos. You can pick up a few souvenirs, eat well for very little money, and take some great photographs. If your stomach is delicate, try the fish tacos at the cleaner, quieter Plaza de Mariscos in the shadow of the giant beige Plaza de Marina that blocks the view of the traditional fish market from the street. ☒ *Ensenada.*

Riviera del Pacífico (*Centro Cívico Social y Cultural Riviera de Ensenada*)

HOUSE | Officially called the Centro Cívico Social y Cultural Riviera de Ensenada, the Riviera is a rambling, white, hacienda-style mansion built in the 1920s. The former casino and hotel was frequented by wealthy U.S. citizens and Mexicans, particularly during Prohibition. You can

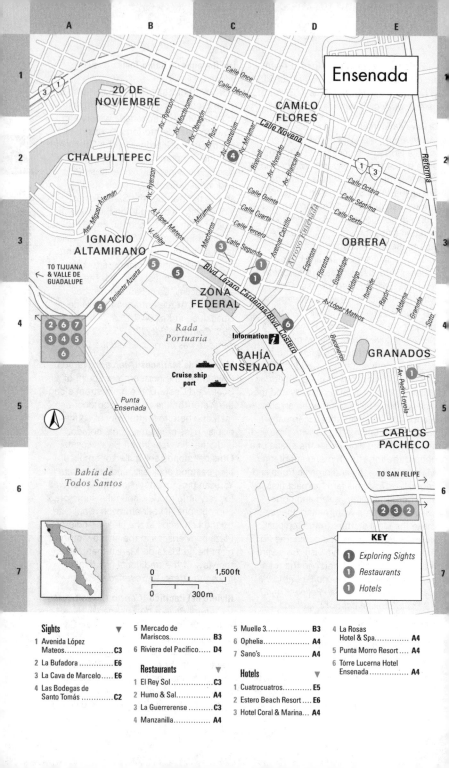

Ensenada

KEY

- ① Exploring Sights
- ① Restaurants
- ① Hotels

visit the café and history museum, and tour the gardens and some of the elegant ballrooms and halls, which occasionally host art shows and civic events. ✉ *Blvd. Lázaro Cárdenas 1421, Centro* ✣ *Blvd. Costero at Av. Riviera* ☎ *646/176–4310* 🌐 *www.rivieradeensenada.com.mx* 🎟 *Building and gardens free; museum entry $2.*

🍴 Restaurants

El Rey Sol
$$ | **FRENCH** | From its chateaubriand *bouquetière* to the savory chicken chipotle cooked with brandy, port wine, and cream, this classy French restaurant has been family-owned since 1947. Louis XIV–style furnishings and an attentive staff make it both comfortable and elegant. **Known for:** French pastries; table-side Caesar salad; first-rate service. [$] *Average main: $20* ✉ *Av. López Mateos 1000, Centro* ☎ *646/178–1733* 🌐 *www.elreysol.com.*

Humo & Sal
$$ | **SEAFOOD** | A trendy offspring of neighboring Sano's Steakhouse, "Smoke and Salt" focuses on local seafood with a twist. Guests of the casual, "reservations essential" hot spot can also order from the more formal steak house next door. **Known for:** fresh oysters; tamarind-mezcal margarita; blue-corn tortillas piled with shrimp and scallops. [$] *Average main: $14* ✉ *Zona Playitas, Carretera Tijuana–Ensenada, Km 108, Zona Playitas* ☎ *646/174–4061* 🌐 *humoysal-baja.negocio.site* ⏲ *Closed Mon.–Wed.*

La Guerrerense
$ | **SEAFOOD** | This food-cart stall off Ensenada's bustling Calle Primera is *the* place where locals get a solid helping of the region's seafood. Established in 1960, La Guerrerense has been featured on international shows like Anthony Bourdain's *No Reservations.* **Known for:** world's best tostadas; fresh ceviche with mango; homemade salsas. [$] *Average main: $10* ✉ *Calle Primera at Alvarado* ☎ *646/206–0445* 🌐 *www.laguerrerense.com* ⏲ *Closed Tues. No dinner.*

Manzanilla
$$ | **ECLECTIC** | Two of the most exciting chef-owners in Baja Norte, Benito Molina and Solange Muris, have taken a truly modern approach to Mexican cuisine at Manzanilla, integrating the freshest catches from the local waters—oysters, mussels, abalone, and clams, for instance—and using ingredients like ginger, saffron, smoked tomato marmalade, and *huitlacoche* (corn truffle). The ahi with ginger strawberry vinaigrette melts in your mouth, and the white clam with Gorgonzola is delicious. **Known for:** fresh Baja seafood; homemade tagliatelli; grilled quail with wild mushrooms. [$] *Average main: $20* ✉ *Recinto Portuario, Teniente Azueta 139, Centro* ☎ *646/175–7073* 🌐 *www.rmanzanilla.com* ⏲ *Closed Mon. and Tues.*

★ **Muelle 3**
$$ | **SEAFOOD** | This marina-front restaurant is a hole in the wall that will blow your mind, starting with the six-course menu for $25. The small patio gives a front-row seat to the boardwalk action where locals stroll, sailboats bob, and seagulls squawk at the day's catch. **Known for:** cozy atmosphere; great prices; fresh-as-can-be house ceviche. [$] *Average main: $12* ✉ *Marina Boardwalk, Teniente Azueta 187-B, Centro* ☎ *646/174–0318* 🌐 *www.muelle-3-restaurant.negocio.site* ⏲ *Closed Sun. and Mon.* ☞ *Reservations recommended.*

Ophelia
$$ | **ECLECTIC** | For a garden escape along Highway 1, check out Ophelia, opened by Rosendo Ramos. It's a favorite among the Ensenada foodie crowd. **Known for:** octopus tacos and shrimp ceviche; Zen vibe in garden patio; fresh yellowfin tuna. [$] *Average main: $16* ✉ *Carretera Tijuana–Ensenada, Km 103* ☎ *646/175–8365* ⏲ *Closed Mon.*

★ Sano's

$$ | **STEAKHOUSE** | This elegant restaurant, with its white linens, open trusses, and soft candlelight is the best steak house in Baja California. Prepared on mesquite wood, the steak is divine and tender, almost as if it's been marinated in butter (though the chef swears salt and a little love are the secret). **Known for:** aged rib eye; dishes cooked to perfection; excellent service. [$] *Average main: $20* ✉ *Carretera Tijuana–Ensenada, Km 108* ✥ *Just after Playitas Club del Mar, heading south to Ensenada* ☎ *646/174–4061* 🌐 *www.sanos.com.mx* ⏲ *Closed Mon.–Wed.*

Hotels

Cuatrocuatros

$$ | **B&B/INN** | Situated among vineyards is this peaceful settlement of 17 luxury tents with creature comforts like air-conditioning, a minibar, fireplace, king-size beds, and private sundecks, plus access to a growing number of on-site activities including a winery, beach club, zipline tours, and horseback riding. **Pros:** the ultimate in Baja "glamping"; great views from hilltop beach club; private beach. **Cons:** 15 minutes from town; restaurant closes at 6 pm and front desk at 8 pm; tents beginning to show some wear. [$] *Rooms from: $200* ✉ *Carretera Transpeninsular, Km 89* ☎ *646/174–6789* 🌐 *www.cuatrocuatros.mx* 🛏 *17 cabañas* 🍴 *No meals.*

Estero Beach Resort

$$ | **RESORT** | **FAMILY** | Families love this long-standing resort on Ensenada's top beach, especially because of its private location and endless activities like horseback riding, tennis, volleyball, kayaking, and Jet Skiing. **Pros:** wonderful breakfasts; right on the beach; good for families. **Cons:** rooms by parking lot aren't great; boat launch fee; food somewhat pricey. [$] *Rooms from: $180* ✉ *Carretera Tijuana–Ensenada, intersection of Lazaro Cardenas and Lupita Novelo, Estero Beach* ✥ *10 km (6 miles) south of Ensenada* ☎ *646/176–6235, 646/176–6225* 🌐 *www.hotelesterobeach.com* 🛏 *96 rooms* 🍴 *No meals.*

Hotel Coral & Marina

$$ | **RESORT** | **FAMILY** | In addition to its own marina and artificial beach, this all-suites resort has indoor-outdoor pools, a spa, tennis courts, a water-sports center, and a sports bar overlooking the bay. **Pros:** guests receive Fast Track Pass for border crossing; spacious rooms; outstanding Sunday brunch. **Cons:** pool can get noisy with kids; patchy Wi-Fi; slow elevator. [$] *Rooms from: $208* ✉ *Carretera Tijuana–Ensenada, Km 103, Zona Playitas* ☎ *646/175–0000, 800/862–9020 in U.S.* 🌐 *www.hotelcoral.com* 🛏 *147 suites* 🍴 *No meals.*

Las Rosas Hotel & Spa

$$ | **RESORT** | This intimate hotel north of Ensenada has rooms facing the ocean, but it's the infinity pool spilling into the sea that will take your breath away. **Pros:** laid-back and relaxing; great ocean views; attentive staff. **Cons:** dated rooms; rocky beach; some street noise; weak Wi-Fi signal in rooms. [$] *Rooms from: $154* ✉ *Carretera Tijuana–Ensenada, Km 105.5, Zona Playitas* ✥ *Just north of Ensenada* ☎ *646/174–4310, 646/174–4360* 🌐 *www.lasrosas.com* 🛏 *48 rooms* 🍴 *No meals.*

Punta Morro Resort

$$ | **RESORT** | In one of Ensenada's most beautiful settings, this 24-room hotel has charm and tranquillity to spare with spacious rooms that have balconies facing the ocean. **Pros:** room rates half off Sun.–Thurs.; great restaurant; personalized service. **Cons:** no bathtubs; uncomfortable couches in rooms; rocky beach not suitable for swimming. [$] *Rooms from: $229* ✉ *Carretera Tijuana–Ensenada, Km 106, Zona Playitas* ☎ *646/178–3507* 🌐 *www.hotelpuntamorro.com* 🛏 *24 rooms* 🍴 *No meals.*

⭐ **Torre Lucerna Hotel Ensenada**

$ | HOTEL | The most upscale hotel in Ensenada has a swanky "Mad Men" vibe, right down to the golden pillars, art deco terrace, and paintings of pin-up girls adorning the lobby and suites. **Pros:** spa, pool, and rooftop restaurant on-site; reasonable rates; underground secured parking. **Cons:** street-facing rooms have traffic noise; loud piano in the lobby; no direct beach access. $ Rooms from: $146 ⌂ Carretera Tijuana–Ensenada, Km 108, Zona Playitas ☎ 646/222–2400 ⊕ www.lucernahoteles.com ⇌ 146 rooms ⦙◌⦙ No meals.

ⓨ Nightlife

When Valle de Guadalupe shuts down for the night, Ensenada is just getting started. The corner of Avenida Ruiz and Avenida López Mateos (Calle Primera) has the most action, with loud music and cheap beers in a cantina setting. For something a bit more refined, there are a few hip microbreweries near the coast.

Agua Mala

BREWPUBS/BEER GARDENS | Don't be fooled by the name "bad water." This artisanal brewery pours a mean oatmeal stout and imperial IPA. Nearly a dozen handcrafted beers are served in the container bar where menu items like octopus tacos and artisanal pizzas pair well with just about everything on tap. ⌂ Carretera Tijuana–Ensenada, Km 104 ☎ 646/174–6068 ⊕ www.aguamala.com.mx.

Cerveceria Transpeninsular

BREWPUBS/BEER GARDENS | This two-story brewery is a game changer for Ensenada, luring locals and travelers alike for craft beers in a warehouse-like setting. They have live music, jam sessions, open-mic night, and NFL Sunday. Check their Facebook page for upcoming events and specials. ⌂ Carretera Tijuana 107 + 240, Zona Playitas ☎ 646/175–2620 ⊕ www.cerveceriatranspeninsular.com.

Hussong's Cantina

BARS/PUBS | Hussong's Cantina has been an Ensenada landmark since 1892, and has changed little since then. Ask anyone here and they'll tell you that this is where the margarita was invented by bartender Don Carlos Orozco in October 1941; however, this is just one of several local establishments that state that claim to fame. Regardless, come by Saturday when you can get two margaritas for the price of one, or two-for-one beers every Tuesday and Thursday. A security guard stands by the front door to handle the often-rowdy crowd. The floor is covered with sawdust, and the noise is usually deafening, pierced by mariachi and ranchera musicians and the whoops and hollers of the pie-eyed. ⌂ Av. Ruíz 113, Centro ☎ 646/178–3210 ⊕ cantinahussongs.com/home.html ⊘ Closed Mon. ⊸ Closed Mon.

⭐ Wendlandt Cervecería

BARS/PUBS | For a casual yet refined bar scene, this chic spot is a favorite of Ensenada's many vintners, chefs, and brewers. Showcasing local beers from the region, as well as wines from nearby Valle del Guadalupe, the friendly owners have literally mastered the craft with their own cervezas that landed them the titles of Mexico's best beer in 2015 and 2019. Beer tastings in their brew pub are available by reservation only. If you're hungry, Wendlandt serves elevated bar food using local ingredients. The nondescript bar is simply marked by their logo and an antique door. ⌂ Blvd. Costero 248, Centro ☎ 646/178–2938 ⊕ www.wendlandt.com.mx ⊸ Closed Mon.

👜 Shopping

Most of the tourist shops hold court along Avenida López Mateos (Calle Primera) beside the hotels and restaurants. There are several two-story shopping arcades, some with empty spaces for rent. Dozens of curio shops line the street, all selling similar selections of pottery, serapes, and tackier trinkets and T-shirts.

Adobe

GIFTS/SOUVENIRS | This modern shopping court is a one-stop shop for all your gift needs, with six vendors selling vanilla, clothing, pottery, jewelry, accessories, and souvenirs from the region. ⊠ *Av. López Mateos 490, Centro* ☉ *Closed Mon.*

Bazar Casa Ramirez

CERAMICS/GLASSWARE | Bazar Casa Ramirez sells high-quality Talavera pottery and other ceramics, paintings by local artists, jewelry from Taxco, wooden carvings, and papier-mâché figurines. Everything here is made in Mexico. Be sure to check out the displays upstairs. ⊠ *Av. López Mateos 498, Centro* ☎ *646/178–8209.*

Casanegra

CLOTHING | This indie boutique specializing in streetwear is the place to go for "cool souvenirs made in Mexico," as owner Juliett puts it. You'll find hats, shirts, jewelry, and vinyl records, plus apothecary products made from coffee and wine extracts. The shop doubles as a café, meaning you can power up, shop, and hit Ensenada full steam ahead. ⊠ *Quintas Papagayo Hotel, Carretera Tijuana–Ensenada, Km 108, Zona Playitas* ☎ *646/117–2772* ⊕ *www.shopcasanegra.com* ☉ *Closed Wed.*

Los Castillo

JEWELRY/ACCESSORIES | Operated by the renowned Sanchez-Macfarland family for more than five decades, this jewelry store has the highest quality and most unique silver pieces from famous designers from the Taxco region. ⊠ *Av. López Mateos 1084, Centro* ☎ *646/156–5274* ⊕ *www.loscastillosilver.com.*

Swap Meet Pórticos

OUTDOOR/FLEA/GREEN MARKETS | Clothing, artwork, collectibles, and food are sprawled across endless rows at Baja's largest swap meet. ⊠ *Blvd. Enlace 2000, at Blvd. Zertuche* ☎ *646/185–9062* ☉ *Closed Mon. and Tues.*

⚙ Activities

SPORTFISHING

The best angling takes place from April through October, with bottom fishing the best in winter. Charter vessels and party boats are available from several outfitters along the boardwalk and off the sportfishing pier. Mexican fishing licenses for the day ($13) are available from charter companies.

Sergio's Sportfishing

FISHING | One of the best sportfishing companies in Ensenada, Sergio's Sportfishing has year-round private charter or open party boats. Whale-watching tours are available from December 15 to April 15. ⊠ *Sportfishing Pier, Blvd. Lázaro Cárdenas 6, Centro* ☎ *646/178–2185, 619/399–7224 in U.S.* ⊕ *www.sergios-fishing.com* ⌧ *Fishing $80 per person on a group boat, including the cost of a license; whale-watching $30 per person.*

WATER SPORTS

Estero Beach and Punta Banda (en route to La Bufadora, south of Ensenada) are both good kayaking areas, although facilities are limited. A small selection of water-sports equipment is available at the Estero Beach Resort.

WHALE-WATCHING

Boats leave the Ensenada sportfishing pier for whale-watching trips from December through March. The gray whales migrating from the north to bays and lagoons in southern Baja pass through Todos Santos Bay, often close to shore. Binoculars and cameras with telephoto capabilities come in handy. The trips last about three hours. Vessels are available from several outfitters at the sportfishing pier. Expect to pay about $30 for a three-hour tour.

Index

Photo Credits

Front Cover: Hemis / Alamy Stock Photo [Description: Mexico, Baja California Sur State, Sea of Cortez, listed as World Heritage by UNESCO, Cabo San Lucas, Sea Kayaking towards El Arco.]. **Back cover, from left to right:** Gary718/Dreamstime.com, Leonardospencer/ Dreamstime.com, Dgirard12/Dreamstime.com. **Spine:** Khewey/Dreamstime.com. **Interior, from left to right:** DavidWitthaus/iStockphoto (1). Sarah_Robson | Dreamstime.com (2). Bruce Herman/Mexico Tourism Board (5). **Chapter 1: Experience Los Cabos:** Frederick Millett/ Shutterstock (6-7). Courtesy of Los Cabos Tourism Board (LCTB) (8). Courtesy of Los Cabos Tourism Board (LCTB) (9). niknikon (9). toddtaulman/ iStockphoto (10). ferrantraite (10). Douglas Peebles Photography / Alamy Stock Photo (10). Courtesy of El Squid Roe (10). Courtesy of Los Cabos Tourism Board (LCTB) (11). Hasselblad H4D (11). Courtesy of Los Cabos Tourism Board (LCTB) (11). Ed-Ni-Photo/iStockphoto (11). francisco estrada PHOTOMEXICO (12). Kartinkin77/Shutterstock (12). Michael Seidl (12). Leswrona | Dreamstime.com (12). Barbara Kraft (13). Courtesy of Los Cabos Tourism Board (LCTB)/ Courtesy of Huerta Los Tamarindos (13). Los Cabos Tourism Board (16). Grey82/Shutterstock (16). Lupe amador/Shutterstock (16). One&Only Palmilla (17). ChavezEd/Shutterstock (17). Tamarindos Mexican Farm to Table (18). Jacopo ventura/Shutterstock (18). Pueblo Bonito (18). carlosrojas20/iStockphoto (18). Restaurante Los Tres Gallos (19). Paul Camhi/La Lupita (19). MielPhotos2008/iStockphoto (19). T.Tseng/CC BY 2.0 (19). San Miguel Glass blowing company. (20). dianeta8/Shutterstock (21). **Chapter 3: Cabo San Lucas:** emperorcosar/Shutterstock (61). Robert Chiasson / age fotostock (69). Kartinkin77/Shutterstock (87). rhfletcher/Shutter-stock (89). Reinhard Dirscherl / age fotostock (92). tonobalaguerf/Shutterstock (94). Larry Dunmire (95). Bruce Herman/Mexico Tourism Board (96). **Chapter 4: The Corridor:** DBSOCAL/Shutterstock (99). Odor Zsolt/Shutterstock (105). Tatiana Koshkina/iStockphoto (108-109). The Esperanza (112). Courtesy of One&Only Palmilla (114). National Geographic Creative / Alamy Stock Photo (119). Jim Russi / age fotostock (120). Kato Inowe/Shutterstock (120). RCPPHOTO/Shutterstock (120). Henry William Fu/Shutterstock (121). Kato Inowe/Shutterstock (122). Bruce Herman/Mexico Tourism Board (124). Kato Inowe/Shutterstock (124). **Chapter 5: San José del Cabo:** karamysh/Shutterstock (127). Gerasimovvv | Dreamstime.com (134-135). Courtesy of Los Cabos Tourism Board (LCTB)/ Courtesy of FloraFarms (137). Khamsai Vang/ Flickr (140). Galina Savina/Shutterstock (144). John Mitchell / Alamy (146). Maria Lourdes Alonso / age fotostock (147). Maria Lourdes Alonso / age fotostock (148). Ken Ross (149). Jane Onstott (149). Ken Ross (149). Ken Ross (149). fontplaydotcom/Flickr (150). patti haskins/Flickr (150). Wonderlane/Flickr (150). Photographer: Jose Zelaya Gallery: ArtedelPueblo.com (150). Jane Onstott. (150). csp/Shutterstock (151). **Chapter 6: Los Cabos Side Trips, Todos Santos, La Paz, and East Cape:** Ryan C Slimak/Shutterstock (155). Shawn Goldberg/Shutterstock (167). San Rostro / age fotostock (170). Matt Gush/Shutterstock (180-181). Joost van Uffelen/Shutterstock (184). Adalberto Rios Szalay / age fotostock (187). Michael S. Nolan (188). gary718/Shutterstock (188). Ryan Harvey/Flickr (189). Leonardo Gonzalez/Shutterstock (191). **Chapter 7: Baja California With Ensenada and the Valle de Guadalupe Wine Region:** Priscilia Sa-llinas/Shutterstock (199). VG Foto/Shutterstock (205). Sherry V Smith/Shutterstock (209).Adobe Guadalupe (214). Tomas Castelazo/wikipedia. org (214). Adobe Guadalupe (214). Maria Lourdes Alonso (215). Adobe Guadalupe (216). Adobe Guadalupe (216). Sherry V Smith/Shutterstock (219). **About Our Writers:** All photos are courtesy of the writers.

*Every effort has been made to trace the copyright holders, and we apologize in advance for any accidental errors. We would be happy to apply the corrections in the following edition of this publication.

Notes

Notes

Notes

Notes

Notes

Fodor's LOS CABOS

Publisher: Stephen Horowitz, *General Manager*

Editorial: Douglas Stallings, *Editorial Director*; Jill Fergus, Amanda Sadlowski, *Senior Editors*; Kayla Becker, Alexis Kelly, *Editors*

Design: Tina Malaney, *Director of Design and Production*; Jessica Gonzalez, *Graphic Designer*; Mariana Tabares, *Design & Production Intern*

Production: Jennifer DePrima, *Editorial Production Manager*; Elyse Rozelle, *Senior Production Editor*; Monica White, *Production Editor*

Maps: Rebecca Baer, *Senior Map Editor*; David Lindroth, Mark Stroud (Moon Street Cartography), *Cartographers*

Photography: Viviane Teles, *Senior Photo Editor*; Namrata Aggarwal, Ashok Kumar, *Photo Editors*; Rebecca Rimmer, *Photo Intern*

Business & Operations: Chuck Hoover, *Chief Marketing Officer*; Robert Ames, *Group General Manager*; Devin Duckworth, *Director of Print Publishing*; Victor Bernal, *Business Analyst*

Public Relations and Marketing: Joe Ewaskiw, *Senior Director Communications & Public Relations*

Fodors.com: Jeremy Tarr, *Editorial Director*; Rachael Levitt, *Managing Editor*

Technology: Jon Atkinson, *Director of Technology*; Rudresh Teotia, *Lead Developer*; Jacob Ashpis, *Content Operations Manager*

Writers: Luis Domínguez, Marlise Kast-Myers, Chris Sands

Editor: Kayla Becker

Production Editor: Monica White

6th Edition

ISBN 978-1-64097-345-9

ISSN 2326–4152

All details in this book are based on information supplied to us at press time. Always confirm information when it matters, especially if you're making a detour to visit a specific place. Fodor's expressly disclaims any liability, loss, or risk, personal or otherwise, that is incurred as a consequence of the use of any of the contents of this book.

SPECIAL SALES

This book is available at special discounts for bulk purchases for sales promotions or premiums. For more information, e-mail SpecialMarkets@fodors.com.

PRINTED IN CANADA

10 9 8 7 6 5 4 3 2

MIX
Paper from responsible sources
FSC® C016245

About Our Writers

Luis Domínguez is a Riviera Maya-based freelance writer and independent journalist interested in travel, art, books, history, philosophy, politics, and sports. He has written for *Fodor's Travel*, *Yahoo!*, *Sports Illustrated*, *Telemundo*, and *Homeschool Spanish Academy*, among other digital and print publications in North America and Europe. Luis updated the San José del Cabo and Corridor chapters of this guide.

Journalist and author **Marlise Kast-Myers** has traveled to more than 80 countries and has lived in Switzerland, Dominican Republic, Spain, and Costa Rica. Before settling in Southern California, she completed a surfing and snowboarding expedition across the world. Following the release of her memoir, *Tabloid Prodigy*, Marlise co-authored over 25 Fodor's Travel Guides including books on Cancun, San Diego, Panama, Puerto Rico, Peru, Los Cabos, Corsica, Riviera Maya, Sardinia, Vietnam, and Costa Rica. She served as a photojournalist for *Surf Guide to Costa Rica* and authored *Day and Overnight Hikes on the Pacific Crest Trail*. Based in San Diego County, she writes travel features for *The San Diego Union Tribune* and other publications. She lives at the historic Betty Crocker Estate where she and her husband, Benjamin operate an antique business, Brick n Barn. Her website is ⊕ *www.marlisekast.com*.

Chris Sands is the Cabo San Lucas and Side Trips writer for *Fodor's Los Cabos* as well as the local Cabo San Lucas expert for *USA Today's* travel website, 10 Best, and a contributor to numerous websites and publications, including *Marriott Bonvoy Traveler*, *Forbes Travel Guide*, *Porthole Cruise*, and *Cabo Living*. He is also the co-founder of CaboViVO, a website dedicated to promoting the best of Los Cabos. He is a full-time resident of Cabo San Lucas.